SAVING LIVES IN AUSCHWITZ

The Prisoners' Hospital in Buna-Monowitz

Ewa K. Bacon

Purdue University Press
West Lafayette, Indiana

Hardback ISBN: 978-1-55753-824-6

The Library of Congress has cataloged the earlier paperback edition as follows:

Names: Bacon, Ewa K., author.
Title: Saving Lives in Auschwitz: The Prisoners' Hospital in Buna-Monowitz / Ewa K. Bacon.
Description: West Lafayette, Indiana: Purdue University Press, [2017] | Series: Shofar Supplements in Jewish Studies | Includes bibliographical references and index.
Identifiers:
LCCN 2017012197
ISBN 9781557537799 (pbk.: alk. paper)
ISBN 9781612494920 (epdf)
ISBN 9781612494937 (epub)
Subjects: LCSH: Budziaszek, Stefan. | Auschwitz (Concentration camp) | Jewish physicians—Medical care. | Concentration camp inmates—Medical care. | World War, 1939–1945—Prisoners and prisons, Polish. | Holocaust, Jewish (1939–1945)
Classification: LCC D806 .B33 2017 | DDC 940.53/18092 [B] —dc23
LC record available at https://lccn.loc.gov/2017012197

Cover: The image used on the cover is a never-before-published artifact from within the prison, taken from a hand-drawn gift card, a name-day card, given to Stefan by a fellow prisoner. As only art can and with the candor of dark prison humor, it speaks to the complex double-bind of doing no harm, while assisting the SS and saving lives in Auschwitz. The full image appears and is discussed here publicly for the first time.

To Stefan's great-grandchildren:

Evelyn, Charlotte, Eleanor, and Katherine,

the fourth generation.

CONTENTS

PREFACE

My father had a tattoo. It was a faint blue line on his left forearm, 20526. Growing up in Germany, I saw that many adults around me also had a tattoo. My parents and I were displaced persons stranded outside of Poland in the British occupation zone of Germany. I spoke Polish at home and German in school. I knew the term "DP" ("Displaced Persons") and I knew that we weren't really "home," that we lived, as the Poles would say, "outside the border." Many DPs were scattering, moving away from Germany. I was not at all aware of the difference between those DPs with tattoos who were Roman Catholic and those with tattoos who were Jewish.

My father, Stefan Budziaszek, was a doctor and my mother, Ewa Irena, was a nurse. They met and married in the chaos of postwar Germany in 1945 and their marriage had disintegrated by 1954. It was perhaps not an uncommon event, but it represented an enormous break in my life. Both parents immediately remarried and my mother and I and my step-father, Jerzy Kujawski, left Germany for Sweden and three years later, in 1957, for the United States. My father married a German Jewish woman, had a son, Stevie, and stayed in Germany. I didn't see him again or meet his new family until I was 19, a student at Stanford University, and traveling back to Germany for the first time.

He still had the tattoo and I now knew that meant he had been a prisoner in a concentration camp. It was accepted and not a matter for discussion, even in the family. Neither he nor his friends talked about those years. It was much like other veterans of other wars: it was better not to bring it up. It was not until 2002, some eight years after my father's death in 1994, when I received a large carton of documents from Germany, that I had access to any information about those war years. By now I was a historian. Since I am a native speaker of both Polish and German, I specialized in Central European history. But I had no research agenda that dwelled on Auschwitz. In the United States, when I mentioned the tattoo and Auschwitz, I had to repeatedly explain that yes, my father had been in Auschwitz, and, no, he didn't die there. No, we were not Jews, and yes, many other non-Jews were also in the concentration camps.

The terms "Holocaust" and "genocide" were now in wide currency. The enormity of the Jewish Shoah became the subject of intense study. Scholars listened to Holocaust survivors and documented their stories. There was not, however, a collective noun for non-Jewish survivors or victims. There still is not. Those Holocaust survivors who formed families raised children who were identified as "second generation" victims, as in Art Spiegelman's graphic novel, *Maus.* I also belong to a second generation, but I do not share in the level of trauma of the Jewish cohort. Non-Jewish victims of Nazi atrocities are only labeled by their nation: Poles, Dutch, French, and so on, and thus were subsumed by a political identity.

I found a deeply fascinating document among my father's papers: a transcript of his oral testimony to the museum and research center established in Auschwitz after the war. This was the first time that I had access to a coherent narrative of his war experiences, and I found it startling and exciting on many levels. First, it was part of my family history and formed the subtext to my upbringing. Second, it was a primary historical document, a rare and valuable source to a working historian. Third, it was like nothing that I could have imagined. Here was the full story of political intrigue, of arrests and beatings, of transfer to the notorious death site, Auschwitz, of some place called "Buna," of improbable achievements, and finally of rescue and survival. I was determined to translate this Polish document into English, a language that my children could read, so they could share this story.

I am thus writing for the third generation of survivors. As a historian I am familiar with the context of the war and its perpetrators and understand the rise of Nazis in Germany and the vast cast of characters involved. But I quickly realized that my third generation children and their compatriots do not have any great familiarity with this information. The names and places and details of my father Stefan's story needed a context.

Who were these Nazis and why did they attack Poland? What was their attitude toward Slavs? Why did they arrest educated people? Why would a world-famous German company decide to build a factory near Auschwitz? Who were the Auschwitz inmates? Who were the jailors? Who were the prisoners? How was Auschwitz managed? Why did conditions in Auschwitz change? What is the difference between a labor camp and an extermination camp? How was Auschwitz different for Jewish inmates? How was it possible to survive what more than one survivor called the *anus mundi*? Fundamentally, was Stefan's story verifiable? Who could substantiate his narrative?

Many of my stereotypical assumptions about Auschwitz were shattered as I assimilated Stefan's story. Fundamentally, Auschwitz was a political prison and a labor camp. It was not planned with gas chambers and crematoria; those instruments of genocide developed over time. Stefan and his fellow long-term prisoners were distinct from the vast multitude of Jewish families swept up across Europe and shipped to Auschwitz to be exterminated. Prison laborers, both gentile and Jewish, had to deal with quotidian details: food, shelter, clothing, health, fellow prisoners, and jobs. Skills mattered, giving working prisoners a level of agency in a brutal system. Nazis used prisoners who were carpenters or electricians to build the camps. They also used prisoners who were doctors to deal with injuries and diseases.

Only one piece of paper survived from my father's long imprisonment in Auschwitz. I found it in the green file folder labeled

"20526," his Auschwitz number. It is a small, stiff piece of paper, a hand-lettered greeting card from the camp carpenters, to honor Stefan's name-day celebration. It is the equivalent of a "Hallmark" production. In Auschwitz? In the death camp? I realized that I had a lot to learn about what it meant to be a long-term prisoner. Who were these carpenters and why were they sending Stefan a card? Who had the time, energy and supplies to provide this card? Was there a party?

The story of the prisoner hospital in the third large camp built in Auschwitz, the Buna camp, exists within a complex history. Prisoners not only managed to survive enormous privations in Auschwitz, but they also exhibited vigorous agency to protect one another. My children and grandchildren and others who might venture to read this story are not likely to be historians. I hope that I have provided them, the third and fourth generation, with enough detail that they can understand the forces which disrupted so many lives in the middle of the twentieth century.

INTRODUCTION

Some seventy years have passed since the collapse of Adolf Hitler's Third Reich. Allied soldiers forced open the gates of concentration camps in 1945, liberating a dazed and traumatized group of surviving prisoners into civil society. Jew and gentile, they emerged into a Europe indifferent to their suffering. Everyone had suffered and they were not seen as unique. Jewish victims told their individual stories over a decade before they became defined as the collective experience of Shoah, the Holocaust. The assembly of painful eyewitness stories such as those of Primo Levi, Elie Wiesel, or Olga Lengyel defined an event whose horror seemed only manageable by using the vocabulary of an apocalypse. The glare of an atomic explosion in Japan and its mushroom clouds was matched by the glare of the cauldrons of extermination camps and their billows of crematoria smoke.

Dazed by the stories of the Holocaust, its witnesses and its historians engaged in a form of history called presentism in which the historical context of the event is lost.[1] The late European historian Tony Judt called this "layers of mis-memory."[2] Marci Shore, an intellectual historian, refers to the collapse of a historical event such as this into a single narrative as the teleological deceptions of retrospect.[3] This is the argument that hindsight, knowing the outcome of an event, obscures the ambiguities and confusion of the actual historical process. Amos Tversky, the prominent behavioral economist and cognitive psychologist, points out that this is a cognitive bias all historians face. They know the outcome and create confident and neat stories. This obscures the chaos and uncertainties of the event itself.[4] Once survivors and witnesses understood the dimensions of the Shoah, the Holocaust, they began explaining the events in the camps only in terms of genocide. It is as if the possible narratives of Nazi atrocities collapsed into the dominant vision of extermination that drove other possible narratives into the shadows. The result is a loss of the full dimension of the Nazi camps. Morris Dickstein, a cultural historian, expressed the dilemma: "Many writers took their inspiration from philosopher Theodor Adorno's dictum that to write poetry after Auschwitz is barbaric. They are convinced that the enormity of the Holocaust opened up a rift in human consciousness that cannot be bridged by conventional forms of discourse."[5]

Yet this void, this rift in the historical narrative, is being filled through the patient work of historians who are reconstructing the historical context of both the Jewish and gentile experiences. Dickstein, reviewing the twenty-first-century text *Rethinking the Holocaust*,[6] states that Shoah scholar Yehuda Bauer's writing is "altogether free from the fear and trembling of those who approach the subject in the spirit of Adorno or Wiesel."[7] Far from diminishing the significance of the Holocaust, a wider scrutiny adds to our understanding.

A historical analysis should reject a view of the Nazi Holocaust as sui generis and provide instead a context for the acute episode of the Holocaust (the concentration camps and the extermination camps) within the history of the Third Reich's utilitarian labor needs and its policies for terrorizing enemies. This applies equally to the *Altreich,* the "old Germany," and to the conquered territories. Concentration camp survivor and historian Tadeusz Dębski is blunt: "the Camps were an organizational tool, intended to serve many purposes. Had Hitler realized some of his terrifying dreams and killed all Jews in Germany and the conquered countries, the Camps would not have disappeared. They would have continued to contain the enemies of the Nazis, function as a new kind of school to teach the populations of the conquered countries obedience, and house a great reservoir of slave workers who could be used everywhere according to the needs of the state."[8] The concentration camps were central to the issues of terror and labor.[9] Incarceration and survival were as real as the fact of genocide, and survivors and victims deserve to have their experiences made known.

This historical approach to the Auschwitz concentration camps in particular is evident in Yehuda Bauer's work, as well as in current German research from the *Institut für Zeitgeschichte.*[10] Post-Cold War archival research provides social history perspectives to understand such organizations as the Auschwitz camps. This research about the creation of the concentration camps, their growth, and their relationship to Nazi labor policies provides notable contributions to the extensive Auschwitz literature. There was a twisted logic in Nazi labor policies, their use of slave labor, and the camp system.

The work I am presenting is a contribution to the social history of long-term prisoners in Auschwitz, particularly the medical workers in the Auschwitz III camp, Buna-Monowitz. These are the men who spent years surviving the prison and labor camp system of the Third Reich, unlike those millions of men, women and children who were murdered in extermination sites at the time of their arrival.[11] The insightful chronicler of the Auschwitz experience, the prisoner Hermann Langbein, writes in the introduction to Tibor Wohl's book, *Arbeit Macht tot*: "Every prisoner saw [Auschwitz] from his own, unique point of view. Therefore each report functions like a single stone in a mosaic. From all of them together we can create an approximate picture of the reality that was the Auschwitz extermination camp. No one can ever understand it fully—and that is good."[12]

To examine how long-term prisoners understood and manipulated their prison experiences, I will use an oral history collected in 1974.[13] Tadeusz Iwaszko interviewed Dr. Stefan Buthner (Budziaszek) (1913–1994) on behalf of the Auschwitz Museum (*Archiwum Państwowego Muzeum w Oświęcimiu*) as part of the museum's effort to collect the memories of survivors. This oral history speaks of one man's survival: his June 1941 arrest by the SS, his imprisonment in the Krakow Montelupich prison, his February 1942 transfer to Auschwitz I, his labor at the Buna factory, his September 1942 transfer to the Jawischowitz labor subcamp, his June 1943 transfer to the new Auschwitz III-Monowitz camp, the January 1945 evacuation of Auschwitz to KL Buchenwald, and his immediate postwar experience.

Stefan's testimony is published here intact, with no transpositions or deletions. The flow of memories is chronological, but it is neither systematic nor organized. His testimony is more than stream-of-consciousness, but he does not remember his experiences in order. He has clearly been prompted by his interviewer to remember as many people as possible. Stefan circles around some difficult and tense topics—his conflicts with other prisoner groups, hospital selection events—and returns to them numerous times.

Stefan's most significant experience took place in the Auschwitz III-Monowitz camp, a labor camp. For 19 months, he was the senior prisoner in charge of its prisoner hospital. This hospital served to maintain the working capability of the slave force used by the IG Farben Corporation to build a huge industrial complex. This factory was expected to produce synthetic fuel and a synthetic rubber, known as Buna, for the German war effort. In 1943 prisoners reorganized an existing camp clinic into a hospital which protected them from some of the effects of injuries, disease, and concentration camp terror. Over forty physicians from various European countries, Jews and gentiles, worked to create an oasis in the Buna-Monowitz hospital amid the tempest of the labor camp. Stefan's experiences shed light on the role of chance as well as the strategies of survival which served him and many others. As the German war effort churned forward and created unprecedented demands on forced and slave labor, the Nazi leadership instituted changes in the camp system. Random killings and beatings were curbed. New SS physicians were installed to prevent heavy labor losses. The impact on Buna-Monowitz is clear, and these administrative changes are part of the story of survival as well. More than

30,000 men entered the KL Auschwitz III-Monowitz camp. That nearly a third of them survived the brutal conditions was due in part to the efforts of physicians at the camp hospital. The physicians provided medical aid and creatively manipulated the available resources.

"Auschwitz" cannot be a catch-all for the varied experiences of all of its victims. Auschwitz was part of the huge SS-managed labor camp system that exploited captive people. Prisoners in the labor camps had to negotiate a complex set of interactions and often treacherous conflicts. As Auschwitz grew and its economic potential looked limitless, well-established German corporations like Krupp and IG Farbenindustrie settled around Auschwitz in order to use their prisoners as workers. The interaction between the demands of the factory owners and the SS authorities running the labor camps influenced the chances for a prisoner worker's survival. In 1940 the original camp, Auschwitz I, had been planned for 10,000 prisoners. In March 1942 the far larger Auschwitz II camp, Birkenau (first planned for 100,000), was operative and Auschwitz III, Buna-Monowitz (10,000 more), designated solely for the use of the Buna factory was almost finished. All of them were work camps, but each had unique characteristics and dangers. Prisoners were always in danger from starvation, disease, or random violence, but Auschwitz II, Birkenau is notorious as the extermination site of hundreds of thousands genocide victims.

"Auschwitz" was also a long-term prison for criminal and political offenders. Many of the criminals had the advantage of earlier experiences of prison life; the political prisoners, on the other hand, had to adapt to prison culture, and adapt quickly, to survive. Prisoners wore colored triangles on their shirts to distinguish them. They struggled among themselves for influence: the greatest tension developed between "greens" (green triangles on their shirts denoted criminal prisoners) and "reds" (red triangles denoted political prisoners). Furthermore, the "reds" competed with each other since they consisted of rival political groups: Polish socialists, communists, and nationalists. After the war, this struggle becomes interpreted by some as part of a racial story. Many communist political prisoners were Jews and some of them later interpreted camp struggles not as political battles but as antisemitism.

As the war expanded to the Soviet Union in 1941, the camps took on the functions of extermination sites. Concentration camp historian Nikolaus Wachsmann states that as deadly as the camps were, "No KL was designated as a place for killing large numbers of Jews until 1942."[14] While Nazi German squads, *Einsatzgruppen,* murdered Jews in the Soviet-held territories, Polish ghetto Jews and Jews from occupied Europe were shipped in boxcars to the extermination sites. Auschwitz gas chambers and crematoria are the emblem of a wide-ranging Holocaust.

For those who were selected for work, the "Auschwitz" story is the complex interaction of labor issues, its availability and cost; the surprising relationship of German big business leaders and the SS leaders; "Auschwitz" as a prison for criminals as well as for political prisoners; competition among groups in Auschwitz; and institutional changes in the camp itself across time. Prisoners rarely knew about changes at higher levels and could exert virtually no influence to protect themselves from institutional changes.

Holocaust literature centered on Auschwitz has on the whole emphasized the fate of nearly one million Jews who never made it past the ramp. Danuta Czech, a researcher in the *Oświęcim Muzeum,* compiled the daily events of the main camp in the prodigious *Auschwitz Chronicle, 1939–1945.* It makes clear that prisoners were lost to disease, maltreatment, and murder in Auschwitz. However, there were survivors.

Just what are the parameters that allowed tens of thousands to become "long-term" prisoners who survived the first three months? The following conditions appear to be critical: finding a support system in the camp (such as fellow nationals); securing a job useful to the camp (so-called *Funktionshäftlinge*); maintaining contact with the outside (such as with letters or food packages); defining the concentration experience as a war effort (resistance to Germans); having passable understanding of the camp languages (Polish, since most of the early prisoners were Poles, and German); having had a previous experience of regimentation to lessen the shock of camp life (military service, previous imprisonment); and adjusting to the loss of one's prewar "self" in order to adapt to the roles and norms of prison culture.[15]

Even if one were lucky enough to find friends, maintain contact with family, find a job as perhaps a shoemaker or a surgeon, and learn to deal with the chaos of camp life, one still faced the threat of typhus, an enraged SS man with a gun, physical and psychological exhaustion, and just plain bad luck. No repertoire of behaviors could guarantee survival, but hundreds of thousands managed to survive the gauntlet of the concentration camps. This number is dwarfed by the legions of victims who had no opportunity, no strategy, and no power to escape the walk into the gas chambers.

NOTES

1. Jonathan Clark, *Our Shadowed Present* (Stanford: Stanford University Press, 2004), 2.
2. Tony Judt, *Postwar: A History of Europe Since 1945* (New York: Penguin Books, 2005), 821.
3. Marci Shore, "The Jewish Hero History Forgot," *The New York Times*, April 18, 2013.
4. Michael Lewis, *The Undoing Project: A Friendship That Changed Our Minds* (New York: W. W. Norton and Co., 2017), 206–08.
5. Morris Dickstein, "Sounds of Silence," *The New York Times Book Review*, January 28, 2001, 10.
6. Yehuda Bauer, *Rethinking the Holocaust* (New Haven: Yale University Press, 2001).
7. Dickstein, "Sounds of Silence," 10.
8. Tadeusz Debski, *A Battlefield of Ideas: Nazi Concentration Camps and Their Polish Prisoners* (Boulder, East European Monographs, 2001), 11.
9. The term in German is *Konzentrationslager*, abbreviated KL in German and often KZ in Polish. *Vernichtungslager* is the mid-1941 transformation of the designated camps into extermination sites.

10. The following two are relevant publications from the *Institut für Zeitgeschichte:* Sybille Steinbacher *"Musterstadt" Auschwitz: Germanisierungspolitik und Judenmord in Oberschlesien* (Munich: KG Saur Verlag, 2000); and Bernd C. Wagner, *IG Auschwitz: Zwangsarbeit und Vernichtung von Häftlingen des Lagers Monowitz 1941–1945* (Munich: KG Saur Verlag, 2000).
11. I will additionally use excerpts from several first-person narratives of prisoners in Auschwitz who survived their long incarcerations: Czesław Wincenty Jaworski, *Apel Skazanych: wspomnienia z Oświęcimia* [*Roll Call of the Condemned: Memories of Auschwitz*] (Warsaw: Instytut Wydawniczy PAX, 1962); Antoni Makowski, *Organization, Entwicklung und Tätigkeit des Häftlingskrankenbau in Monowitz* (*KL Auschwitz III*) [Organization, Development and Function of the Prisoner Hospital in Monowitz-KL Auschwitz III], in *Hefte von Auschwitz* 15 (1975) 113–81; Mieczysław Zając, *Powrót Niepożądany* [No Return Required] (Krakow: Wydawnictro Literackie, 1986); Tibor Wohl, *Arbeit Macht tot: Eine Jugend in Auschwitz.* [Work Kills. Youth in Auschwitz] (Frankfurt am Main: Fischer Verlag, 1990). I will also use works in English by such well known figures as Primo Levi, Elie Wiesel, Olga Lengyel, and Imre Kertesz. However, they did not arrive in Auschwitz until 1944.
12. Wohl, *Arbeit Macht tot,* 9. Wohl's title is a play on the iconic camp gate "Arbeit macht frei." Wohl is saying that in Auschwitz work kills you.
13. I have translated the text of the Auschwitz statement from Polish. All other translation from both Polish and German texts are also my own. I received the Auschwitz interview in 2002. The document bears the Oświęcim Museum file # IV–8520–227/4091/73.
14. Nikolaus Wachsmann, *KL: A History of the Nazi Concentration Camps* (New York: Farrar, Straus and Giroux, 2015), 288.
15. Ewa Bacon, "The Other Auschwitz Prisoners: Long Term Survival at KL Auschwitz III," in *Emerging Issues in Holocaust Education*, edited by Kathleen McShary (Seton Hill University National Center for Holocaust Education: 2010), 161–87.

1

1939: GERMANIZATION

All is mine, but nothing owned,
Nothing owned for memory,
And mine only while I look.

Wszystko moje, nic własnością
nic własnością dla pamięci,
A moje, dopóki patrzę[1]

In the late eighteenth century the Kingdom of Poland failed as a state. It had neither the resources nor the will to oppose the takeover by three predatory empires. In 1772 Catherine the Great of Russia, Frederick the Great of Prussia, and Maria Theresia, the Habsburg empress of Austria, started the partitioning of Poland. Poland ceased to exist as an independent political state in 1795. The Polish community was now divided by the government and language of either Prussia (Germany after 1871), Russia, or Austria (Austro-Hungary after 1867). Various attempts in the nineteenth century to reconstitute the Polish nation failed. It was not until World War I, the defeat of Germany, and the 1917 Russian revolutions that Poles could hope for a state of their own. This hope was realized during the Paris Peace Conference, when Poland was recognized as an independent state. The rubble of the Austro-Hungarian Empire also saw the creation of Czechoslovakia, Hungary, and Yugoslavia by the peace-makers. The new states of Central Europe faced formidable problems, the most severe of which was the Great Depression of 1929.

Imperial Germany was replaced by the German Weimar Republic. Under Friedrich Ebert, it became a parliamentary republic led by the Social Democratic Party. This disappointed the hopes of German communists on the left as well as the stalwart right-wingers outraged by the dissolution of the German Empire. The temporary formation of a Soviet Republic in Munich galvanized the extreme right-wing groups. Paramilitary groups like the *Freikorp* resorted to violence and joined new political parties such as the National Socialist Workers Party. The new German state appeared doomed by hyperinflation between 1921 and 1923, a 1923 attempted takeover of Munich by the Nazis, and 1927 Berlin street fighting between the Nazi paramilitary wing, the *Sturmabteilung* (SA) and the communists.

However, the Weimar Republic also experienced both civic and fiscal stability between 1923 and 1929. Both employers and workers benefited from a revived and productive economy. German industrial dominance in the nineteenth century's "second industrial revolution," in both chemicals and steel production, was laid low by World War I, but recovered smartly. The currency was stabilized and war reparations benefited from the 1924 Dawes plan—a loan agreement between US banks and the Weimar Republic. The capital, Berlin, experienced an explosion of avant-garde creativity. Jazz, the American import, delighted hip Berliners and outraged staid traditionalists. The flapper's makeup and racy short skirt, public smoking, and the outre cafes and cabarets offended some. However, Berlin became a destination for Europeans and Americans who wanted to hear Josephine Baker perform in Berlin in 1925 or see a new Bertold Brecht play. Architectural enthusiasts came to admire the new Bauhaus style or to find a canvas by prewar German expressionists of the *Blaue Reiter* school.

Nothing could have prepared Germany—or for that matter capitalist states—for the debacle created by the October 1929 Wall Street stock market crash. Germany was especially hard hit since its economy was closely linked to US banks. As Americans catastrophically demanded swift loan repayments, the German economy could not maintain normal employment levels. Within a year of the crash, unemployment rose to 15.9% and topped 30.8% in mid-1932. Germans began voting for right-wing parties which promised a restoration of German dignity as well as jobs. In 1933 Adolf Hitler and the Nazi party won a plurality of the votes and Hitler edged into the chancellorship. The Nazis promised a new kind of Germany. Hitler delivered this new state by dismantling the Weimar Republic and creating a fascist and racist dictatorship in short order, the Third Reich. He re-armed the German army, contrary to the Versailles accord, and challenged Europe by systematically dismantling peace provisions as well as the new map of Europe. By 1938 Austria and portions of Czechoslovakia were incorporated into Hitler's Third Reich. He then set his sights on the lost eastern provinces: the new western portions of Poland. The Allies of World War I guaranteed the new borders they had drawn in Central Europe, so Hitler anticipated a war with France and England. What he wanted to avoid was a two-front war, fighting to the west and the east, which he saw as the critical German error in World War I. To have a free hand in Poland, Hitler approached the Soviet Union. Fascists and communists were sworn ideological enemies. However, Josef Stalin, the leader of the USSR, had given up hope that the democratic states had the fortitude to resist Hitler. Stalin decided that he could protect the USSR best by allying himself with Hitler.

When the Soviet Russians and the Nazi Germans stunned the world with their August 1939 Non-Aggression Pact, they were negating the vision of Europe developed at the Versailles Peace Conference. In 1939, "new" Europe was returning to an older map: the Polish state would disappear again. The invasion of Poland by Germany on September 1, 1939, ended—from the German-Austrian point of view—the anomaly of good Prussian and Silesian land and people under Polish administration. Wachsmann refers to the German invasion of Poland as Hitler's first racial war. Special troops consisting of SS men and police forces followed the army. They targeted "politicians, state officials, priests, and noblemen as well as local Jews."[2] Tens of thousands of Poles fell victim to this early rampage. Germans cultivated a negative stereotype of Poles. They were labeled as "sly, brutal, primitive; along with Jews, they posed the greatest danger to Germany." Poles were now seen as a race of Slavs, inferior to the race of Aryans.[3]

The Germans wanted to identify German-Aryan folk among the masses of inferior Slavic stock. Ethnic Germans could sign a list, the *Volksliste*, to differentiate themselves from the Slavic masses and, of course, the Jewish Polish minority. These *Volksdeutsche* would become a new privileged group. Looking at the newly Germanized city of Auschwitz, Polish Oświęcim, the director of the Schlesien-Benzin enterprise stated: "Culturally and in terms of civilization this region is totally open. Each German who comes here is therefore a colonist."[4] In order to fulfill the economic potential of the new acquisition, they needed only to remove the natives.

This fourth partition of Poland in 1939 added 20 million people to the German Reich, 1.7 million of whom were Jews. The new Nazi political administration of Polish territories distinguished between territories previously ruled by Germany or Austria and the rest of the Polish state created at the negotiation tables at Versailles and League of Nations plebiscites. German Upper Silesia was joined by four new administrative units: the new East Upper Silesia, the Eastern Zone (which included Auschwitz), Warthel-and, and Danzig-West Prussia. The city of Krakow remained part of the "General Gouvernament," the remnant of the Polish state, now under German administration.[5] The Soviet Union seized the eastern remnant of Poland.

By the turn of the twentieth century the provincial town of Auschwitz was already developing strongly, thanks to its favorable location as a railroad junction: among other railroads, the three lines of the Emperor Ferdinand Northern Railway connected Krakow, the coal mining town of Katowice, with the imperial capital, Vienna. This was the new industrial belt of Upper Silesia. It would become an important economic region for interwar Poland and an attractive target for Hitler. Newly annexed to the Third Reich in 1939, Auschwitz became a desirable location for German corporations seeking to integrate these new territories into the German economy. Hitler himself was open about his vision of the German expansion eastward (*der Drang nach Osten*). By 1939 Hitler had already absorbed Czechoslovakia and Austria and thereby created the Great Germany (*Großdeutschland*), which Otto von Bismarck, the chancellor of the Wilhelmine Empire, had rejected as untenable in the nineteenth century.

After September 1939, Poles in the new German provinces and districts which had been Western Poland for the previous twenty-odd years were faced with aggressive German policies to create a racially pure Aryan state. Germans had decided to expel all Jews and most Poles and resettle the territories with Germans and with local *Volksdeutsche*. Early in October 1939, Hitler placed Heinrich Himmler in charge of this transformation. The new East Upper Silesia proved easier to Germanize than the Eastern Zone, which had become almost exclusively Polish and Jewish in the twentieth century.[6] Together, the newly reclaimed territories fulfilled Hitler's promise to Germans to reverse the territorial losses of World War I and to expand Germany eastward—the promise of a new *Lebensraum*, the notion of German manifest destiny.

The Polish army was not capable of defending Poland—and its diplomatic agreements with friendly states failed to bring aid. The German occupation of Poland reawakened among Poles a sense of their historic mission to resist the German and Russian occupiers. This historic mission and the idea of a Catholic Polish state was the creation of nineteenth-century Polish romantic nationalists. This vision of Poland inspired the ardor of young Poles to create a resistance movement in 1939 against the occupation, and Polish university students became active in a host of clandestine organizations. In 1940, resistance fighters pledged themselves to fight the Nazis with the following oath:

> In the presence of the Almighty God, the most sacred Holy Mother Mary, the royal crown of Poland, I place my hand on the Holy Cross, the symbol of suffering and redemption, and

> swear, that I'll be true to and faithful to Poland's honor, and that I will fight with all my strength and to the death to free her from captivity. I will obey all orders from the organization and guard its secrets.[7]

One young man reciting this oath was a second-year student of chemistry at the University in Krakow, Mieczysław Zając. Just before the outbreak of the war, the message he heard at school was, "If the Germans attack, don't forget they are our eternal enemies."[8] For these young men, and tens of thousands like them, the struggle during the occupation had an overwhelmingly political and historic character. Poles saw that they were being incarcerated and shot by Nazis as part of the policy to destroy the leaders of interwar Poland, even as they also witnessed the German's bestial attitude toward Polish Jews.

The German occupation was carried out in the first instance by the military. Within weeks after the collapse of the Polish state, German civilian administrators followed. German bureaucrats swiftly organized the newly annexed territories of (*Gaus*) Danzig-West Prussia, the Wartheland, and Upper Silesia, as well as the Polish state remnant, the General Gouvernament. Historian Mary Fulbrook's *A Small Town near Auschwitz* is a detailed look at the German administration on the level of county government, with a focus on the career of the *Landrat* Udo Klausa. As early as November 12, 1939, the directive addressing *Landräte* in the Warthegau stated that all Jews should be deported to effect the *Judenrein* (clearance of Jews) objective. Additionally there were unresolved questions about the Polish population as the Germans tried to identify the *Volksdeutsche,* ethnic Germans. However, one category of Poles subject to immediate control was those "who either belong to the intelligentsia or who, by virtue of their Polish national ties, might represent a danger for the instigation and establishment of Germanness."[9] The term "intelligentsia" in the context of Eastern European societies identified a specific social class (about 10%): those with university education, leaders in the artistic community, and those whom we could call public intellectuals today.[10] This sweeping category encompassed not only the politically active, but also all potential opponents to the Nazi agenda.

In 1939, the SS had the authority "to murder members of the intelligentsia, the clergy, the nobility as well as Jews and the mentally ill."[11] Their systematic roundups instituted a rule by terror. The collapse of the Polish state had been sudden, but the collapse of independent Polish identity did not follow suit. The terror quickly encompassed the Polish Jewish community. United by their synagogues, neighborhoods, and schools, Jewish communities convulsed under the early impact of deportations, street terror, and the loss of homes, work, and property. On November 19, 1939, the Nazis ordered prominent Jews to organize into local councils designed to carry out German directives. The *Judenräte* were to provide housing and food, culture, and education for Jews.[12] These Jewish councils began frantic efforts to appease the unappeasable German regime.

The rule of terror extended to Polish civil society, because Poles needed to be convinced that they were an inferior race suitable only as a workforce in a new expanded German state. Poles refused to speak German and did not acknowledge the superiority of German culture. Fulbrook quotes an implausible German police report of June 9, 1940 from Sosnowicz, just north of Auschwitz: "A people with such a low level of culture as the Polish are not worthy of gentle treatment . . . the Polish subhuman species [*Untermenschen*] still has at its disposal innumerable weapons, and uses these ruthlessly."[13] Thus, reasoned the police, the Poles must be ruled with iron fists.

The regular German army, the *Wehrmacht,* overran Poland in the *Blitzkrieg* of 1939. However, the subjugation of the population was under the purview of a special organization, the *Schutzstaffel,* the SS. In their intimidating uniforms, often jack booted and in sinister black, always with the two lightning bolt insignias, the men of the SS stood for terror in the Third Reich. At the outset of the Nazi state, the SS were Hitler's personal body guards. Heinrich Himmler was instrumental in the growth of the SS and had convinced Hitler to declare the SS a clandestine, highly elite military organization in

1938. As the German state expanded, the SS's parent organization, the Reich Security Main Office, grew enormously and was in charge of intelligence gathering, the Gestapo (the German secret police), the concentration camps, and the extermination camps.[14]

The resistance movement which developed in Poland was fraught with confusion. Prewar Polish political parties ranged from the Christian Democratic Labor Party, the strong urban National Democratic Party, and the anti-Soviet Polish Socialist Party. The Poles formed a government-in-exile which ended up in London after the fall of France in June 1940. Władysław Sikorski assumed command of Polish affairs. But how to coordinate groups working in Poland? The political infighting of the prewar years did not end. Numerous spontaneous and poorly led anti-Nazi groups formed with fanciful names like the "White Eagles" and the "Musketeers."[15] These rivalries would impact the lives of camp prisoners. Sikorski formed an umbrella organization for the resistance movements: the *Armja Krajowa*, the AK, the home army.

The Poles, then, were at war with the Germans. Poles were arrested, beaten, tortured, jailed, and finally sent off to prisons and camps like Auschwitz. Poles were shot in the streets, hung from lampposts, subjected to lethal injections, and starved. The attack on educated Poles was relentless: 45% of Polish physicians and dentists, 40% of university professors, 57% of attorneys, 30% of technicians, 25% of Catholic priests, and more than half of opinion makers and journalists were arrested by the Nazis.[16] In the month of September 1939 alone, 16,000 Poles were executed.[17] For many of the long-term prisoners, the war and the German occupation, not racist ideology, were the salient characteristics of the conflict and the reason for their imprisonment.

In August 1942, resistance fighter Mieczysław Zając, the college chemistry student, learned of Sikorski's reorganization of the resistance into the AK. On the ground in Krakow, however, these organizational changes did not protect individual resistance fighters or even ordinary citizens. Zając reports: "In the city, the Gestapo raged. They [were] busy arresting the intelligentsia: doctors, lawyers, and retired military officers. Sometime in the middle of April [1942] about 200 people were arrested at the Plastyków Café. Some dozen were shot at Montelupich [prison] and the rest were shipped to Auschwitz."[18] Danuta Czech reports that the Auschwitz log for April 24, 1942, reads: "198 prisoners were sent by the Sipo and SD from Montelupich Prison . . . These inmates were arrested in Krakow Artists' Café at 3 Łobzowska Street on April 16, 1942. The 198 detainees include artists, painters, actors, etc. They are arrested in retaliation for the attack on a high-level SS commander at the Krakow airport."[19] The Auschwitz chronicle for May 27, 1942, reads: "168 prisoners are shot at the execution wall in the courtyard of block 11. They belong to a group of painters, artists, and actors who were arrested on April 16 . . . and sent to Auschwitz on April 24 and 25 . . . The prisoners are taken to the courtyard four at a time and shot. The block senior utters the following sentence: 'For the murder of the head of the Luftwaffe in Krakow, you are condemned to death.' Then they are killed with individual shots from a small-caliber weapon. Present at the execution are the Director of the Political Department [the camp Gestapo unit], Maximilian Grabner, Protective Custody Commander Hans Aumeier, and the Labor Deployment Director, Heinrich Schwarz."[20] Poles were witnessing the destruction of their society.

NOTES

1. Wisława Szymborska, *Sounds, Feelings, Thoughts: Seventy Poems by Wisława Szymborska*, translated by Magnus J. Krynski and Robert A. Maguire (Princeton University Press, 1981), 42–43.
2. Wachsmann, *KL*, 192.
3. Ulrich Herbert, *Hitler's Foreign Worker* (New York: Cambridge University Press, 1997), 69.
4. Wagner, *IG Auschwitz*, 45.
5. Sybille Steinbacher, *Auschwitz, A History* (New York: Harper Collins, 2005), 18.
6. Ibid., 20.
7. Zając, *Powrót Niepożądany*, 43.

8. "*Jeżeli Niemcy napadną na nas, nie zapominajcie, że jest to odwieczny nasz wróg.*" Zając, 12.
9. Mary Fulbrook, *A Small Town near Auschwitz* (Oxford University Press, 2012), 81.
10. Alicja Iwańka, *Polish Intelligentsia in Nazi Concentration Camps and American Exile* (Lewiston, NY: The Edwin Mellon Press, 1998), 7.
11. Peter Longerich, *Holocaust: The Nazi Persecution and Murder of the Jews* (Oxford University Press, 2010), 144.
12. Ibid., 161.
13. Fulbrook, *A Small Town near Auschwitz*, 102.
14. Michael Wildt, *An Uncompromising Generation* (Madison: University of Wisconsin Press, 2009), 131. See also Rudolph Höss, *Death Dealer: The Memoirs of the SS Kommandant at Auschwitz,* edited by Steven Paskuly (Buffalo, NY: Prometheus Books, 1996), 171n4.
15. Richard Lukas, editor, *Forgotten Survivors: Polish Christians Remember the Nazi Occupation* (Lawrence, Kansas: University Press of Kansas, 2004), 53.
16. Ibid., 5.
17. Longerich, *Holocaust*, 144.
18. Zając, *Powrót Niepożądany*, 55. Zając was captured in mid-1942 and sent to Montelupich Prison.
19. Danuta Czech, *Auschwitz Chronicle 1939–1945* (New York: Henry Holt, 1997), 159.
20. Ibid., 171.

2

STEFAN'S ARREST AND MONTELUPICH PRISON

Threatened
By his own non-existence
From all sides
At every instant.

Narażony
za nieobecność swoją
zewsząd
A każdej chwili.[1]

Stefan Budziaszek was born in January 1913 in Andrychów, a small Austro-Hungarian town between Krakow and Oświęcim (Auschwitz) in the province of Galicia. His father, Florian, was employed by the imperial and royal railroad and served in the Austro-Hungarian army in World War I. Florian Budziaszek and his Polish contemporaries benefited from the 1866 statute which gave Galicia extensive rights of self-government, including the right to have school taught in the Polish language.[2] By the time Stefan entered elementary school, he and his brothers and sister were Polish citizens in a new state negotiated into existence at the peace conferences of World War I. The old German empire of William II ceded its eastern provinces to become the western portion of the new Poland. To the south, the defunct Austro-Hungarian empire surrendered Galicia to the Poles. The Russian empire had collapsed before the war's end. Its Soviet successor state was unable to hold its Polish-speaking regions and these lands became eastern Poland. By 1939 Stefan had completed medical school at the Jagiellonian University in Krakow and was working at the St. Lazarus clinic in Krakow. Like many of his contemporaries, especially university graduates, he felt threatened by Nazi roundups. And like many patriotic young men, he joined groups which expressed anti-Nazi sentiments, read underground newspapers, and listened to clandestine broadcasts from the West.

In May and June of 1941 the Gestapo was particularly active, arresting identified and suspected members of the resistance in Krakow. In Stefan's 1974 oral statement to the Oświęcim Museum, he describes the crisis point that led to his arrest. He was by no means a prominent member of the local resistance, but he was sufficiently engaged to provide himself with an alternative name to protect his identity. The use of pseudonyms was a common strategy. Zając switched his own several times. Stefan wrote a far more detailed report on his arrest in 1949 (see appendix). The problem with remembering pseudonyms is keeping the language straight. He remembered calling himself "Szewc," the Polish word for shoemaker, but in 1949 he remembered it as "Szuster," the German word, in Polish spelling. Stefan relates how he was under increasing surveillance and finally hunted by the Nazi authorities:

> I was arrested on June 21, 1941, in Krosno. I was hiding in Krosno under the false name Mieczysław Szewc. I fled Krakow and hid in Krosno fearing arrest by the [Nazi] authorities. I escaped at virtually the last possible moment. While working at the clinic of St. Lazarus in Krakow I was told that the Gestapo was looking for me. As soon as I heard, I immediately ran through the garden and managed to reach Grzegòrzecka Street. Having been outed in Krakow, I had to leave the city quickly and was helped by a surgeon in Krakow (whose name I can't remember right now) who drove me to Krosno by car.

The Gestapo were targeting social networks, as Stefan discovered. There is no indication of any particular political posture in this group other than its anti-German activities. Stefan's nephew, Tadeusz Budziaszek, remembers that Stefan was in a relationship with the niece of Fr. Skarbka, a local priest who owned a radio.[3]

> As concerns belonging to a conspiracy, as a student (in 1939 I completed my medical studies in Krakow) early on I joined a group led by Fr. Skarbka of St. Anne's in Krakow, which before the war had been the academic church. Today I find it hard to describe the character of this group since those were the early days of the occupation. Among other things, Fr. Skarbka disseminated political news gathered from foreign radio stations and provided false documentations for people who for various reasons had to change their names. Unfortunately the Gestapo discovered the activities of this organization. I don't know the particulars of this matter. I know Fr. Skarbka's two sisters were both arrested (they lived near St. Anne's), though Fr. Skarbka managed to escape and hid near Bochno at the home of a parish priest, his friend. (I do not recall the name of either the parish priest or the town.) I visited Fr. Skarbka there and gave him news and information relevant to our business.

This "conspiracy" was neither well organized nor well connected. Sikorski, in London, had no control over these types of local anti-German activities. The German occupation authorities, however, were very much concerned with local resistance. From the Nazi point of view, Poles acting locally in Krakow could coordinate with those in Warsaw. The Sikorski strategy of forming the Home Army (AK) in August of 1942 was precisely what was needed for a united resistance front. Fr. Skarbka's cell of anti-Nazi activities consisted primarily of supplying news from abroad. This was not a case of a clandestine radio station which could bring Poles into radio communication with Poles in London.[4] Stefan's participation, however, was not as passive as he described later. His false identification papers (which never proved useful) indicate that he was engaged in dangerous anti-Nazi activities. Fr. Skarbka monitored prohibited foreign radio stations, but then he also organized a printing operation. Stefan worked at this underground press and helped to distribute news flyers. This was a clear act of active resistance of the type that the Gestapo were intent on stopping. This small group was betrayed to the Gestapo by a fellow Pole. Stefan was arrested along with several Catholic priests. Their destination was the harsh Krakow prison: Montelupich. This was the first stop on the road to Auschwitz for many Poles.

> My arrest in Krosno was in a sense an accident. Soon after I left Krakow for the apartment at the Clinic for Internal Medicine, a man I knew, a railroader from Oświęcim, was caught in a roundup and arrested by the Gestapo.
>
> Under interrogation and torture, he allowed that if I had escaped then I had probably fled to Krosno. Naturally the Gestapo used this clue and quickly arranged for my return to Krakow: this time as a prisoner.

Citizens of Krakow had no illusions about the severity and ruthlessness of the German occupation. On November 6, 1939, 184 professors, other academics and university staff were lured to a lecture at the Jagiellonian University supposedly on German plans for Polish education under the new regime. They were summarily arrested. Their first stop was Krakow's Montelupich prison. Criminals, resistance members, political prisoners, Poles, Jews, and criminal SS men spent time there, a diverse army of "enemies" and "suspects."[5] This urban prison was once the manor house of the sixteenth-century Italian merchant family, the Montelupi. Clandestine photographs from the 1940s reveal an imposing four-story stucco façade with tall, regularly spaced windows.[6] But rather than movable shutters, large opaque plates had been affixed to cover 22 windows on the second and third story. These were the cells for prisoners. The first-story windows were unencumbered by this concealment. The photographer's viewpoint from an upper story site across the street revealed the ominous scene behind the tall brick wall, crowned with barbed wire, which screened the

Montelupich courtyard from the street. Some seventy men stood waiting in a long line facing the building's wall. Two cars—a convertible and a sedan—and seven jack-booted Nazis completed the picture. The interrogation rooms, their windows flush with the sidewalk, formed the lowest floor.

> After my arrest and transfer to Krakow, I was placed in the Montelupich prison, where I remained from June 1941 until the beginning of February 1942. In this prison there were interrogations along with torture. Captain (*SS Hauptscharführer*)[7] Siebert directed the interrogations using an ethnic German (*Volksdeutscher*) named Protzner as his translator. This translator combined his functions with that of torturer and understood his work well. He was one of the most awful and callous of SS men. The interrogations took place on the ground floor of the Montelupich prison. On those days we were taken to the so-called "open cell" and held for several hours without nourishment awaiting the interrogations.

The systematic use of violence by the German occupation was standard policy.[8] The aim was terror on a level which would immobilize resistance and demoralize the civilian population. In the small towns of the newly Germanized western Poland as well as in large towns like Krakow, resistance to German rules was punished severely. The interrogation process in prisons like Pawiak in Warsaw and Montelupich in Krakow depended on physical brutality. The aim was to discover the names and participants of resistance groups. Zając was interrogated in Montelupich he was beaten with a rubber hose, and he describes that he was forced to lie down and that the "Gestapo man hit systematically, like a machine."[9] Konstanty Piekarski reports that after Gestapo interrogations at the Pawiak Prison in Warsaw, "men had been coming back with smashed testicles."[10] After the war, Stefan received monthly indemnity payments from the West German government for injuries he sustained at the hands of the Gestapo.

> As I refused to respond to questions, they began to beat me. I received strong punches in the stomach as well as blows against my lower legs with a square-cut wooden stave—often broken-off chair legs. They also beat my groin with a hammer, causing the crushing and destruction of one testicle. In spite of these awful tortures, I didn't break down. I held out and didn't spill anything. Other prisoners suffered such tortures, a number of priests among them. I know one of them came from Bobrek near Oświęcim, another from Oświęcim, who might even have been a relative of Fr. Skarbka's, and was well-known for his lovely tenor voice; there was also a priest from near Bochno, and still some others. Unfortunately I can't remember their names right now, though we were all transported by truck at the beginning of February to the Auschwitz concentration camp. There were between 15 and 20 prisoners in this transport.

Germans targeted Polish Catholic clerics specifically since in Germany Catholic clerics formed various anti-Nazi groups.[11] Reporting from the Dachau concentration camp, Father Bedrich Hoffman stated that Germans filled camps with priests. Nazis considered Polish priests as part of the intelligentsia and a potent source of resistance. "The Gestapo feared that they would raise the consciousness of the common people and strengthen them in their resistance against the German Reich."[12]

> But returning to the time spent in the Montelupich prison, the process of the interrogation and torture, the nightly selections for executions demoralized the prisoners. As each evening and night approached everyone was tense waiting to see who would be ordered to leave the cell. As I learned later, the selected prisoners were driven to the vicinity of the village Mogiła, where they were shot to death. Later, when the Nazis decided to exploit my medical training to treat prisoners, I was able to get to know various sections of the prison, including the cellars—mostly Jewish prisoners were held there. The worst conditions were there.

The imprisonment at Montelupich served to harden naïve civilians and thereby ironically helped to protect them from the acute dangers of the concentration camp, Auschwitz. The most dangerous time for prisoners arriving in the complex and rapidly lethal Auschwitz camps was the first weeks. The shock of arbitrary violence, inadequate food, depersonalization, and brutal regimes of marching and work were enough to condemn newcomers to rapid decline and death. Historian Bernd Wagner, whose work focuses on Auschwitz III, Buna-Monowitz, a labor camp, summarizes the conclusion of former long-term prisoners: "Depending on their adaptability and life experience, the introductory phase could vary in length. Those who could not absorb the rules of camp life in a couple of days, or at most weeks, ended up in Birkenau."[13] To end up in Birkenau implied a death sentence by shooting, injection, or gassing. The critical phrase here is "life experience." In one sense, the first step to survival in Auschwitz was survival in Montelupich.

> The food in the prison was so poor and the amount so meager that within a short period the process of starvation began. The prisoners also had too little space. What used to be single cells were now routinely occupied by four to seven prisoners, sleeping on the floor as there were no bunks.

The total daily food ration for each Montelupich prisoner consisted on one quarter kilogram of bread, three quarters of a liter of thin soup and a half liter of a coffee substitute.[14] The nutrition in Auschwitz was far worse because prisoners performed strenuous work on these meager rations. While Montelupich prisoners had access to Red Cross supplies, such supplements were unavailable in the concentration camp.

One notable inmate in Montelupich was Józef Cyrankiewicz (1911–1989), a prewar lawyer and journalist, who served as prime minister in the postwar Polish state (1947–1952 and 1954–1970). Long-term concentration camp prisoner and one of its most informed inmates, Hermann Langbein, identified Cyrankiewicz as part of the Polish communist resistance movement in Auschwitz.[15]

Cyrankiewicz made numerous attempts to escape Nazi custody both in Montelupich and later in Auschwitz. Resistance fighters and other prisoners tried to maintain contact with compatriots. The sense that Nazi prisoners in either prisons or concentration camps were totally isolated from civilian society cannot be confirmed by the history of long-term prisoners.

> In spite of the strict isolation of Montelupich prisoners they nonetheless got news from the outside. Such contacts were maintained by such current prisoners as, for example, Józef Cyrankiewicz and the doctor from Chrzanowa, Dr. Garbień. This was possible thanks to the attempt by the Red Cross to supply prisoners at Montelupich with weekly deliveries (on Fridays) of a paste consisting of white cheese, sardines, and radishes, as well as bread. Thanks to the people of the Red Cross, opportunities arose for outside contacts, especially for those people occupying the so-called open cells. But the main point of contact was the laundry room, where women prisoners from the nearby Helcel prison came to work. The same building also held a prison for SS men.
>
> Women prisoners from Helcel who came daily to the Montelupich prison kitchen and laundry acted as contacts, bringing in and picking up information and sending it on to persons on the outside. As concerns Józef Cyrankiewicz, I saw him often, since as an inmate of a collection cell he was forced, among other things, to wash floors and corridors. Prisoners also communicated through doors but with extreme caution due to the danger of being overheard by informers.
>
> In late summer, perhaps fall, of 1941, Józef Cyrankiewicz and Dr. Garbień were caught preparing to escape, an escape which was to have been aided by SS men. In any case, the escapees were supposed to leave the prison through the gate. After being caught they were beaten dreadfully. They were put in chains and kept in darkness. It needs to be explained that Dr. Garbień had previously been able to gain the confidence of the Montelupich prison commander (whose name I can't remember). That had happened by accident. When this commander

> broke his leg, Dr. Garbień had had the opportunity to meet him in his function as a physician. At any rate, this accidental contact allowed a relationship based on gratitude towards an imprisoned doctor and perhaps even sympathy. This was very important for Dr. Garbień, since after a long period of imprisonment in the dark he was released to an open cell and subsequently released from the prison, thanks to the prison commander's intervention. Dr. Garbień was moved to the open cell in February, 1942.

Stefan learned an important aspect of the relationship between prisoner doctors and the SS. A relationship between two men of vastly unequal power could occur and bring benefits. In the far more dangerous and volatile Auschwitz camp, Stefan worked hard to maintain such contacts. Stefan's clinical experience gave him a useful skill. In both Montelupich and later in various Auschwitz units, his training was obvious to his jailers. In German parlance, he could perform a function in the prison (*Funktionshäftling*). Clinics and prisoner-run hospitals in the concentration camps were coveted sites that offered protection to inmates from the danger of brute physical labor on a construction site. Even at Montelupich, Stefan's situation improved when he received a work assignment at the nearby women's prison, Helcel. Not only was he in a quieter, safer prison, but his access to food and to information improved. The months at Montelupich served as inoculation against the shock of the significantly more severe challenge of Auschwitz. He learned how to survive as a prisoner.

> After the incident with Dr. Garbień, the prison doctor was changed. Dr. Garbień was replaced in Montelupich prison by Dr. Nadolski. He was a strange person. Different stories about him circulated among the prisoners but I don't want to repeat them since the stories were never investigated. These events also changed my situation as I became the prisoner doctor of the women prisoners in Helcel. I was moved there and housed in a large communal hall which held about 20 prisoners. This was a general collection cell for various ex-SS men and

> *Volksdeutsche*, some of whom had death sentences for various crimes such as swindling or illegal trade. This cell also held a Ukrainian who had held a high position in occupied Krakow. I don't remember his name. He was an epileptic and suffered frequent seizures. Being housed in this cell, besides the negative effects (my isolation from other Polish prisoners) it also had some positives, such as decent food and relative quiet. My cellmates spent evenings playing cards while I remained by myself in a corner. We slept on beds and had changes of bed linen. In a word, these conditions were diametrically different from those of other prisoners.
>
> Among my duties as a prisoner physician was treating those seeking help. I was, of course, overseen by German female prison guards (*Aufseherinnen*), usually very simple women aged between 20 and 30. They weren't the worst in their relations to the women prisoners. As a doctor I had the opportunity to treat the women prisoners who had undergone torture during interrogations, since they needed bandaging. These women had numerous wounds on their breasts and lower legs which had been caused by beatings with canes. There were large bleeding wounds and painful bruises. These young girls, between 17 and 25, were very brave during these questionings and tortures. I learned about this in fragmentary conversations I had with these women prisoners. Fr. Skarbka's two sisters were also held in this prison—they worked in either the kitchen or the laundry. Occasionally we could exchange a few words.

Stefan witnessed the atrocities at Montelupich as a 28-year-old. He had started medical school in the fall of 1933 at 20. His memories of this time period, some 30 years earlier, strive to be analytical and factual. For all his medical training, he was shocked by what he witnessed. Auschwitz would be worse. These were still early days in the construction of the Third Reich, a thousand-year-long plan. The German plan to decapitate Polish resistance worked on many levels at Montelupich prison. However, here, as in other sites of Nazi coercion, community ties remained intact. Both at

Montelupich and subsequently at Auschwitz, Stefan met people he had known at the university or in other social contexts. Poles had a significant advantage in these camps in comparison to prisoners shipped in from other corners of Europe who were isolated by language from other prisoners and by distance from social support. Stefan, for instance, recognized one of his teachers and attempted to ameliorate his suffering. Both of them ended up in Auschwitz. Most Poles from former German or Austrian regions had a working knowledge of German—a critical survival trait.

Nazi fixation on Jewish prisoners was abundantly evident even in the city prison. The prison had not only German guards and administration, but also German prisoners, including members of the elite SS. The German SS prisoners brutalized Jewish inmates specifically. During Zając's imprisonment in Montelupich, some months after Stefan was shipped out, he reports that two Jewish women were shot to death on the street as they were being transferred from Helcel to trucks going to Auschwitz.[16] Stefan also witnessed torture of Poles, both gentiles and Jews:

> I experienced a tragic event in the basement of Helcel prison. One day I was taken to the basement and I saw some (12 to 14) naked prisoners standing in cold water showers. This was one of the tortures inflicted on members of the resistance. To my utter horror, I recognized my old professor Gieszczykiewicz among them.[17] I tried to help him somehow. I visited him daily on the pretext that he was sick, bringing him some food and medicine every time. I met the professor later in the Auschwitz concentration camp, where he was lost in the courtyard of block 11 [executed by shooting].
>
> I was also a witness of the inhuman torment of Jews by the SS men prisoners.[18] Among these SS men prisoners I remember the name of one—he was Count von Knige, whose family estate was somewhere in the vicinity of Hanover. He and other SS men prisoners formed a gauntlet, in the presence of the guards, through which the Jewish prisoners had to pass. Those

passing through were tormented mercilessly. It's difficult to believe that normal, even educated, people could treat others, even fellow prisoners, so vilely. One of these tormenters, an officer in the *Wehrmacht*, was not much later himself enchained and shipped out to execution. Among the Jewish prisoners, one caught my special interest. He was a well-built, noble-looking man who was beaten daily. In the evening I was called in to determine if he was still alive. The things that I witnessed were so horrifying that I will never be able to forget them.

In December 1941 a typhus epidemic erupted in Montelupich prison. Typhus was spread in the prison by people arrested in the provinces, where typhus had already been an epidemic for some time. Because of this I was given the order to examine prisoners in their cells. We did this work with the previously mentioned Dr. Nadolski. It's at this moment that I was led to the dark rooms and basements and saw the shackled Drs. Grabień and Cyrankiewicz. They were both holding themselves bravely, thanks to their fundamentally good physical condition.

Looking through these cells I had the opportunity to see one of the secret holes in Montelupich. In one of these cellars a man (whose name I can't recall) was being held. At any rate, he was a well-known prewar lawyer in Krakow who was arrested trying to flee to the Soviet Union. Previously he and I had shared a cell. He was a Jew. Because of where he was arrested or because of other issues, he was often taken out of our cell (this was at the time when we shared a cell) for interrogations. After these he returned in a pitiable state. One day he told me that the Gestapo got all the information they needed from him. After the next interrogation he did not return to our cell. A couple of months later, during the cell inspections during the typhus epidemic (though these efforts to find the characteristic skin eruptions made no sense, as they appear late in the course of the disease—the first symptom is high fever), I saw the lawyer in one of the basement cells. I barely recognized him. His hair had turned gray and his face was

> wan; he was completely exhausted. My first impulse was to say a few words to him, but the lack of expression on his face and his lack of reaction in seeing me made clear that nothing was reaching this prisoner any more. He didn't even recognize me. These examples serve as witness to the tragedies which took place in the cellars of the prison building to which ordinary prisoners had no access. Dr. Grabień would have been able to reveal a great deal but unfortunately he died after the war.
>
> At the beginning of 1942 I heard from one of the SS men prisoners (working in the Helcel kitchen) that I would be released. On some day in February 1942 I was transferred [back] to the Montelupich prison. I supposed that the rumors of my release had been true. After all, during my interrogations I had not admitted anything and the Gestapo had no convincing proof of anything—so my thoughts about a release seemed realistic. At the end of the investigation, no verdict was announced; I received no sentence. I had also not signed the interrogation protocol. I had never seen my arrest warrant (*Schutzheftbefehl*). Before I was moved from Helcel they gave me back my personal belongings, but didn't include my case of medical instruments. The SS man who returned my belongings said to me briefly that I wouldn't need my medical gear "over there." ("*Es hatt alles drüben was es nötig hat*"). I remember I was very concerned what the word "*drüben*" [over there] meant. The next day I was transferred to KL Auschwitz where, indeed, I would have no use for them.

Stefan was an inmate of the Montelupich prison almost eight months. He would spend over three years in Nazi concentration camps. Sociologist Erving Goffman has analyzed such "total institutions" to determine how they change inmates. Cut off from the outside world and regimented by rules, prisoners lose all control over daily life: eating, sleeping, working, socializing. The guards impose all the rules.[19] In Nazi concentration camps, inmates have to contend not just with normal guards, but with highly dangerous, hostile, and frequently deadly guards, the SS men. In Goffman's view, amply supported by concentration camp survivors, there is a sharp demarcation between inmates and staff in total institutions. The social distance between the two is even marked by restricted speech, a special tone of voice, and especially in the staff's or guards' control over information. Stefan encountered this reality in Montelupich: he had no clue as to any verdict, didn't know the result of the interrogations and was not told where he was going next.

Critically for his survival in Auschwitz, Stefan had learned prison behaviors. One vital lesson was that performing a function, that is, having a job within the prison, brought serious benefits. While he was exposed to horrifying sights as a prison functionary, he was also able to gain respite (better sleep, additional food, periods of quiet) working in the women's prison. The shock of moving from the Krakow Montelupich prison to the far more brutal Auschwitz camp was considerable. However, the camp was now not a totally new experience. Montelupich was a critical learning experience: he had arrived as a civilian, was stripped of power and identity, found a role as a prison physician, but was also fundamentally powerless.

NOTES

1. Szymborska, *Seventy Poems*, 74–75.
2. Sybille Steinbacher, *Auschwitz, A History*, 18.
3. Private letter, June 11, 2006.
4. Lukas, *Forgotten Holocaust,* 88.
5. Zając, *Powrőt Niepożąndany*, 104.
6. Two photographs of Montelupich are available on the United States Holocaust Memorial Museum website.
7. Italicized words in the text of the oral testimony reflect a word in German in the original Polish language manuscript. This transcript is presented as recorded by Iwaszko with no deletions or transpositions.
8. Fulbrook, *A Small Town near Auschwitz,* 115.
9. Zając, *Powrőt Niepożąndany*, 69.

10. K. Piekarski, Foreword, March, 1989, http://members.shaw.ca/escapinghell/00-kon.htm.
11. Herbert, *Hitler's Foreign Workers,* 65.
12. Bedrich Hoffman, *And Who Will Kill You* (Inez, Texas, privately published, 1994) (ISBN 83-7014-223-0).
13. Wagner, *IG Auschwitz,* 37.
14. Zając, *Powrőt Niepożąndany*, 63.
15. Hermann Langbein, *People in Auschwitz* (Chapel Hill: University of North Carolina Press, 2004), 42.
16. Zając, *Powrót Niepożądany,* 121.
17. Stefan's transcript from the Jagiellonian University shows that he had had Gieszczykiewicz's classes in microbiology and bacteriology in 1936.
18. The SS men were probably convicted of various thefts, usually for not turning over confiscated property.
19. Erving Goffman, *Asylums: Essays on the Social Situation of Mental Patients and Other Inmates* (New York: Anchor Books, 1961), 6.

3

CONCENTRATION CAMPS, THE NEW ENTERPRISE ZONE

> Fierce tenants elbow their way through history
> Legions of sword-fodder
>
> *Rozpychają się w dziejach dzicy lokatorzy*
> *Zastępy mięsa mieczowego*[1]

The city of Oświęcim had no German schools or churches, and no German organizations or newspapers, in 1939. In the interwar years it had become a Polish town of some 14,000, about half of them Jewish. This little town was incorporated by plebiscite in the revived Poland in 1921, but was remembered by the Germans to the west as being part of *Ostoberschlesien*, East Upper Silesia.[2] The town was part of the railroad network that served this region rich in coal mines. The Sixth Polish Cavalry division barracks were located in Oświęcim. The town was seized on September 4, 1939, and a week later the town square was renamed "Adolf-Hitler-Platz." It is important to realize that Auschwitz was annexed to Germany. It was no longer in Poland. Its development was to serve as a prototype of the Germanization planned for Slavic regions. Today we would use the term "ethnic cleansing" for the process of removing Jews and Poles. Only the *Volksdeutsche* were left in place and the new government wanted to attract German settlers. This little, newly Germanized city was going to house people working at new German factories as well as at the new German labor camp, Auschwitz.[3] The small

Polish town, Oświęcim, and the villages of Brzezinka and Monowice became Auschwitz, Birkenau, and Monowitz, respectively.

The plans for Germanization made by Adolf Hitler and Heinrich Himmler, the new Reich Commissar for the Strengthening of German Nationhood, ran into a logistical problem: a scarcity of local Germans, *Volksdeutsche,* or of immigrating Germans. The Nazis created a special administration zone for this territory: Auschwitz was part of the Eastern Zone *(Oststreifen)* of East Upper Silesia. This became a new land of opportunity for Germans. Careers in government as well as business ventures appeared limitless. Ambitions ran riot: "War euphoria, confidence in victory, and a pioneering spirit turned into a lack of moral inhibition, and personal enrichment became the rule among the Germans in the East."[4]

To exploit these new frontiers, Germans had to subdue the natives. The Nazi government had experience in intimidation and control. Since their 1933 takeover of Germany they had built a system of concentration camps to control political and ideological dissidents.[5] The dilapidated cavalry barracks just south of the town Auschwitz became the nucleus of a new camp that came into operation in May 1940. Its design was to control the subjugated Poles. In its five-and-a-half years of operation, the camp grew monstrously and expanded to administer close to 50 subcamps.

The Polish men and women in emerging resistance movements in such centers as Warsaw and Krakow knew that, if captured, their final destination was this newly established German concentration camp. Polish resistance and the Polish home army knew of the executions in Montelupich prison in Krakow or Pawiak prison in Warsaw. More of the same took place at the execution grounds of block 11 in the Auschwitz concentration camp. As late as the spring of 1942, Auschwitz prisoners were still overwhelmingly Poles. "Today Auschwitz is synonymous with the Holocaust, but it was built to impose German rule over Poland."[6]

But Auschwitz was also a labor camp, attractive to German big business. It had an economic function which was part of the vision of the exploitation of the conquered territories. Bernd Wagner titles his book *IG Auschwitz*, pointedly referencing the factory name "IG Farbenindustrie." The initials *IG* stand for *Interessengemeinschaft*, which is fundamentally a corporation, but could be translated as "a community with a common interest." The "common interest" in "IG Auschwitz" is cheap labor. In the eyes of corporate Germany, the potential of the eastward expansion of Germany was the acquisition of new labor sources. The appeal of the Nazi regime to big business in Germany was partially based on Hitler's promises in 1933 to end the horrific economic depression of Germany, when unemployment figures reached six million. One in four workers was unemployed. By 1940, Hitler's labor programs and military expansion reversed the situation: German industry was experiencing labor shortages and was looking eastward to find workers, the cheaper the better.

Forced labor was not invented by the Nazis. During World War I, what had been Polish seasonal migrant labor in Germany was converted into forced labor. By 1915 Poles were not permitted to return home from their seasonal farm work. Poles were now labeled with identification badges.[7] The Nazis returned to the use of badges for Polish forced laborers in March 1940. They were used as the pattern for the iconic Jewish star badges introduced in September 1941.[8] Labor and raw materials shortages in the industrial and the farming sector were acute in Germany as early as 1936. Historian Ulrich Herbert identifies "the catastrophic overheating of the German war economy [which posed] a serious threat to the preparation for war which hinged on the armament industry."[9] As World War II developed and Nazi Germany subjugated Europe to the west and to the east, the war economy became dependent on workers brought into Germany as forced labor. By August 1944, more than 7.6 million foreign workers were registered in "Greater Germany."

Even before the war broke out, one group was targeted for forced labor by the racist Nazi state: the Jews. As Jews were deprived of the legal right for normal work, the Nazi state created programs of forced labor to provide some income for Jews. This policy began with menial public works jobs such as street cleaning and sanitation. However, by early 1939, some German cities sought to create Jewish labor camps for local road construction.[10] These often temporary camps were administered by municipal or forestry officials, quite separate from the SS. As the Nazis expanded into Poland, so did the use of Jewish forced labor such as the Schmelt system.

There is a distinction between the terms "forced labor" and "slave labor." Forced laborers received some compensation for their work but slave labors essentially did not. Unfortunately, the two terms are often used interchangeably. It's a distinction worth preserving. For instance, the slave laborers in Auschwitz often worked side by side with forced laborers. The slaves returned to Auschwitz as prisoners; the forced laborers had separate camps with no barbed wires or manic SS guards. Forced labor became an essential part of the German war economy.

German historian Götz Aly's groundbreaking 2005 book, *Hitler's Beneficiaries*, turned a laser-bright focus on still other German profits during World War II.[11] In 1940, Western European states were the first to experience not only subjugation but also outright plunder. The glaring looting of major museums in conquered nations was only the most obvious transfer of wealth to the Third Reich. Nazi banks and industry profited, but so did ordinary Germans. Most Germans felt satisfaction with the Nazi government because citizens did in fact benefit from the plunder of Europe.[12] Aly defines the Third Reich as a kind of racist-totalitarian welfare state. He argues that German anti-Semitism is not a sufficient explanation for the Nazi regime.

Hitler paid close attention to lower-class Germans and shared war loot and plunder with them.[13] German armies in Western Europe transferred wealth which the state used to shield ordinary Germans from the cost of war. Nazi policies improved the material welfare of Germans. Food, furniture, and clothing were far from the only advantage the German people received as war booty. The use of forced labor was another significant form of plunder. The most straightforward transfer of wealth was the Nazi expropriation of 60 to 70 percent of the wages paid to foreign laborers in the Nazi industrial system. Between 1941 and 1945, the German state earned $150 billion (in 2006 dollars) from forced labor. Companies which used forced labor (Krupp, IG Farben, etc.) benefited greatly, but so did the German state and its citizens.[14] The billions in state revenues from forced labor took a significant load off ordinary German taxpayers. Forced labor became an integral part of the Nazi war economy. Foreign workers in Germany were an acceptable alternative to placing a heavier work load on Germans who were working triple shifts and overtime producing material for the military.[15]

The Nazi war machine had subjugated all of Western Europe but was not able to overcome Great Britain. By mid-1940 the Germans began looking systematically at their territories in the east to support long-term warfare. October 15, 1940, Heinrich Himmler appointed Albrecht Schmelt *Reichsführer* SS for Non-German Labor Deployment in Upper Silesia. His job was to organize forced Jewish labor and to keep the costs of this workforce as low as possible.[16] The Schmelt system operating in the newly annexed Polish territories forced 6,500 Jews in 25 camps to build an expressway (*Autobahn*) between Berlin and Krakow. Another 8,500 Jews were forced to labor in mines and industrial plants. The SS management collected fees (RM 6 for skilled workers and RM 4.50 for unskilled) which went to support both the SS and Schmelt himself.[17] Between November 1940 and June 1941 Jews were told to provide workers to 546 different retail stores and small workshops and were paid a flat rate of RM 3.50 daily, of which Schmelt kept RM 0.60. Schmelt also collected fees from organizations that used Jewish labor. Ultimately, the German tax authorities profited from the forced labor of Polish Jews. The tax office collected 18% of gross wages from factories using Jewish workers. Historian Stephen Lehnstaedt argues that labor exploitation in East Upper Silesia was more tolerable to the local Jews than forced labor in the Warthegau or the General Gouvernament and certainly preferable to a transfer to the Auschwitz camp as slave laborers.[18]

The Jews in the Schmelt system did not live in the closed urban ghettos such as Warsaw, Krakow, and Łódz. While Nazis did not permit Jews in the small towns of western Poland to work independently or to own their own shops, they still lived in their homes but were forced to work for Schmelt or face destitution. Schmelt pioneered one feature which would dominate the lives of prisoners in Auschwitz: selections for death. "Schmelt's Jewish laborers were a great economic prize, and those who could not work burdened his system. Pioneering the process of selections that would come to characterize the life-or-death entry point at Auschwitz, Schmelt, starting in late fall 1941, sent all Jews in his camps who could no longer work [*arbeitsunfähig*] to be murdered in the newly created gas chambers of Crematorium I in Auschwitz. They were the first Jews to be killed in that installation."[19] The Schmelt system collapsed as Nazi policy towards Jews changed from labor exploitation to systematic racial extermination around May 1942.

Historians have searched for the critical moment, the defining document that details the Final Solution. The concept of a pure German racial state, cleared of Jews, was a foundational tenet of Nazism. The process of creating a community free from Jews, *Judenrein*, however, changed over time. Historian Peter Longerich shows the erratic, disjointed series of decisions which culminated in the attempted extermination of European Jews.[20] The decisive turning point for the decision to engage in genocide was the subjugation of Poland in the fall of 1939. The smoking gun detected later at the Wannsee Conference (January 20, 1942) only finalized the ongoing process of ghettoization, extermination through work, and the camp mass murders. European Jews started arriving in Auschwitz in unimaginable numbers in March 1942.[21]

Once the Nazi decision to exterminate the Jewish "race" was finalized by 1942, even economically useful populations were condemned to death. Eighty-five thousand Jews from Upper East Silesia, the backbone of the Schmelt Jewish labor system, perished in Auschwitz.[22] The slave labor camp, KL Auschwitz, however, was a significantly different type of labor organization from Schmelt's.

It was on a much larger scale, centralized into a giant camp and organized to provide labor for future large factories and to control Poles, both Jew and gentile, with terror. The workers were no longer forced laborers; they were slaves.

The favorable location of Auschwitz in relation to railroad lines and existing mines and industry was obvious to the German business community immediately. In September 1939, a week after the outbreak of the war, planners at IG Farbenindustrie talked seriously about moving industry into the newly conquered territory. Eight major chemical and pharmaceutical companies formed IG Farbenindustrie in 1925, creating what was the largest chemical industry conglomerate in the world.[23] The company's director, Carl Bosch, a Nobel-Prize winning chemist, had perfected the Bergius-Bosch process of converting coal to oil to create a synthetic oil. Hitler and many others felt that Germany had lost the First World War because they could not control the raw material pipeline essential for the military. When the Nazis came to power in 1933, Hitler was convinced that the chemical processes that produced synthetic oil and rubber, though very expensive, were nonetheless the key to the problem of self-sufficiency. By 1928, Bosch had achieved a process for creating a synthetic rubber, Buna. By 1938, the government provided financial support to IG Farbenindustrie to produce almost all the synthetic oil, synthetic rubber, poison gases, magnesium, lubrication oil, explosives, methanol, sera, plasticizers, dyestuffs, nickel, and thousands of other items critical to the Nazi military.[24]

The first full-scale Buna factory was begun in late fall 1935; the second in June 1936. The financial support of the Nazi government was critical. To appease Hitler, IG Farbenindustrie management ousted all Jewish directors and scientists, to the dismay of men like Bosch who claimed these men very critical to the success of IG Farben. In 1937, all directors of IG Farben were party members.[25]

A third Buna plant was planned in 1939. IG Farben's first choice had been a site near Breslau, Rattwitz. The unexpectedly quick defeat of France, however, made it look like a short war and an assured German victory, and planning eastward was halted.

However, the failure to defeat England in the fall of 1940 caused a reassessment by both the government and the factory administration. The decision was made that a major Buna production site was needed far enough east to be safe from allied bombing.[26]

The final decision to place the Buna production unit in Auschwitz, the first such factory in the newly annexed territories, was influenced by the proximity of the concentration camp Auschwitz. The labor camp guaranteed a steady, reliable source of cheap labor. In addition, the region, the East Zone, was heavily settled, so civilian local *Volksdeutsche* could be employed as well as those "colonist" Germans who would come to the newly Germanized, newly vacant little town of Auschwitz.[27] Thus the Auschwitz concentration camp, the place designed to house political dissidents, became enmeshed in the German industrial complex. It would grow significantly as a labor camp to the extent that eventually (November 1943) the main camp, Auschwitz I, expanded into two more, Auschwitz II-Birkenau, the site of the gas chambers, and Auschwitz III-Monowitz, dedicated solely to supplying workers for IG Farbenindustrie. This Buna plant was intended to be the largest ever built, with the potential of serving entirely new markets in the Soviet Union and Asia. IG Farbenindustrie committed 900 million Reichsmarks to that end. The Nazi state would supply labor for the building of this giant plant. In 1941, IG Farbenindustrie demanded between 8,000 and 12,000 workers. These slave laborers were the concentration camp inmates in the conveniently located Auschwitz.[28] Big business provided the factory and money; government added labor and administration.

The Nazi *Schutzstaffel,* the SS, managed and ran these new camps. They had previous experience in organizing camps: Dachau, opened in 1933, became the model.[29] By 1937, professional criminals and such regime resisters as the Jehovah's Witnesses joined the political inmates. The number of political prisoners increased exponentially with the conquest of Czechoslovakia, the *Anschluß* of Austria and then, of course, the conquest of Poland. In the spring of 1942 yet another phase of the camps developed: Jewish transports began arriving in Auschwitz. Their destiny was extermination, not labor, except for a select few.

The mental model for the camps was twofold: military organizations and prison organizations. The military use of roll calls, the marching units, the command structure of the camps, all these would have felt familiar to those prisoners who had been in a military unit. Other camp features derived from the European prison system. On May 20, 1940, the first command group to arrive in Auschwitz consisted of 30 professional criminals from Sachsenhausen, chosen by Rudolf Höss. Fifteen SS men of the SS cavalry, transferred from Krakow, joined them.[30] In the concentration camps, barracks, or "blocks," which ranged in size from 200 to 2,000 men, were run by a senior inmate, the elder, who maintained order. This was a replication of European prisons in which the elder in the large cells created a parallel governance structure wherein the senior criminal had more influence than the nominal prison guard. The recruited criminal prisoners maintained strict order among the incoming Polish prisoners.[31] They had a fairly free hand, including the power to kill the disobedient. Most of the guards were willing helpers of the SS, enthusiastically beating and killing their subjects.[32] Those who became *Blockälteste,* the barracks elders, maintained the familiar traditions of prison life.[33]

These barracks elders were prisoner functionaries, prisoners who had an assigned camp task and were not assigned work in the factories and farms that used Auschwitz laborers. When prisoners left for work, they were under the control of another type of prisoner functionary, the capo (also spelled "kapo"). Capos supervised units of prisoners in the various work sites in the extensive grounds of Auschwitz. In the Buna factory, capos controlled workers carrying heavy cement sacks, digging ditches, and doing brute labor as well as more technical jobs like the chemistry lab detail. Serving under a brutal capo in a physically demanding job was a death sentence. The Germans called it *Vernichtung durch Arbeit,* extermination through labor.

The category of other functionaries was extensive. Auschwitz needed secretaries for the administrative SS staff, but also janitors in each of the blocks. Tens of thousands of men needed to be fed: the camp kitchens proved a highly desirable site for work. Carpenters, painters, and electricians were in demand. Auschwitz had a printing press, and a bordello. The infirmaries for prisoners needed orderlies, nurses, dentists, and doctors. For those prisoners who survived in the long-term, gaining access to a prisoner functionary job was critical for survival. Access to these jobs was often predicated on knowing someone who was already in the system. The network of people you knew and who could help you was essential in gaining access to perhaps a little more food, in avoiding a physically exhausting job, or in actually using some of your professional skills to become a valued prisoner rather than an expendable one.

Integration into the camps, however, proved a horrendous ordeal. Those prisoners who could not navigate the gauntlet of Nazi brutality did not live long.[34] A survivor explains: "Most of the prisoners in the camp perished within the first three months after their arrival. The reason was that the devitalizing nature of the system hit an unprepared human being with enormous force and, as it were, crushed him intellectually, so that he was ready for impending death."[35] Between April 15 and July 17, 1942, of the Jews chosen for work (thus it does not refer to men, women, and children consigned to death), 3.06% died in the first week; 5.32% in the second; 6.2% in the third; 11.32% in the fourth; 11.04% in the fifth; and 10.75% in the sixth. After the sixth week, percentages decreased, and after the twelfth week, less than 2% died per week as prisoners acclimated to the Auschwitz environment.[36] Camp survivor Tadeusz Dębski writes in *A Battlefield of Ideas* that the shock of the brutality of the camp stunned the new arrivals. For some, the impact resulted in collapse. They could not cope and were soon consigned to death. Primo Levi called them the flotsam and jetsam of the camps. For men with military or prison experience, however, the regimentation, the brutality, the use of foul language in Auschwitz were recognizable from previous experience. These men had a better adjustment.[37]

NOTES

1. Szymborska, *Seventy Poems*, 76–77.
2. Steinbacher, *Auschwitz*, 12–13.
3. Ibid., 17.
4. Ibid., 21.
5. In 1940, the other concentration camps were Dachau (the prototype, established in 1933), Sachsenhausen, Buchenwald, Flossenbürg, Mauthausen, and Ravensbrück. The facility at Auschwitz thus formed the seventh major, but far from the last, camp. See Wachsmann, *KL*, 628.
6. Wachsmann, *KL*, 203.
7. Herbert, *Hitler's Foreign Workers*, 26.
8. Ibid., 72.
9. Ibid., 34.
10. Wolf Gruner, *Jewish Forced Labor under the Nazis: Economic Needs and Racial Aims, 1938–1944* (New York: Cambridge University Press, 2006), xiv–xv.
11. Götz Aly, *Hitler's Beneficiaries: Plunder, Racial War, and the Nazi Welfare State*, translated by Jefferson Chase (New York: Metropolitan Books, Henry Holt, 2005).
12. Ibid., 2.
13. Ibid., 7.
14. Ibid., 162. Wachsmann's figures in German currency are 200 million RM in 1943; 400 million RM in 1944 (Wachsmann, 410).
15. Herbert, *Hitler's Foreign Workers*, 39.
16. Stephen Lehnstaedt, "Coercion and Incentive: Jewish Ghetto Labor in East Upper Silesia," *Holocaust and Genocide Studies* 23, no. 3 (2010): 407.
17. Ibid., 411.
18. Lehnstaedt, 418.
19. Deborah Dwork and Robert Jan van Pelt, "Sala's World, 1939–1945, Sosnowiec, Schmelt's Camps and the Holocaust" in *Letters to Sala: A Young Woman's Life in Nazi Labor Camps*, edited by Ann Kirschner (New York: New York Public Library, 2006), 68.
20. Longerich, *Holocaust*, 5.
21. Ibid., 422.
22. Lehnstaedt, "Coercion and Incentive," 420.

23. Joseph Borkin, *The Crime and Punishment of I.G. Farben* (New York: The Free Press, 1979), 54.
24. Ibid., 95.
25. Ibid., 91.
26. Wagner, *IG Auschwitz,* 44–45.
27. Ibid., 47.
28. Borkin, *The Crime and Punishment of I.G. Farben,* 148.
29. Tadeusz Dębski, *A Battlefield of Ideas* (New York: Columbia University Press, East European Monographs, 2001), 20.
30. Czech, *Auschwitz Chronicle,* 10.
31. Dębski, *A Battlefield of Ideas*, 27: "Every [large prison] cell had an elder, normally recognized as such by the prison guards and the prison warden . . . In many prisons order was maintained chiefly by these elders, and some of them could proudly affirm that they and not the warden or the guards were the real rulers of the prison."
32. Ibid., 110: "The SS brought to Auschwitz a band of professional criminals from KL Sachsenhausen, choosing big, strong, energetic, cruel men who gladly tortured and killed people."
33. Ibid., 28
34. Wagner, *IG Auschwitz,* 137.
35. Langbein, *People in Auschwitz,* 57.
36. Ibid., 57.
37. Dębski, *A Battlefield of Ideas*, 175.

4

AUSCHWITZ CAMPS DEVELOP

> I have a body that's unique, immutable,
> I'm here but once to the marrow of my bones.
>
> *Man ciało pojedyncze, niepremienne w nic,*
> *Jestem jednorazowa aż do szpiku kości.*[1]

Stefan Budziaszek's prisoner number was 20,526, tattooed on his forearm. He received this new identity when he arrived in Auschwitz on February 10, 1942, along with 23 other prisoners sent from Montelupich.[2] The first days, sometimes the first hours, were critical. Stefan, arriving after months in Montelupich prison, had been acculturated to some extent to what was coming, but it was still a matter of luck that he found a place in the prison hospital in the early phase of his incarceration. Finding a network, finding friends with more experience of the camp, was critical for long-term survival in the camps.

> I don't remember the exact date of my transfer to KL-Auschwitz. It was probably mid-February 1942. A truck carrying about 20 prisoners from Montelupich in Krakow passed the camp gate with the motto *Arbeit Macht Frei* and halted nearby. The truck gate was opened and we had to jump down (there was no step-stool provided). Nearby SS men fell on us, cursing, shouting and kicking at random. After I had been in the camp longer, I realized that they always did this when the transport included priests. And in our transport, there were priests wearing cassocks! I, too, wasn't spared the "pleasure" of

> a welcome by the boots of SS men. I got a couple of kicks until we got to the barracks, where we were stripped, washed, and photographed. During the wash the newly arrived prisoners were superficially examined by the SS camp doctor (SS *Lagerarzt*), Dr. Entress.

Stefan had encountered one of the significant players in Auschwitz. Dr. Friedrich Karl Hermann Entress, with the rank of captain (*SS Hauptsturmführer*), was born in 1914 in Posen, Germany, a city which would become Poznan, Poland, after World War I. He served as the camp physician at the main Auschwitz camp from December, 11, 1941 until October 20, 1943. SS physicians did not typically reside in some part of the camp but rather in housing appropriated for their use in the town of Auschwitz now designated for German settlers. He set up an operating room in block 21 to practice surgeries. He was active in murders by injecting phenol into the heart and participated in the largest selection in the medical block (August 29, 1942) in which convalescent patients, typhus infected patients, prisoner doctors, and medical personnel were liquidated in the gas chamber. SS Dr. Entress received payment from the Bayer pharmaceutical subsidiary of IG Farben for testing experimental drugs against typhus and tuberculosis.[3] Dr. Entress subsequently became the camp physician (March 1943–October 20, 1943) in the Auschwitz III camp, Buna-Monowitz, during the time Stefan worked there as a prisoner doctor.[4]

Stefan's first day in Auschwitz continued to get worse:

> As I was leaving the showers I felt a pain in my hand (due to a kick) and additionally I slipped on the wet, soapy floorboards, fell, and broke my left hand. While being examined by the SS doctor I turned to him and said, "I believe I've fractured my lower arm" ("*Ich glaube das ich mein Unterarm fraktuirt habe*"), to which he replied, "I think so, too. You're going to the station" ("*Ich glaube auch. Sie kommen zu Revier*"). After the showers we were taken to the identification office (*Erkennungsdienst*), where the photographing took place. There were a couple of prisoners—BVers (*Berufsverbrecher*, professional

> criminals) [green triangle prisoners]—who were playing nasty games with us. The trick worked as follows: each prisoner was seated on a camp stool to be photographed. This stool was maneuvered from a distance by a long metal brace. At the conclusion of the photography, they yelled "Stand!" while simultaneously pulling the metal brace, causing each person being photographed to fall to the floor. After these "games" I reported to the hospital barrack, number 28. Prisoner doctor (*Häftlingsarzt*) Diem examined my hand and said, "It's a good thing you broke your hand, because you wouldn't last long in the camp."

Dr. Rudolf Diem was a Polish Protestant prisoner doctor (as distinguished from a German Nazi SS doctor) who held a key position in the Outpatient Department. He advised newcomers such as Stefan and found protected work positions for incoming prisoner physicians. Dr. Diem himself ran afoul of the SS, possibly because of political tensions among prisoners who controlled desirable, safer work sites such as prisoner hospitals. Diem was locked up in the bunker by the camp Gestapo as a result of a quarrel with the influential camp elder Ludwig Wörl.[5] Stefan would later also experience competition for influence among prisoner functionaries, but was more successful in maintaining calm relationships with his SS superiors.

Critical networks functioned in the camps. Stefan, like other new camp prisoners, needed to find allies such as old colleagues, coreligionists, political allies, or friends from other prisons. Stefan's broken hand brought him into contact with such allies at this dangerous juncture. To survive, prisoners had to be alert. Prisoners who had a functionary role in Montelupich, for instance, arrived in Auschwitz with a reputation. If they had abused their privileges in Montelupich, they could face prisoner reprisal in Auschwitz.[6] Officially, the SS men ran the camps, but rivalries, whether political or for resources, created vital and dangerous networks of influence. This is a constantly recurring theme of camp life, but not one well-articulated in the various witness narratives.

Stefan entered this political maze and was fortunate to meet friends:

> From this outpatient clinic I was directed to the surgery, barracks number 21, which stood opposite. Here I encountered colleagues who were filling positions as nurses, Drs. Zabicki and Zbozien. A plaster cast was applied and I was given a place on a sack of straw. The sanitary and hygienic conditions in the prisoner hospital were at that time terrible. Bandages were only exchanged twice a week. The phlegmon[7] division was run by Dr. Zbozien from Krakow (who, due to his wife's efforts, was later released from the camp)—a very decent man. I was a patient in the hospital for about two weeks, and these colleagues arranged for me to work in the laboratory, which was located on the ground floor of barracks number 28. In this lab I performed normal tests for hospital use: blood, urine, and sputum. The lab was equipped with basic equipment such as microscopes, for example. The director was a young man whose name I don't remember (he was shot to death in Birkenau). As nurses, we slept in one of the rooms across from the lab. One of the prisoners who had traveled far abroad before the war told us of his adventures—unfortunately, I can't remember his name. He spoke in a lovely, literary language. We listened to his stories before falling asleep.[8] In a word, given the general conditions in the camp, my lot was pretty easy. But it did not save me from contracting typhus, which happened about a month after I arrived in the camp. It wasn't difficult to get infected, given the epidemic conditions prevailing there.

Typhus was endemic in the overcrowded camps and posed a serious concern for the SS physicians, It is an infectious bacterial disease well known since the Middle Ages as "spotted fever." Another common name was "jail fever," as it often infested prisons. The agent of transmission is lice. Until the wide use of pesticides like DDT, the prevention of typhus depended on hygiene. In July of 1940, the Nazis used Zyklon B, a hydrocyanic acid, to fumigate Auschwitz buildings.[9] The stripping, showering, and shaving of prisoners was part of lice control measures. These delousing rituals were not sufficient. The barracks were infested with lice. The symptoms of typhus started with fever and chills and presented a rash in about a week. It was a deadly disease readily spread from prisoners to guards. In the conditions of the camp only underlying sound health—virtually unsustainable in the prison—provided a chance for survival.

> After getting sick, I was transferred to the section for infected patients, barracks number 20, where the prisoner Stössel[10] acted as block elder (*Blockältester*)[11] and Stanisław Kłodziński and others served as nurses. The patients were housed on three-level plank beds covered with gray blankets—totally flea-ridden. During this time the first transports of women prisoners arrived and they were housed in a part of the camp separated from the men's section with a wall. Typhus killed many. Additionally, we were subject to some kind of experiment: we were smeared with some kind of red paste. I myself was forced to take tablets with a special mark which started with the letter "B." After I took these tablets, I vomited. I was in a bad state, lost consciousness, and was lucky to survive. I was in the hospital some four to five weeks, until May 1942. At this time many of the sick died, done in by a SS man acting as orderly (SDG, *Sanitätsdienstgrad*) named Klehr and other helpers such as Stössel.
>
> When I recovered I did not return to work in the lab but was moved to one of the front barracks in the first row—across from the commandant's office. I had swollen feet and was extremely thin. Had they done a selection at this time I would surely have been a candidate for a death sentence.

The use of prisoners for experiments by SS physicians is well known. SS Dr. Josef Mengele (1911–1979) was the most notorious among them. He was a member of the Nazi Institute for Hereditary Biology and Race Hygiene and volunteered for the Waffen SS. Injured, he then volunteered to work in Auschwitz in 1943, where his work focused on twins and dwarfism to determine the heritability of traits. His coworker, SS Dr. Eduard Wirths, assessed his work in Auschwitz in August 1944 claiming that, "in his work on the analysis of the scientific materials available to him by virtue of his position [in Auschwitz], he has made a valuable contribution to anthropological science."[12] The more quotidian "research" efforts had more practical objectives: dealing with common infectious camp diseases like typhus. Zając, the young chemistry student from Krakow, reports an incident (June 1943) in the main camp: he and other young prisoners were chosen to report to barracks number 28, where they were asked by an SS doctor if they had or were suffering from an infectious disease, specifically typhus. If the prisoner declared himself healthy, the SS doctor instructed an orderly in a white uniform to inject them. "He injected everyone in the left chest with a brown liquid."[13] Zając then developed typhus.

Prisoners with medical training banded together to create some alternatives to the SS sponsored medical facilities if only to avoid the dubious attention of medical orderlies. The role of the "orderly in a white uniform" was often that of an active agent of murder. The SS medical orderly Joseph Klehr whom Stefan met also performed phenol injections. A syringe of phenol to the heart produced instant death. After the war, Klehr received 475 life sentences at the Frankfurt trials for murders committed "on his own initiative and with special malice."[14] Dr. Jaworski also mentioned Klehr's participation in selections of prisoners for gassing and calls him a well known executioner.[15]

Stefan encountered his boyhood friend from Andrychów, Stefan Hommé, in the main camp. Hommé was a trained pharmacist who had served in the Polish army. The Nazis arrested him and put him in Pawiak prison in Warsaw. He was transferred to Auschwitz in mid-1942,[16] and would become an important contact and resource in the prisoner network of health care.

The second Auschwitz camp, Birkenau, opened in October 1941, about two kilometers from the main camp. Birkenau was first planned to house a workforce of 30,000, though expectations were that it would be significantly expanded in the future. This was part of Himmler's grand scheme for the development at Auschwitz to lay "a stable foundation for a German future in the East."[17] The influx of prisoners began with some 10,000 Soviet POWs in early October, 1941, as the German army swept into the USSR. This new camp developed more slowly than planned due to a lack of construction materials. By August 1942 the first women's section was operational. New groups were added: in September 1943 a Terezienstadt family camp (Section BII6) was organized. The doomed Gypsy Family Camp (BIIe) lasted from from February 1943 until August 2, 1944, when 20,000 Gypsies were killed. One of the single largest groups sent into Birkenau were the Jews of Hungary who were transported to Auschwitz-Birkenau in June of 1944.[18]

But Auschwitz-Birkenau, Auschwitz II, is infamous not for its prisoners but for its role as an extermination center. The main camp, Auschwitz I, began as a site to terrorize local Poles and as a transit camp for forced labor shipped to Germany. The main camp had a prison block, block 11, and a crematorium to expedite camp hygiene.[19] But Birkenau had a special extermination task like the stationary death camps, the "Reinhard camps," Belzec, Sobibor, and Treblinka, which were set up between March and July of 1942.[20] This new function mandated the building of both gas chambers and industrial-sized crematoria. While the slave laborers of Auschwitz worked in munitions factories, mines, and chemical factories, Jews were dying in a root-and-branch genocide in Birkenau. Workers debilitated by disease or injuries were sent to their death in Birkenau by the thousands; Jews from Polish ghettos and from occupied Europe were funneled into mock shower rooms, gassed to death, and, once dead, incinerated by the hundreds of thousands. By July 1942, the machinery of the Birkenau camp was operational. Himmler himself visited the concentration camp complex, witnessed a selection of Jews from the Netherlands at the railroad ramp, and saw a bunker cleared of the dead.[21]

The victims had to abandon their suitcases and were stripped of their clothing before entering the gas chambers. The property stripped from the Jews became profits for the SS. Nazi records reveal that in February 1943, 824 boxcars of goods left the camp to line the coffers of the SS. But before they were shipped out, the valuables from the stripped victims ended up in the warehouse called "Canada." This warehouse began as three barracks, but expanded to more than thirty. The name was derived from Polish slang as some far-off, very rich place.[22] The plunder thus collected was sorted for resale, and as Stefan attested, was also a source of corruption for the SS men handling Canada goods. The concentration camp as labor camp was planned to provide profits from labor and plunder. Himmler was straightforward in his speeches; in 1942 he asserted, "We are not conceivable without the SS economic enterprises . . . if I do not get the money from some place or other. No one gives me the money as a present."[23] Slave labor was on the agenda, but so was the confiscation and sale of prisoner property.

Stefan saw this system at work:

> The camp gardeners were housed in the basement of barracks number 25, and among them was my colleague from Andrychów, named Hommé. There is where we organized a kind of clinic in which we treated prisoners who were in a state of panic, fearing a visit to the official hospital. At this time I served as one of the men pulling a camp gurney. We did a number of things. Among other things, our gurney was sent to the camp in Birkenau, where we picked up suitcases filled with valuables from some building.[24] Naturally, we were accompanied by SS guards. Our capo, whose name I don't recall, stole some of these and tried to use them to buy things in the camp. We went to Birkenau daily, and on a daily basis we brought back more than a dozen suitcases filled with valuables and unloaded them in the building which housed the *Geldverwaltung*, a one-story building next to the commandant's office of the main camp. We also transported other things but I can't recall them in detail.

One of the major work sites for the ordinary Auschwitz workers from the main camp was the IG Farben Buna factory complex, under construction some six kilometers from the main camp. The expected influx of German workers into the *Oststreifen* did not materialize and IG Farben management had to rely more on prison labor than planned. Initially, prisoners marched daily at 4 a.m. from the main camp to the Buna grounds. The prisoner laborers were thus exhausted before the beginning of the work day and a solution was sought: in July 1941, railroad transport from the main camp to the factory grounds started.[25] Stefan became part of this workforce. At the same time, a more efficient solution was planned. Rather than transporting workers, a permanent camp for Auschwitz workers close to the factory was already under construction. Auschwitz III, Buna-Monowitz opened on October 25, 1942.

More than 200 kommandos—work gangs—with between 20 and 300 workers each, came daily to the Buna factory site. In the fall of 1942, an 18-year-old, Tibor Wohl, was transported by the Nazis from the Czech ghetto Terezienstadt to labor in Buna-Monowitz, building the factory facilities. With no connections with any groups within the camp, with no professional training, Wohl became an ordinary worker: "We worked with shovels. We carried cement and iron rods. We shoved tubs and wheel-barrows. We shook in the rain, frost, and wind. Stomachs were swollen, limbs scrawny, the face swollen in the morning and hollow in the evening."[26] Underfed and overworked, prisoners could not sustain this effort. In contrast to this dangerous situation, Stefan's medical training gave him laboratory skills and, with the help of friends, changed his situation from laborer to technical worker:

> In May 1942 I was moved to Buna. This happened due to the support and intervention of colleagues. The majority of prison laborers at Buna had to do terribly difficult physical labor, but as my luck would have it, I ended up in the eight-person *Materialkontrolle,* industrial quality control. Our capo was a very sympathetic man, an educated, certified engineer. Unfortunately I can't remember his name or that of the others working with me there.

> At this time the prisoners were delivered to Buna by train. I would estimate that 2,000 prisoners worked there. We were awakened very early, and left the camp around 6 a.m. The conditions of the transport were awful. We were moved in covered railroad cars filled to the limit. We were packed in so closely that it was hard to breathe. Only those who were lucky could find a place near the small window. The other prisoners fought for air with difficulty, only waiting for the doors to open. Many fainted; there were even some deaths by suffocation. Equally macabre were the returns in the evening under the heat of the sun. The high temperature made the return even worse. Several times I got out of the wagon barely alive. My parents knew that the prisoner transport passed through the Oświęcim station daily, and came out to the platform hoping to see me. Likewise I tried to get a spot by the small window and more than once glimpsed them. My mother waved her handkerchief at me in greeting, and I raised my hand. Sometimes one of my younger siblings stood next to my mother. Sometimes the train even stopped in the station. The brief moments of contact were possible because one day while the train was standing in the Oświęcim station, I spotted an acquaintance and shouted to him to give my parents information when the train was scheduled to drive through the station. This acquaintance (whose name I cannot remember) told my parents and thus I had at least this way of experiencing the joy of seeing those nearest and dearest to me.

Most Auschwitz prisoners in 1941 and early 1942 were still Poles. Stefan clearly benefited psychologically from this brief contact and it would lead to further contact the next two years. His family was close by and aware of his situation. This contact was a surcease denied to other prisoners as inmates from all over Europe were aggregated in this eastern concentration camp over the coming years.

> The prisoners employed at Buna had the most difficult physical labor, with only a shovel and pickax for tools. This heavy labor naturally accelerated the exhaustion of the prisoners. I was lucky enough, as I mentioned earlier, to work

> in a lab which tested, among other things, the quality of arriving building materials, mainly bricks and cement. We performed various stress tests. Naturally this kind of work demanded some familiarity and technical skills and as a former medical student I knew something about lab work (I had graduated in 1938 and passed my [medical] exams in 1939). The beginning of the war prevented the completion of those exams. I took some exams secretly with Professors Młodinski, Gieszczykiewicz, and Walter. I did receive my diploma and was employed in the St. Lazarus Hospital's Clinic of Internal Medicine in Krakow.

Stefan had begun his medical studies in Krakow's Jagiellonian University's medical faculty on October 7, 1933. The university was organized into trimesters. Stefan's transcript is a 5 by 7-inch book which lists each class Stefan took and the number of hours per class and bears the signature of each professor. This register bears the number L. 3696. He studied without interruption until May 30, 1939, when his classroom work was completed. In the fall, the university was closed by the Germans. The university went underground. Professors continued to teach students such as Stefan to make sure that all final exams and internships were completed.[27]

> A German civilian master worker also worked in the lab. He was a decent man and I asked him to get in touch with my parents, who at that time were living in railroad property near the Oświęcim station. He was able to do so and through his efforts I got news of my parents and even food. Unfortunately I don't remember his name. He was the lab director. In a word, thanks to my quiet work environment and my ability to maintain contact with my parents, I was in a much more favorable position than hundreds of other workers performing physical labor.

Prisoners received letters. The SS were unable to hermetically seal the camps from outside contacts. Prisoners at the factory even worked next to civilian workers. The daily transports offered opportunities to develop human contact. Stefan's family was local and maintained communication and eventually even visits. Poles in

Auschwitz had the psychological and practical advantage of family and friends close by who could send packages and receive mail. Prisoners were forced to send formulaic monthly post cards to their home address. Two German sentences were allowed: "I am healthy. I feel fine."[28] Essentially these cards were a way of proving to those at home that you were still alive. The political theorist and philosopher Hannah Arendt emphatically believed the camps created total isolation: "The real horror of the concentration and extermination camps lies in the fact that the inmates, even if they happen to keep alive, are more effectively cut off from the world of the living than if they died, because terror enforces oblivion."[29] The prisoner narratives do not always support this view.

Some prisoners, Polish prisoners in particular, received food. Food packages served three functions: incoming food was more nutritious than the miserable camp rations, food could be used to bribe the SS and other prisoners, and food could be shared with friends to build community. Many prisoners could survive thanks to the extra nutrition they received, even if it was not large.[30] In contrast, inadequate camp food led to malnutrition and starvation. Men performing physical labor were daily fed 150–200 grams of bread, soup cooked with potatoes and meat remnants, a little bit of marmalade, and a poor grade of cheese or margarine. Jan Sehn, a judge in the postwar Nazi war crimes trials in Poland, reports that the Nazis claimed that heavy workers got 2,150 calories and medium workers 1,738 calories. The actual amounts were 1,744 calories for heavy workers and 1,302 for medium workers. The League of Nations published statistics showing that the minimum number of calories needed to sustain health was 4,800 daily calories for heavy workers and 3,600 for medium workers.[31] Camp inmates were on starvation rations. Getting packages did not automatically mean a windfall of food since they were subject to "inspections" during which some items disappeared.[32] Maximilian Grabner, Gestapo chief in Auschwitz, admitted to large scale thefts in the camp parcel office, but fortunately, enough came through to make a difference to prisoners.[33]

Stefan, a physician, was vitally concerned with food and its distribution:

> The worksite of the prisoners was surrounded by SS guards and a barbed wire fence. The prisoners working at Buna got some soup at midday, which tasted better and probably was a little higher in calories than the soup in the camp. If I remember correctly, we brought the soup kettles with us and had to carry them back.[34]

> In the afternoon we returned from work. Our work unit (*Kommando*) was one of the last to return at the end of the day. Unfortunately I can't judge the death rate in our group. I don't know who the group leader was. On the other hand, the Obercapo position was held by a Polish prisoner—Bolek Pressen.[35] He was known for being good humored and I can't recall that he treated the prisoners badly. Naturally, as we were lining up he could push someone, but he didn't beat us like other prisoner functionaries. He didn't have a good reputation among his peers. It was said that he signed the *Volksliste* and associated with various people. But one has to realize that a man in his position was a subject of great interest and one could always find someone with an opinion. Most of the prisoner functionaries (the capos) in Buna were almost exclusively Germans, the majority of whom had passed through the KL Sachsenhausen, where probably 70% of the prisoners wore the green triangle [criminals], actually the same was true at the main camp [Auschwitz I].
>
> I worked at Buna to the end of July or perhaps the beginning of August, 1942. The spreading epidemic crossed the wires of the camp and the victims now were not only the prisoners but also the SS men. Even one of the SS doctors, named something like Szwalbe, died of typhus. Fearing that the epidemic would spread to the civilian workers employed by IG Farbenindustrie, the supply of prisoners was interrupted.

In 1942 the epidemic affected the town of Auschwitz and killed some SS personnel and their families. Commandant Höss ordered strict quarantine of SS men and their dependents in July. Swimming and washing in the Sola River was prohibited. The Auschwitz SS leadership faced a massive problem trying to control this typhus outbreak. On May 10, 1942, the typhus epidemic killed the Garrison SS Captain, Dr. Siegfried Schwela.[36] Between August and November, 1942, no Auschwitz prisoners were allowed to work at Buna. This was a significant problem for the factory management. Prisoner labor was important to meet construction time tables.

The conditions in Auschwitz as a whole were changing dramatically. On February 15, 1942, the first transport of Jews had arrived to be murdered, never registered, never part of the routine of labor. The extermination camp period had begun.[37] The level of daily danger in Auschwitz increased for the long-term prisoners. The camps became more violent and deadly. During the month of March 1942, there are records of 2,397 deaths. On the single day of Sunday, March 15, 1942, drunken SS guards shot 131 men before the morning roll call. The total for the entire day was 103 Russian POWs murdered, as well as 198 Poles, 68 Jews, 20 Czech, 8 Germans, and 2 Yugoslavs.[38] Deaths by shooting and beating were routine, but now the typhus epidemic became an additional scourge.

Typhus struck the women's section of the main camp on March 27, 1942. An attempt to treat the outbreak with Lysol baths didn't affect the lice but instead spread the disease more rapidly.[39] The monthly death rate figures climbed to 500 men during 1942. Not only were men dying of typhus, but also those who were ill were being killed with phenol injections to contain the epidemic.[40] A new garrison physician, SS Dr. Kurt Uhlenbrock, was installed on August 17 but was forced to leave on October, 2, 1942—ill with typhus.[41] Further attempts to halt the spread of the epidemic now involved gassings: on August 29, 746 prisoners were gassed to death; another general gassing took place on October 10, 1942.[42] The August 29, 1942, selection, which Stefan witnessed, was announced as a transfer to Birkenau from the infirmary in the main Auschwitz camp. Prisoner doctor Antoni Makowski explained that the Nazi policy was "to kill the sick, as well as those in contact with them, with the gas Zyklon B." He listed death selections due to typhus continuing in January and February 1943.[43] The acute phase of the epidemic did not abate until later in the spring of 1943. Typhus remained endemic and remained a threat to any prisoner. The information Danuta Czech was able to collect about the daily events at Auschwitz relies on records found or reconstructed. The total picture is incomplete because the registers for the women in the camp (first in the main Auschwitz camp and later in Birkenau) were destroyed by the Nazis.[44]

> During the period when we were shipped to Monowitz, we had the opportunity to meet groups of women (at this time women prisoners were still housed at the main camp). We saw the tragic sight of young and pretty women transformed into ruined objects with gray skin, wrinkled faces and gray, shorn hair. Even if we could come to terms that we men were incarcerated in the camps—after all, we thought of war as a usual fate for men—even so it enraged us that women were treated as badly as we were.[45] We heard of the SS men's attempts to use gas in the first crematorium, during which Slovakian Jewish women were killed. Once, as we were being transported to work, we could see a crowd of women and men driven towards the old crematorium. This was probably in July 1942. All of this had a terrifically depressive impact on our psyches.
>
> As the transports to Buna were halted [due to the typhus outbreak], the prisoners were organized into different work units. Since I knew this was happening, I asked colleagues for help to get assigned to the prison hospital. The intervention of my colleagues Zbozień and Zabicki got me the new work assignment as a nurse in the surgical barracks number 21, on the first floor where my colleague Zbozień was in charge. As hospital workers in this period, we lived through more than one tragedy. The camp authorities took the task of liquidating the camp typhus outbreak literally: they sent all of the typhus patients in barracks number 20 to be gassed. One day they drove up to barracks number 20 with a truck on which they loaded the sick and drove

> them off to Birkenau. Among them was one of our colleagues (I don't remember the name) who had an inflammation of his saliva glands and was directed to barracks number 20, where he met his fate. This colleague stepped on the platform of the car in tears and no one could help him or even raise a voice in protest. In the choice of sick people many SS doctors from the main camp participated. Their leader was the camp doctor (*Lagerarzt*) Entress.

Dr. Jaworski adds a poignant note to the image of desperate and terrified prisoners. While he was ill in the prisoner hospital in the Auschwitz III camp, Buna-Monowitz, he noted the danger: "If a prisoner happened to seek treatment in the clinic on a day of transport, they were taken, too, even without being examined by the *Lagerarzt* [camp SS doctor], only by the SDG [medical orderly] Klehr. Sometimes completely healthy people came to the hospital just to change their work units and paid with their lives [as they were added to the Birkenau gas chamber transport]."[46]

NOTES

1. Szymborska, *Seventy Poems*, 30–31.
2. Czech, *Auschwitz Chronicle*, 133.
3. Dixon, *Commanders of Auschwitz*, 83–84. Entress was tried for war crimes in March 1946 and was hanged at Landsberg-am-Pech Prison on May 27, 1947.
4. Langbein, *People of Auschwitz*, 34; Makowski, *Häftlingskrankenbau in Monowitz*, 129.
5. Langbein, *People of Auschwitz*, 221.
6. Zając, *Powrót Niepożądany*, 119.
7. Phlegmons are subcutaneous staph bacterial abscesses.
8. Zając recalls (*Powrót Niepożądany*, 106) similar moments at Montelupich: "I talked Julek into reciting for us in the evening, after roll call, fragments of Sienkiewicz's *Trilogy*."
9. Deborah Dwork and Robert Jan van Pelt, *Auschwitz 1270 to the Present* (New York: W. W. Norton, 1996), 219.

10. Langbein (*People in Auschwitz,* 183–84) mentions Polish officer Alfred Stössel, block elder of the infirmary, as a prisoner functionary in barracks number 20 who was eventually shot by the SS at the Black Wall in March 1943 but was also implicated in the phenol injection killings.
11. Prisoner functionaries were designated with the term "-älteste" meaning roughly "senior" or "eldest" thus often a long-term prisoner or one placed in a superior position. Prisoner functionary positions were, for example, *Lagerälteste* (camp eldest, responsible to the SS), and *Blockälteste* (barracks eldest, responsible for order in the barracks). Positions manned by the SS usually contain the term *-führer*, that is, "leader," such as *Lagerführer* (SS officers with authority over prisoners but not guards or other SS men) and *Blockführer* (the SS chief of one *Block* or barracks (Debski, *A Battlefield of Ideas,* 265–66).
12. Quoted in Czech, *Auschwitz Chronicle,* 819.
13. Zając, *Powrót Niepożądany,* 137.
14. Langbein, *People in Auschwitz,* 392.
15. Jaworski, *Apel Skazanych,* 120.
16. Leon Wanat, *Za Murami Pawiaka* (Warsaw: Książka I Wiedza, 1967), 423. Hommé survived Auschwitz and immigrated to the US in the 1950s.
17. Dwork and van Pelt, *Auschwitz,* 254.
18. Steinbacher, *Auschwitz, A History,* 90–91: 1944 map of Auschwitz II-Birkenau.
19. Dwork and van Pelt, *Auschwitz,* 174. Block 11's underground cells were used to try out Zykon B on September 3, 1942 (292).
20. Wachsmann, *KL,* 293.
21. Dwork and van Pelt, *Auschwitz,* 319.
22. Gunrun Schwarz, "Frauen in Konzentrationslager—Täterinnen und Zuschauerinnen," in *Die Nationalsozialistischen Konzentrationslager,* edited by Ulrich Herbert, Karin Orth, Christopher Dieckmann, vol. 2 (Frankfurt am Main: Fischer Verlag, 2002), 803.
23. Quoted in Michael Thad Allen, *The Business of Genocide: The SS, Slave Labor, and the Concentration Camps* (Chapel Hill: University of North Carolina Press, 2002), 140.
24. Stefan is referring to "Canada."

25. Wagner, *IG Auschwitz,* 69.
26. Tibor Wohl, *Arbeit mach tot: Eine Jugend in Auschwitz* (Frankfurt am Main: Fischer Taschenbuch Verlag, 1990), 37.
27. Jan Oswald, *Die Ermittlung im Fall "4 Js 798/64" Handlungsspielräume von Funktionshäftlingen in nationalsozialistischen Konzentrationslagern am Beispiel des Monowitzer Revierältesten Stefan Budziaszek alias Stefan Buthner* (dissertation, printed on demand, GRIN Verlag, 2006), 55.
28. Jaworski, *Apel Skazanych,* 85.
29. Quoted in Debski, *A Battlefield of Ideas,* 28–29.
30. Ibid., 147.
31. Jan Sehn, LL.D., *Concentration Camp Oświęcim-Brzezinka (Auschwitz-Birkenau)* (Warszawa: Wydawnictwo Prawnicze, 1957), 53. Jan Sehn was on the Commission for the Investigation of Nazi Crimes in Poland.
32. Zając, *Powrót Niepożądany,* 73.
33. Langbein, *People in Auschwitz,* 26.
34. Zając recalls that a "buna soup" was provided by the factory. It was thin and unfortunately extremely salty (Zając, *Powrót Niepożądany,* 142). Wagner reports that the "buna soup" was provided in addition to the camp food and consisted of vegetable ends and occasional pieces of potato peelings, and after the spring 1943 expansion of the Monowitz kitchens, it was prepared there and transported in thermoses to the factory (Wagner, *IG Auschwitz,* 129–30). Jaworski (*Apel Skazanych,* 60) also comments on the soup as being more nutritious but also very salty.
35. Jaworski writes of Bolek Pressen: "The position of the Buna Capo was newly given to a young, energetic, Polish, red-triangle prisoner [i.e., political], said to have been an actor in Warsaw." Jaworski, *Apel Skazanych,* 54.
36. Czech, *Auschwitz Chronicle,* 165.
37. Ibid., 135.
38. Ibid., 143.
39. Ibid., 150.
40. Ibid., 182.
41. Ibid., 220.
42. Ibid., 229, 251.

43. Makowski, *Häftlingskrankenbau in Monowitz,* 117.
44. Czech, *Auschwitz Chronicle,* 151.
45. The Polish prisoners, those civilians who had identified with the Polish resistance to the Nazi occupation, saw their imprisonments in Montelupich prison in Krakow or the Pawiak prison in Warsaw, and their transfer to labor camps like Auschwitz, as part of the bitter fortunes of a lost war.
46. Jaworski, *Apel Skazanych,* 171.

5

THE JAWISCHOWITZ SUBCAMP

Falling from the roof
I can safely land on green grass.

Spadajęc z dachu
Umiem spaść miękko w zielone.[1]

One of the objectives of interviewing survivors such as Stefan 30 years after the war was to collect as many names and episodes as possible. Stefan was able to remember Polish colleagues as well as some of the notorious Nazis whom he encountered at Montelupich and Auschwitz. His clearest recollections deal with his coworkers, men with whom he had daily contact. One aspect of long-term survival was the help of such social support groups within the camp. Historian Wagner writes: "Only membership in a larger prisoner group, which had a measure of influence in the camp, meaningfully increased one's chances of surviving."[2] Prisoners witnessed an unending series of atrocities, often of strangers, sometimes of colleagues.

One of Stefan's university professors had been arrested and arrived in Auschwitz on July 30, 1942. Dr. Marian Gieszczykiewicz, professor of bacteriology at Jagiellonian University, encountered some of his students in the infirmary. They tried to protect him by claiming a sham illness, to no avail. "At 9:00 a.m. roll call Leader Palitzsch issued an order to bring Gieszczykiewicz to the bunker of block 11 [execution chamber], regardless of his physical condition. They put the completely healthy professor on a stretcher and covered him with a blanket. Roll Call Leader Palitzsch pulls back the blanket, checks the number, and kills Professor Gieszczykiewicz with two shots to the head."[3] Gerhard Palitzsch was one of the original thirty "green triangle" criminals recruited from KL Sachsenhausen on August 20, 1940. Longtime concentration camp prisoner Langbein writes: "He was one of the few who looked the way Nazi propaganda loved to present SS men: athletic, blond, well built. His wife, with whom he lived in the camp area, died of typhus in the fall of 1942. This was an indication that Palitzsch had 'organized' clothes for her from the Canada warehouse because this was the only way the woman could have come in contact with an infected louse."[4] Palitzsch did not consider theft an ethical problem. Neither was murder. His most important role was that of block 11 executioner. On November 11, 1941, for instance, he shot 151 Polish political prisoners using small-caliber weapons fired point-blank at the base of the neck.[5]

After the war, Höss, the Kommandant of Auschwitz, tried to exonerate himself from the crimes at Auschwitz by blaming Palitzsch: "It is mainly Palitzsch's fault that there were such depraved violations and inhuman mistreatment of the prisoners. As duty officer he was in the position to prevent most of it, but to the contrary, he wanted this to happen in order to feed his hunger for power. It was also his doing that allowed the kapos to rule, which caused such a disaster in Auschwitz."[6] Palitzsch was subsequently arrested by the SS for race defilement, *Rassenschande,* for having sex with Jewish inmates.[7] Stefan also mentions Hans Aumeier, the deputy to the camp commander, Höss. Aumeier arrived in Auschwitz on February 1, 1942. Though virtually uneducated and almost illiterate, he had attained the rank of major: *SS-Sturmbahnführer der Waffen SS.* "He was responsible for many draconian methods, including tortures, beatings and executions."[8] In 1943 he was transferred out of Auschwitz for unspecified "violations" and was ultimately executed in Montelupich in 1947.[9]

> Besides such experience there were others, equally tragic. Among them were the deaths, the executions. Those slated for execution knew about it for many hours, since their numbers were called during roll call and they were ordered to remain in the camp after their morning roll call and to report to the chancellery (*Schreibstube*). When the workers marched out of the camp, the condemned were forbidden to leave their barracks, and then groups of the condemned, escorted by SS men and the recorder (*Rapportführer*) Palitzsch and the camp leader (*Lagerführer*) Aumeier, were taken towards barracks number 11. I personally suffered deeply the execution of people I knew, especially that of Prof. Gieszczykiewicz, my colleague Stefan Źabicki, and many others that I knew. It was so demoralizing that I asked myself each morning if this was going to be my last day.
>
> Besides all this, there was the liquidation of ill and exhausted prisoners with phenol injections.[10] Emaciated, starving prisoners suffering from a lack of albumin approached organic collapse and became what were called "Musselmen." This state was accelerated by long-term imprisonment (*Haftpsychose*) and psychological breakdowns. The SS doctor Entress made initial selections already in the outpatient clinic in barracks number 28. Prisoners selected for execution were led to the basement of this barracks. From there they were taken to the building opposite the outpatient clinic. There they were injected with phenol and corpse carriers (*Leichenträger*) circled by for hours with stretchers carrying out the remains of the murdered prisoners.[11]

The image of a prisoner verging on collapse is repeated often in prisoner narratives. As mentioned previously, the enormous stress of the adjustment to concentration camp life described by Dębski and others overwhelmed prisoners with no support system and no previous regimented experience and who were exhausted by the unremittingly hard labor, in some work units under starvation diets. The Nobel-Prize-winning Hungarian novelist (and camp survivor) Imre Kertész describes the character Georg in *Fatelessness* as one of these lost souls: consumed with hunger, bedeviled by apathy, and no longer in contact with reality.[12] Why they are called *Musselmänner* [Moslem men] is entirely obscure. It is probable that this camp jargon reflected some European stereotype of the appearance of Muslims as having inexpressive faces. Stefan had recognized this debilitated state already in the lawyer in Montelupich who lacked affect or responsiveness after SS torture. In a later part of his testimony, Stefan mentions the vulnerability of Dutch Jews. They were psychologically unprepared.

The prisoner hospital in Auschwitz I, the main camp, manned by functionary prisoners and controlled by SS physicians, consisted of barracks numbers 9, 19, 20 (infectious diseases), 21, and 28 (the ambulatorium, i.e., the outpatient unit).[13] These barracks should have represented a site of respite or healing, but instead, prisoners avoided them assiduously because serious debilitation meant a death sentence. Prisoners were fully aware that the SS physician (*Lagerarzt*) would send seriously ill patients either to be gassed or be injected with "a syringe of 100 cc of 40% phenol" directly into the heart.[14] SS Dr. Friedrich Entress organized this system of murder. Since his arrival in Auschwitz in December, 1941, Entress perfected the methodology of these syringe deaths as well as in the selection process of the victims.[15] The courtyard of block 11, another killing ground, targeted ordinary prisoners. The *Auschwitz Chronicle* compiled by Danuta Czech enumerates the daily executions by pistol fire in numbing profusion.

From his vantage point in the prisoner hospital block 21, Stefan also saw these executions.

> We could observe massive numbers of executions from the attics of barracks number 21. Personally I couldn't force myself to watch them. I only witnessed the death of one prisoner who was executed by Palitzsch. Any windows facing barracks number 11 were nailed over with boards but one could see the executions through cracks between the boards. The executions hit principally prisoners—mainly Poles. But it also happened that

> civilians were transported in to be executed. One transport consisted of Jewish women dressed in furs; at another time the transport consisted of Polish village children where some soldier or perhaps SS man was killed. At least that was being said in the camp. There were also massive executions of Soviet prisoners of war, who were treated bestially by the SS men (ironically, towards the end of the war, German officers and soldiers who were rebelling on the Eastern Front were liquidated in KL Auschwitz. I saw a large number of German uniforms).

The Auschwitz health system was in a state of crisis. A new player was recruited. SS Dr. Eduard Wirths, the new Auschwitz garrison physician, arrived in Auschwitz on September 6, 1942. Eduard Wirths (1909–1945) got his doctorate in medicine in 1936 from the University of Würzburg. He joined the Nazi party in May 1933 and in 1936 he became an SS man, which led him to join the Waffen SS in September 1939. His field of study was "racial science" and in particular, gynecological surgery. He served on the Soviet front and was pulled back to work in concentration camps (April 1942) for health reasons.[16]

His first assignment was Dachau, and there his amanuensis was the long-term concentration camp prisoner, Hermann Langbein. Langbein's book, *People of Auschwitz,* is a substantial source for information about the staffing and inmates of Auschwitz. SS Dr. Wirths was a complex individual. Langbein's depiction of him vacillates between admiration and condemnation. SS Dr. Wirths arrived during the debilitating typhus epidemic which was striking both inmates and the SS men and their families. He arrived with a high reputation and was mandated to halt the typhus epidemic and in particular to deal with loss of labor. Prisoners were no longer allowed to go to Buna to work for fear of infecting civilians at Buna, but this also meant that the SS was not earning income from hiring out prison labor and the Buna factory was not meeting its building schedule.

SS Dr. Wirths was responsible for the health of all the Auschwitz camps and subcamps. He arrived as a reformer and immediately began reassigning personnel to create a more effective medical service. He also ordered the phenol injection killings stopped and transferred Entress and his confederate Klehr. When the typhus epidemic waned in spring of 1943, the commandant Höss lauded Wirths's work.[17] Hermann Langbein devoted a section of his book to the contradictory character of SS Dr. Wirths.[18] Langbein had previously worked as Wirths's secretary in Dachau. They met again in Auschwitz and Wirths re-engaged Langbein.[19]

Stefan met SS Dr. Wirths in Auschwitz I, the main camp, and the encounter changed the trajectory of Stefan's life.

> Unexpectedly, at the beginning of September 1942, the SS main camp doctor (*SS-Standortartz*) Dr. Wirths showed up in the hospital barracks and ordered a meeting of all the prisoner physicians. I didn't know what this meeting was going to be about. Wirths walked along the row of standing doctors, asked "*Wer sind Sie*?" ["Who are you?"], and walked on. He asked me the same question. He then gestured in my direction, saying, "*Sie komm mit. Alles mitnehmen. Sanka ist unten. Verlegung nach Jawischowitz.*" ["You come along. Bring everything. The ambulance is below. Transfer to Jawiszowic"]. The order "to bring everything" was especially amusing in my situation, since as a prisoner I didn't even have a handkerchief. Disoriented with all this, I heard the current senior prisoner or "camp elder" (*Lagerälteste*) of the HKB [*Häftlingskrankenbau*, i.e., the prison hospital], whose name was Hans Bock and was called "Daddy," say to me, "*Na ja, du wirst doch besser haben*" ["Well, it will be better for you there"]. In this way, quite unexpectedly, I found myself in the subcamp Jawischowitz.

Stefan came to Wirths's attention because Wirths needed more medically trained prisoners for the reorganization of health services in the camps. However, Stefan only hints at the political and ideological maneuvering changing the way the camp was being run. It is likely that he was unaware of conflicts at the upper levels at this time.

The battle for camp influence among the old hand criminal green triangles and the incoming political and resistance oriented red triangles was an enduring subtext of camp life. Stefan was still on the margins in these struggles and was going to spend the next nine months in a remote subcamp, Jawiszowice, before returning to Auschwitz III, the new Buna-Monowitz labor camp.

The term "Auschwitz" is iconic but hopelessly imprecise. The Oświęcim/Auschwitz Museum has identified a total of 50 labor camps in the Auschwitz system. Auschwitz I, II (Birkenau), and III (Buna-Monowitz) were only the major units. Factories such as Siemens and DAW (*Deutsche Ausrüstungswerke, GmbH*), a munitions factory, used slave labor as did farm sites (vegetable farms, fish farms, poultry, and rabbit farms) on behest of the SS Economic Administration Office (*SS-WVHA, Wirtschaftsverwaltungshauptamt*). Fundamentally, the enormous Auschwitz complex was run as a for-profit enterprise which hired out labor (prisoners) locally.

Twelve kilometers west of Auschwitz I was the small village of Jawiszowice, a long-time mining town. The Jawischowitz subcamp was established there to serve the Brzeszcze-Jawischowitz coal mine, *Reichswerke Hermann Göring*. This mine formed part of the immense loot accumulated by the Nazi kleptocrat, Hermann Göring, better known for emptying European museums. The Jawischowitz camp opened on August 15, 1942, under the directorship of Sergeant Wilhelm Kowol. About 700 prisoners were housed in barracks near the mine by the end of 1942.[20] Stefan arrived to work here in September, 1942, and would find a measure of respite from the unremitting tension of the main camp:

> Subcamp Jawischowitz was opened in the summer of 1942. It turned out that my transfer was related to the situation in their clinic, to which two Jewish Czech doctors had been assigned. One of them was Wojciech Albert (he died after the war in Koszyce). The two of them, frightened, didn't know how to run this clinic under the control of the medical orderly staff sergeant (SDG *SS-Oberscharführer*) Wloka, an older man who himself didn't quite know how he ended up in the SS.[21] As I learned later, neither of these prisoner doctors wanted to

come to this newly opened facility (apparently there had been discussions about this), so my completely accidental transfer there worked to my benefit.

The subcamp Jawischowitz was a couple of kilometers from the main camp. Its wooden barracks were drowning in seas of green, which stood in stark contrast to the dense set of buildings in the main camp. Also, the subcamp lacked a crematorium and the infamous barracks number 11—and therefore lacked the whole atmosphere of terror which acted so perniciously on our psyches while in the KL Auschwitz [Auschwitz I].

In the subcamp Jawischowitz, the camp leader (*Lagerführer*) was the SS man Kowal, who existed in an unending alcoholic fog. He was dangerous and easily enraged, and known for his lack of concern for and maltreatment of prisoners. I don't remember the name of the prisoner functionaries but they were exclusively Germans wearing green triangles.

My relationship to the camp elder (*Lagerälteste*)—he was a German criminal—was awful. Actually, we didn't even talk to each other. The *Lagerälteste* was irritated by, among other things, that as a prisoner doctor I was not obligated to show up at roll call and I did not allow him any influence in the clinic. There were about 500 prisoners in the subcamp at this time.

Named as the *Lagerälteste* of the sick rooms in Jawischowitz, I set to work enthusiastically. I gave a list to Wloka of essential medicines and instruments needed to treat the most common injuries among the prisoners (cuts and bruises suffered working in the low mine shafts, occasional burns, etc.). Prisoners who had suffered more serious injuries had to be sent to the main camp. It was an unbelievably curious thing, but they were all returned to Jawischowitz after treatment.

As far as their nationalities are concerned, I remember there were not a few prisoner groups from Yugoslavia, Slovenes, tall and well-built men who had worked as miners in their homeland. I don't know why they ended up in this camp. There were

> few Poles. There were more Jews—one group from Antwerp, Holland (diamond cutters), Polish Jews from, for instance, Płonska, Jews from Greece.
>
> It should be made clear that mass arrivals of Jews didn't begin until April 1942 and from the same period more Jewish prisoner doctors ended up in the hospital. Later they began shipping Jews to KL Auschwitz from other concentration camps within the Reich, clearing those camps of Jews. These last transports held Jews who had been imprisoned for years, who ended up in concentration camps due to their political views, principally communists. The largest group arrived from KL Buchenwald and numbers of them took on prisoner functions in KL Auschwitz.

On August 20, 1942, Austrian and German political prisoners transferred in from Dachau. This transport included, as previously mentioned, Hermann Langbein, Karl Lill, and Ludwig Wörl, who soon become active in the camp resistance organization.[22] Stefan needed to deal with these men for the remainder of the Auschwitz years. Dachau, like Buchenwald and Sachsenhausen, was an *Altreich* concentration camp in which dense political networks formed especially among socialist and communist political prisoners. The arrival of Hermann Langbein and his compatriots added a sharp political dimension to decisions about who would control various safe functionary jobs in the various parts of Auschwitz. These changes in the main camp would impact Stefan after his nine month stint in Jawischowitz.

> Even though there was less terror evidenced in the subcamp Jawischowitz than in the main camp, and the prisoners had fewer nasty tricks played on them, there were nonetheless suicides, as prisoners threw themselves against the high tension wire fences. At least twice a night we'd hear shots. The *Lagerführer* Kowal became alarmed and told me to discover the fate of the prisoners who were shot. Anyway, Kowal was short tempered and beat prisoners with little cause. Another man who

> expressed himself by beatings was the *Lagerälteste* of the subcamp; I saw the effects of these beatings as I bandaged the wounds of the beaten prisoners.

These routine beatings took place in every Auschwitz unit. Zając relates that short-tempered SS men would curse and beat a prisoner for not removing his cap or for not answering correctly in German. They would force the prisoners to run and then shoot them in the back. SS guards would kill "prisoners trying to escape" to earn a couple of days of vacation.[23] Danuta Czech records virtually daily reports of these types of shootings which served not only for SS men amusement but were also one of the desperate strategies of prisoners seeking a quick death.[24]

> The clinic rooms in subcamp Jawischowitz consisted of one wooden barracks in which an outpatient clinic was located, as well as a hall of perhaps 15 beds. There was also a dental station manned by a Jewish prisoner from Frankfurt (I don't remember his name), a very cultured man. At the time when KL Auschwitz was receiving transports from Greece, they sent a Greek laryngologist to Jawischowitz. His name was Cuenka;[25] we're still friends to this day. He lives in Lausanne. He had attempted suicide during the transport by cutting his wrists. They clearly saved him and brought him bloody but alive to Jawischowitz. At the subcamp he fell ill with jaundice, but with care and nursing he returned to his health and to himself. We got to know each other and after I was later transferred to the Monowitz camp I attempted to have him transferred, too—him and the previously mentioned Dr. Wojciech Albert. Six doctors worked in the Jawischowitz clinic. Their names, except for those I mentioned, I cannot recall.

Stefan's gradual development of this outpost clinic served as important experience for his subsequent work in the Buna-Monowitz prisoner hospital. He brought prisoner doctors together and fostered the formation of groups. In this subcamp he had encountered Jewish doctors from Germany and Greece. This was only the beginning of what would become a major recruitment effort when he was moved to Auschwitz III, the large Buna-Monowitz labor camp.

> I can't remember if any executions took place while I worked in Jawischowitz—there were also no [organized] escape attempts. With time I gained some influence over the *Lagerführer* Kowal. Nonetheless I was enormously astonished to be called to his apartment where my mother was waiting for me. I don't know what influence she had or through whom she arranged a meeting under such circumstances. I had maintained contact with my parents using miners working next to prisoners as go-betweens. Unfortunately I don't remember the names of these people, and I didn't want to remember the names, either, in case of trouble.

As already noted, the close proximity of his parents allowed Stefan to maintain at least visual contact with his family even while he was on the transport train from Auschwitz I to the Buna factory. The benefit to his mental well-being was enormous. Eventually Stefan's father would bring needed medical supplies for the use of the Buna-Monowitz prison hospital. These were contacts tragically unavailable to those prisoners who arrived in Auschwitz from the various parts of Europe under Nazi control. The Buna-Monowitz camp, in particular, was a sieve, not a sealed site, since on a daily basis prisoners worked in proximity of nonprisoner workers. Historian Wagner notes: "The daily contact between the camp and the factory made it impossible for the SS to attain their goal of building a sealed camp universe."[26] This was even more true for the more distant subcamps like Jawischowitz.

Stefan continued to have opportunities to contact his colleagues in the main camp:

> Once a month I was driven to the KL Auschwitz pharmacy to replenish the small pharmacy at Jawischowitz. On these occasions I met with colleagues and acquaintances, among them Józef Cyrankiewicz and Stanisław Kłodziński.[27]

Occasionally I even stayed overnight in the camp [Auschwitz I]. I had a set-to with the *Lagerälteste* of the HKB [prisoner hospital], Hans Bock, about the text written on my sash. It said "*L. Ä. Häftlingsarzt*" ["*Lagerälteste* prisoner doctor"]. Bock claimed that only SS men could be doctors while prisoners could at best be labeled nurses or caretakers. His opinion didn't concern me since I was following rules which forced me to use the language printed on my sash.

In a word, my situation in the subcamp developed very positively in terms of work in the sick room quarters as well as in the atmosphere there in general. I know that the current mine director was interested in prisoner issues and even got us some benefits. I don't recall that he ever caused prisoners any injuries. He was actually a rather ordinary mine director. When I gave testimony a couple of years ago in Frankfurt am Main, I was asked a couple of questions about him (I don't remember this director's name) and the prosecutor had no particular evidence against him.[28]

Returning again to *Lagerführer* Kowal, I want to explain that he was demoted from his position as punishment (this happened after I was transferred to Monowitz) and became a simple SS man serving in KL Monowitz. Later he disappeared somewhere and I don't know what happened to him. At any rate, he was an exceptionally negative type.

Trading on my correct relationship with him, I attempted to influence him to forbid the beating of prisoners by functionaries. Our talk didn't eliminate them but to some degree controlled them.

Stefan used the term "correct relationship." This is one of the central questions of Stefan's ability to exert agency in Jawischowitz and later in the Buna-Monowitz prisoner hospital. How much freedom of action does a functionary prisoner have in relationship to his SS jailers? Political scientist Jan Oswald makes the point that the technical knowledge of prisoner physicians gave them leverage in their interaction with the SS. Once prisoner functionaries were needed for their skill, their room to maneuver (*Handlungsspielräume*) expanded. Men like Stefan and his cohort in the prisoner hospital had more independence and were less subject to punishments.[29]

> Once a month the subcamp Jawischowitz was personally visited by SS *Standortarzt* Wirths and weekly by one of the SS doctors. These visits were usually to ascertain if we had any typhus outbreaks. Naturally they themselves didn't examine the prisoners—I had to do that myself. As the prisoners returned from work I checked their temperature by touch but I'd stress that these weren't selections since in the Jawischowitz subcamp one didn't encounter occurrences of total exhaustion (*Körperschwäche*). There were also only a few cases of typhus. Actually the SS authorities didn't allow the transfer to KL Auschwitz of sick Jewish prisoners—would that it had been possible—so I had to operate in place when I encountered acute appendix inflammations. I operated under incredibly primitive conditions, on an ordinary table, having only an ordinary spoon and two [undecipherable] which had been sterilized in the kitchen. All the operations went well and none of my patients died. I assume that my work and ingenuity called attention to me and that it was probably the reason that I was transferred to the position of *Lagerälteste* in the prisoner hospital in KL Auschwitz III-Monowitz.
>
> I was informed about the upcoming transfer by SDG-Wloka, who said, "You are being moved to Buna" ("*Sie werden verlegt nach Buna*"), adding that Buna was experiencing significant losses and that I would replace the current *Lagerälteste* in that hospital. I was taken aback by this news and if I had had any choice I would surely have remained at Jawischowitz, which was a small camp in which I was in familiar surroundings, acculturated, and where I had contact with my parents. Unfortunately, as a prisoner, I had no influence on the decision. On a day in June 1943, the *SS-Standortarzt* Wirths arrived at Jawischowitz in his own car. This was a couple of days after the

> talk with Wloka. Wirths told me to get in the car and in this "luxurious" fashion I was driven to Monowitz. On the way, the *Standortarzt* informed me that Hans Bock, the previous *Lagerälteste* of the prisoner hospital in the main camp, was now at Monowitz. Wirths added that Bock was now an ordinary nurse and had no authority over me.

The internal frictions that developed in the camp pitting the criminal inmates, the greens, against political inmates, the red triangles, was overt on the personal level such as the sharp exchange about terms printed on Stefan's sash. Hans Bock challenged Stefan, but it was the SS Dr. Wirths who would seriously limit Bock's influence in Auschwitz I: "When Bock had been 'busted' as a camp elder in March 1943, the garrison physician [Dr. Wirths] chose for the first time an inmate with the red triangle of a 'political' for the influential position of the HKB [prisoner hospital] of the main camp."[30] This was Stefan. Dr. Wirths was choosing among all the people available for medical positions, not just old established prisoners. But functionary prisoner positions in the hospitals and clinics were highly desirable since these men were in safer, protected environments within a murderous system.

Langbein, who had arrived from Dachau just as Stefan was transferred to Jawischowitz, regained his influential position as SS Dr. Wirths's secretary when Wirths arrived in September 1942. Langbein was also highly politically active among prisoners on behalf of communist and politically left-leaning resistance movement inmates. He had placed his compatriot Ludwig Wörl, an x-ray technician without an x-ray machine, in the safe position as the camp elder in the newly constructed Buna-Monowitz prisoner hospital. Langbein, however, was only a secretary, even if one who had the confidence of his boss, SS Dr. Wirths. The decision to move Stefan from Jawischowitz to the Buna-Monowitz camp was not at all to Langbein's liking. Langbein lost influence when Stefan was placed in Buna-Monowitz. The men who worked within the small subset of the medical units in the various camps had to deal with rivalries and old grudges as well as the constant shortages and dangers of camp life.

While Stefan was urging Jawischowitz camp leader Kowal to end the senseless and counterproductive beatings, far more significant decisions began to influence the behavior of the SS men. The head of the SS business administration office in Berlin, Artur Liebehenschel, issued an order on August 19, 1942, to halt the abuse of prisoners. Danuta Czech notes, however, that orders from Berlin were not enough to change the culture of violence: "The order comes too late and results in no change in camp conditions. In Auschwitz, prisoners are constantly abused by fellow prisoners, predominantly by German criminal prisoners, who are encouraged in this by the SS, incited to it, and are never punished."[31] In December 1943, Liebehenschel moved from Berlin to Auschwitz, replaced Höss, and tried to implement a new attitude toward prisoners. Berlin needed workers!

NOTES

1. Szymborska, *Seventy Poems*, 142–43.
2. Wagner, *IG Auschwitz,* 136.
3. Czech, *Auschwitz Chronicle,* 207. Jeremy Dixon, *Commanders of Auschwtiz* (Atglen, PA: Schiffer Military History, 2005), 83, quotes Dr. Friedrich Karl: "On one occasion, on 31 July 1942 a prisoner by the name of Marian Gieszczykiewicz had been shot by *SS-Hauptscharführer* [Captain] Gerhard Palitzsch, the death certificate was signed by Entress and it stated that the victim had died of weakening resulting from intestinal catarrh."
4. Langbein, *People in Auschwitz,* 408–10.
5. Czech, *Auschwitz Chronicle,* 105.
6. Höss, *Death Dealer,* 311.
7. Langbein, *People in Auschwitz,* 409. Palitzsch was demoted to a camp in Brno and was rumored killed in the fight for Budapest in 1944.
8. Dixon, *Commanders of Auschwitz,* 61.
9. Czech, *Auschwitz Chronicle,* 807.
10. Entress organized the system for killing prisoners with phenol injections directly into the heart.
11. Jaworski (*Apel Skazanych*, 73) makes clear that prisoners knew full well what was happening.

12. Imre Kertész, *Fatelessness* (New York: Ransom House, 2004), chapter 7.
13. Steinbacher, *Auschwitz,* 24–25.
14. Jaworski, *Apel Skazanych,* 73 n11.
15. Czech, *Auschwitz Chronicle,* 811.
16. Konrad Beischl, *Dr. med. Eduard Wirths und seine Tätigkeit als SS-Standortarzt im KL Auschwitz* (Würzburg: Verlag Königshausen & Neumann, 2005), 17–18.
17. Dixon, *Commanders of Auschwitz,* 207
18. Langbein, *People of Auschwitz,* 365–85. Hermann Langbein, now Auschwitz prisoner #60355, arrived from Dachau on August 20, 1942 (Czech, *Auschwitz Chronicle,* 224).
19. Ibid., 369.
20. Czech, *Auschwitz Chronicle,* 217.
21. Franz Wloka remained medical orderly in Jawischowitz through October 1942 when he was briefly moved to Buna-Monowitz. SDG Gerhard Neubert replaced him in the Buna-Monowitz prisoner hospital in December 1942 (Makowski, *Häftlingskrankenbau in Monowitz,* 129).
22. Czech, *Auschwitz Chronicle,* 224.
23. Zając, *Powrót Niepożądany,* 141.
24. Czech, *Auschwitz Chronicle,* 164.
25. Dr. Leon Cuenka is listed in Makowski's text *Häflingskrankenbau in Monowitz* (123, 150).
26. Wagner, *IG Auschwitz,* 205.
27. Working in the Auschwitz I infirmary, Kłodzinski as well as Cyrankiewicz were active in the camp resistance movement, according to Langbein who states that they "carried on a continuous correspondence with Crakow" of which 350 letters have been preserved. (Langbein, *People in Auschwitz,* 254).
28. Davin O. Pendas reviews the German anti-Nazi trials in *The Frankfurt Auschwitz Trial, 1963–1965: Genocide, History, and the Limits of the Law* (Cambridge: Cambridge University Press, 2006).
29. Oswald, *Die Ermittlungen im Fall "4 Js 798,"* 26.
30. Langbein, *People of Auschwitz,* 219.
31. Czech, *Auschwitz Chronicle,* 224.

6

SLAVE LABOR ISSUES

> Keep up the good work, if only for a while,
> If only for the twinkling of a tiny galaxy.
>
> *Tylkotak dalej, dalej choć przez chwilę*
> *Bodaj przez mgnienie galaktyki małej.*[1]

In narratives written by Auschwitz prisoners, there is little evidence that they knew of the changes that were taking place in the organization of the camps. Every prisoner knew who the leader of the barracks was, knew his capo in the work unit, and might know the name of the camp commandant, but the actual changes in camp organization were difficult to perceive even by well-placed prisoners. However, changes on the commandant level as well as in the various departments could have an immediate impact on the prisoners.

The original commandant of Auschwitz was Rudolf Höss, who became the head of the new Auschwitz camp on May 4, 1940. He became the SS commandant appointed by Heinrich Himmler on the basis of Höss's experience in the older camps of Dachau and Sachsenhausen. A commandant was in charge of security and the internal camp administration.[2] Auschwitz kept expanding. Höss had to manage an enormous and complicated enterprise. Historian Sybille Steinbacher notes: "By the end of 1940 the camp building site in Auschwitz was so large that a decision had to be made . . . as to the location of the 'protective custody' camp, industrial site, workshops, barracks area, troop stores, SS housing and the agricultural estate. Zone after zone was added to the camp compound; the site was extended to such an extent that the SS soon acquired whole villages, forests, ponds, and farmland. The area was surrounded by warning signs, concrete walls, watchtowers, and double-depth, electrified barbed-wire fences that were illuminated at night."[3] The first year, 1940, the Polish political prisoners, members of the resistance and the intelligentsia, entered a realm of random death as well as systematic executions. However, Auschwitz was changing as it grew larger. For instance, Dr. Diem told the incoming Dr. Jaworski (April 18, 1942, about two months after Stefan) that officially men could no longer be beaten at work, let alone be killed at will, which used be a daily occurrence.[4] Prison labor was necessary for the Nazi war effort.

Dębski suggests that Auschwitz experienced a threefold change beginning in 1942. In the first place, SS men were being reassigned to the eastern front. The offensive against the Soviet Union was in full swing. Since the Barbarossa surprise attack against the USSR began in June 1941, millions of German soldiers were fighting on the new eastern fronts. Germany itself was facing an acute labor shortage and the camp prisoners and their labor were now seen as a valuable part of the war effort. With the SS men at the camp reassigned to more pressing duties on the fronts, the atmosphere in the camps moved away from simple punishment to maximizing the prisoners as workers, that is, fewer random killings.

Second, the camps were becoming overwhelmed with new prisoners. Random acts of brutality had decreased; however, the increase in the number of prisoners in the camp caused serious problems. The barracks were packed and the food grew worse with the arrival of men from conquered nations in Western Europe who were now dumped in the camps in the east. The original camp organization of 1940 was being stressed by the new conditions. Newcomers like SS Dr. Wirths in 1942 and the new Kommandant Liebehenschel in 1943 insisted that Auschwitz had to be run on different principles.

The third change was that in 1942 Auschwitz was designated as an extermination camp.[5] About 20–25 percent of all the Jews killed in the Second World War died in Auschwitz.[6] Nazis emptied the ghettos in Poland and Czechoslovakia and seized Jews in the cities of occupied western Europe. In 1944 the Nazi terror regime reached into both Hungary and Italy, seized the Jews, and transported them to Auschwitz. The vast majority of these men, women and children were never incorporated into the labor camps except for the healthiest and strongest of the men and women.

The impact on long-term prisoners of these profound changes in the size and the function of the camp depended on the functions that they performed. In a sense the manpower shortage of experienced prisoners in this sea of new arrivals increased the value to the camp of those prisoners who showed competence or had needed skills. In overwhelming numbers, prisoners, not SS underlings, became camp bureaucrats. Those prisoners who held positions such as barracks secretaries, central office workers, and hospital administrators were now called "prominent prisoners" to distinguish them from simple prisoners.[7] The hospital personnel at all levels fell into the functionary category and prisoner doctors became prominent prisoners. This is why prisoners sought work in the hospitals and clinics: they found more food, cleaner surroundings, and less stress. Hermann Langbein explained: "As the secretary of the Chief Camp Doctor I did not do heavy work, always had a roof over my head, no hunger, I could wash myself and wear clean clothes."[8]

Langbein was of the opinion that SS Dr. Wirths was an unusual man, more a physician than an SS man. "His reluctance was of the greatest practical importance to the prisoners, for he held the office of SS garrison physician . . . during virtually the entire period in which masses of human beings were murdered—and he accepted the consequence of his attitude as no other physician did." Langbein describes Wirths's behavior in Dachau: "He also makes rounds differently from the other physicians. Every day he walks from bed to bed, sometimes addresses a few friendly words to a patient, and once I even caught him trying to communicate with an old Pole in Polish, something that would never have occurred to any other arrogant SS man."[9] Langbein quotes Höss's memoir: "Wirths often complained to me [Höss] that he could not reconcile the killings demanded of him [by the Political Department headed by Maximilian Grabner] with his conscience as a physician and that this caused him a lot of suffering."[10]

Wirths's transfer to Auschwitz on September 6, 1942[11] was a direct consequence of the raging typhus epidemic. Wirths's function was to keep the prisoners available for work. Prisoners provided income for the SS. Maintaining a stable prisoner workforce meant creating a functioning hospital with actual doctors. In July 1942 an average of 150 prisoners died each day with typhus specifically listed as a cause. This was a familiar story. The same dangers existed in the camps in Germany. "The indifference of SS doctors threatened the entire prison population. Poor hygiene created a breeding ground for infectious diseases, and several epidemics spread through KL in the late 1930s."[12] In Auschwitz, the August epidemic of 1942 also affected the SS. The quarantines, begun the previous month, were again extended in the belief that the typhus was endemic in the city of Auschwitz. Critically, in October 1942 (this had affected Stefan), no men from Auschwitz could be sent out to Buna to work.[13] This hit the SS income stream and it was the obligation of the garrison physician to deal with this crisis.[14] As described above, Wirths recruited Stefan for work in Jawischowitz in September 1942, but as the health crisis in the main camp did not abate, he brought Stefan into the KL Auschwitz III Monowitz camp in June 1943. Wirths's reorganization displaced medically unqualified men who had found sanctuary as functionary prisoners in the hospitals. Stefan arrived in Monowitz in style in Wirths's private car, but his political problems with staffing would never abate.

The head of the SS, Himmler, was a central figure in the development of this Buna site and he strengthened the connection of the SS with German big business by tying IG Farbenindustrie to the Auschwitz "labor pool." The factory received a Nazi subsidy of 36 million *Reichsmark* and tax benefits. IG Farben took over 20.8 square kilometers at 44% below market rates to build their factory.[15] Himmler visited Auschwitz personally and saw his career gaining importance by involving himself as a critical supplier of needed war materials. The fate of the Buna factory and the Auschwitz system camps and subcamps were directly linked to the SS, which was determined to expand and develop the concentration camps. But under wartime conditions building materials were hard to procure. The deal with IG Farben was beneficial to both: the factory got cheap prison labor; Himmler got building material.[16] A deadly quid pro quo was developing as the relationship between camp and factory became more intense.

Heinrich Himmler had a grandiloquent vision of a new German order, a Nazi-run utopia for the master race. In Himmler's schema, the newly Germanized territories of former Poland, the Polish rump state, and the newly conquered Soviet territories existed for exploitation. Historian Michael Thad Allen has analyzed the directorship of the SS and Himmler's role in the configuration of the Nazi regime in the east. The emphasis on a New Order in the east meant that SS policies toward slave labor by the end of 1941 gradually veered toward the preservation of workers.[17] The vast planning needed for this new state suffered early on from management fiascos in the SS. Only in 1941 did a new group of capable bureaucrats rationalize the organization of the SS. In an atmosphere of limited resources, the scarcest resource was labor, especially in the construction sector.

Himmler demanded that Soviet POWs, an "unlimited" supply of labor, be devoted to the building up of camps and industry. The Nazis seized 3,350,000 Russian prisoners from June 1941 until March 1942. Only 5% actually reached Germany to work.[18] A catastrophic regime of mistreatment and a callous policy of starvation and exposure decimated the Soviet POWs. Germans were so critical and outraged about "wasting food" on millions of prisoners that the military reduced rations to starvation levels.[19] Soviet captives did not solve the labor problems in Germany. Hundreds of thousands were expected in Auschwitz. "By the end of the year, however, most of the expected Soviet prisoners perished due to mistreatment, starvation, and exposure before they had even arrived."[20]

On the one hand, Himmler championed the "final solution" of extermination, but on the other hand, the worker crisis only intensified as the war continued. On January 26, 1942, he issued a new order to the Inspector of Concentration Camps, Richard Glück, which would impact the prisoners in Auschwitz. Himmler ordered some Jews be spared for work in the camps: "you must make appropriate arrangements in the concentration camps for 100,000 Jews and up to 50,000 Jewesses. In the next few weeks the concentration camps will be assigned great industrial tasks."[21] One of those "great industrial tasks" was, of course, already ongoing and in competition for labor as well: the Buna factory.

The IG Farbenindustrie Buna factory used prisoners for only part of its personnel. In addition to slave labor, IG Farben recruited civilian laborers. The factory erected eight separate "barracks cities" for various foreign workers. These facilities were Spartan and located in the countryside around the factory installation. In November, 1942, Buna had over 20,000 of these civilian employees of whom only 4,120 were Germans. The ideological master plan for the New Order imagined that Germans would flock to work here. But over 9000 workers were Poles, most of them local, though Ukrainians, Italians, French, Croats, Belgians, and others worked at the factory as well, housed in the newly built barracks by nationality. Concentration camp workers were cheaper and supplemented civilian labor. IG Farbenindustrie paid the SS 4 RM for Auschwitz skilled labor and 3 RM for unskilled labor per day.[22] At the planned full deployment of 10,000 slave laborers, the SS could realize about 35,000 RM daily and a gross of perhaps 10 million RM annually. And this was just one enterprise in a vast system.

The Buna factory director, Walter Dürrfeld, was profoundly concerned that the heavy labor of erecting the new factory was behind schedule. Prisoners too exhausted to work effectively, *arbeitsunfähig*, were killed with phenol injections.[23] The erection of the factory was seriously behind schedule. For instance, of 20,400 piles needed for the factory's foundation, only 6,521 had been driven in by early 1942.[24] Several solutions were tried to avoid worker exhaustion: the first one, as noted, starting on July 29, 1941, involved transporting the prisoners from Auschwitz I to the factory site by boxcars.[25] The German attack on the Soviet Union starting in June 1941, however, caused delays in rail traffic as preferential material was moved eastward. Prisoners could be stranded on the trains waiting for traffic to clear, rather than arriving at work in a timely fashion.[26] The next attempt to solve the problem of moving workers directly from the Auschwitz main camp to the Buna work site was to build a narrow gauge railroad line to connect workers directly to the site. But the ultimate solution was simply to build a totally new camp, next to the factory, on the site of a demolished village: the Monowitz camp.

The typhus epidemic which resulted in the total quarantine and main camp lock down from August to November 1942 was the final impetus to rush to develop the new, separate camp.[27] By September, 1942, this new camp (named "Buna Lager IV" by IG Farben, or "Auschwitz III-Monowitz" by the SS) was ready for the prisoner workers. It only needed barbed wire installed to be complete. The camp was officially opened on October 28, 1942, with 600 men and between 60–100 functionary prisoners who were mostly recruited from the main camp. Its wooden barracks, 26 meters by 8 meters, were designed for 55 civilian workers, but were each used to jam in 250 prisoners.[28] By mid-1943, new barracks could not keep up with the influx, so two huge tents, each holding 1,000 men, were erected.[29]

From the point of view of IG Farbenindustrie, the organization which funded the building of the Monowitz camp, problems continued. The camp existed to provide workers for the Buna factory, but they were not arriving in the numbers that had been promised or expected. The Auschwitz records for February 1943 show that a special officer, SS Lieutenant Colonel Maurer, arrived to investigate why the number of prisoners at the Monowitz camp had significantly decreased.[30] The answer may well be found in the reoccurrence of the typhus epidemic noted in the same month. On March 3, the Commandant Höss received a pointed if remarkable reminder from Berlin that "Jewish armament workers from Berlin must at all costs be kept able-bodied. At the same time, it is ordered that they be transferred directly to the Buna auxiliary camp without being quarantined in Auschwitz."[31] The danger was that the workers could succumb to typhus if they moved through the main camp. The attempts to maintain an adequate level of able-bodied workers continued to be a matter of high-level discussion: on March 19 the Auschwitz concentration camp could not provide the prisoners promised for work in the Buna plant and one thousand non-Polish prisoners were ordered transferred from Mauthausen (an Austrian camp) to Auschwitz so they could be used in the Buna plant.[32] What was the problem?

The Buna plant needed specialized workers who had experience in the construction industry. If not trained, they needed at least able-bodied workers. However, the recruitment of workers was from various other concentration camps and did not produce the required numbers. A transport of 499 men from Dachau to Auschwitz I on October 19, 1942, consisted of men so badly nourished and ill that they were useless for the Buna work. Another transport arrived in the main camp from Buchenwald, supposedly consisting of 163 experienced builders. In the next week, 18 of them died, 3 were hospitalized, 22 were too weak to work, and others suffered from various maladies from frost bites to infections. In the end, 100 could be moved to Buna-Monowitz. Only two of the men in this transport had any actual experience in construction.[33] Since the recruitment of healthy, able workers from other concentration camps was so unsuccessful, the next strategy was to recruit Jews from ghettos. In January of 1943, the order went out to bring workers from Terezienstadt. Of the 5,022 Jews transported from Terezienstadt in late January, however, only 613 men and 316 women survived to work. The other men, women and children were gassed as *arbeitsunfähig*. IG Farben management was outraged and believed that the criteria for "unable to work" were unrealistic in the main camp and demanded that potential workers be delivered directly to the Buna-Monowitz camp. This order was ignored. The manpower shortage was aggravated by the strong competition for able men for work needed in other camps, in other factories, and even in Germany itself. For instance, between March and April 1943, 8,874 Jews arrived in Auschwitz I from Berlin. Only 3,813 people, of them 2,450 men, survived to work. The majority of them were retained in Auschwitz I, the main camp, or in Auschwitz II, Birkenau as workers. No more than 1,700 men were moved over to Auschwitz III, the Buna-Monowitz camp.[34]

Another aspect of the manpower crisis was the reckless policy of working the prisoners to exhaustion. Virtually every prisoner in Monowitz ended up in the Monowitz prisoner hospital for treatment.[35] But the other part of the problem was a short sighted attempt to save money. IG Farbenindustrie and the senior Buna plant administration led by Dürrfeld calculated that the new Monowitz slave labor camp didn't need investment in a clinic or hospital since workers were in an unending supply, cheap and replaceable. The work groups, the *Kommandos*, of the Buna factory involved all kind of physical tasks, but a number of them were frankly labeled *Erschöpfungskommandos*, jobs designed to kill workers by exhausting them. The routine work of carrying 50 kg cement sacks or stacks of roofing tiles had to be performed at a run by these men. Prisoners who collapsed were either beaten back to work or died in place.[36]

The more ordinary jobs were no sinecures: the factory had to be built from the ground up. The slave workers moved concrete and steel alongside the tens of thousands civilian workers employed by IG Farbenindustrie. By the end of 1942 the erection of this enormous complex required workers of greater skill. As more technical jobs had to be staffed, the factory administration realized that they were unable to attract or find German technicians in sufficient numbers. Skilled prisoners became more valuable. At this juncture, really critical workers were protected from gassing—skills provided protection.[37] The Buna camp, Monowitz, had only a single barracks devoted to medical services when it opened in October, 1942, but now the typhus epidemic, the paucity of civilian workers, and the loss of prisoner workers with critical skills mandated that a new medical service be put into play to change the medical facilities at Monowitz to an actual functioning hospital.

Doctors had not in fact been in charge of the hospital. The men who were running the Monowitz *Häftlingskrankenbau* (the HKB), the prisoner hospital, from October 1942 until June 1943 were politically well-connected civilians, not doctors. In March 1943, the political prisoner Ludwig Wörl was the head of the HKB. He had arrived in Auschwitz from Dachau with his ideological compatriot, Hermann Langbein. Langbein was in an excellent position to provide protective functionary positions to his allies. Wörl assumed the *Lagerälteste* position and brought with him Heinrich Schuster, another Austrian political prisoner, who became the next *Lagerälteste* of the HKB. There is no implication here that these men were anything other than well-meaning and diligent, but they were not medically trained. Controlling the HKB position produced desirable functionary positions and was thus valuable, but these men faced a daunting task dealing with prisoner illness and exhaustion. Monowitz came to a new low: 2000 men died in Monowitz between December 1942 and February 1943. The factory managers were alarmed. Despite the fact that the Buna factory executives had made little provision for medical services at Monowitz, Dürrfeld noted the incompetence of medical staff in the prisoner hospital and demanded changes.[38] The IG Farben Corporation did not bear any of the costs of the medical services (that was provided by the SS); however, they were responsible for expanding the hospital facilities. This they did reluctantly.[39]

The Monowitz camp was under the direction of the SS in the main Auschwitz camp, so it was the task of SS Dr. Wirths, the Auschwitz garrison physician recruited to control the typhus outbreak, to also provide improvements in Monowitz health care. In March 1943 he assigned his friend and colleague SS Dr. Horst Fischer to Monowitz. As the *Lagerarzt* at Auschwitz III, the Buna-Monowitz camp, SS Dr. Fischer made selections in the prisoner hospital to send exhausted or ill prisoners to their deaths by phenol injections or Zyklon B gas in Birkenau.[40] Camp lore was emphatic that a selection to Birkenau meant death. There is current evidence, however, that some prisoners were registered as alive in other Auschwitz units after their transfer from the Buna-Monowitz hospital. This would involve less than 10% of transfers. This would not have been known at the time nor was it mentioned at later Nazi trials.[41]

The agenda as determined by SS Dr. Wirths and the IG Farben management, however, was to keep workers on the job. In reality, SS Dr. Fischer in the Buna-Monowitz camp had little control over two major factors leading to prisoner exhaustion: the quality of the food supplied at Buna, and the nature of the work at the factory site (both controlled by IG Farben). On the other hand, the health facilities at the Monowitz camp was a variable that could be improved. SS Dr. Wirths remembered choosing Stefan for work at Jawischowitz in the fall of 1942. The Jawischowitz clinic was actually functioning and providing meaningful services to the mine workers. Satisfied with Stefan's performance at the mine, Wirths transferred Stefan to Monowitz on June 18, 1943.[42] The situation was critical. Stefan understood the medical crisis and, after he was moved to Monowitz, he also began to understand the political crisis.

NOTES

1. Szymborska, *Seventy Poems*, 108–09.
2. Steinbacher, *Auschwitz, a History*, 26.
3. Ibid., 29.
4. Jaworski, *Apel Zkazanych*, 52.
5. Dębski, *A Battlefield of Ideas*, 22.
6. Steinbacher, *Auschwitz, a History*, 133.
7. Dębski, *A Battlefield of Ideas*, 34.
8. Quoted in Dębski, *A Battlefield of Ideas*, 36.
9. Both quotes from Langbein, *People in Auschwitz*, 364.
10. Ibid., 367.
11. Czech, *Auschwitz Chronicle*, 234.
12. Wachsmann, *KL*, 170.
13. Czech, *Auschwitz Chronicle*, 261.

14. Testifying before the Frankfurt judges, Fejkiel [Dr. Władysław Fejkiel, #5647] characterized Wirths as "an intelligent physician and not a bad person. He brought medicines and knew how to combat typhus." Quoted in Langbein, 371.
15. Piotr Setkiewicz, *Z dziejów IG Farben Werk Auschwitz, 1941–1945* (Państwowe Muzeum Auschwitz-Birkenau w Oświęcimui, Oświęcim, 2006), 52.
16. Wagner, *IG Auschwitz,* 63.
17. Michael Thad Allen, *The Business of Genocide: The SS, Slave Labor, and the Concentration Camps* (Chapel Hill: University of North Caroline Press, 2002), 150.
18. Herbert, *Hitler's Foreign Workers,* 117.
19. Ibid., 155.
20. Allen, *The Business of Genocide,* 150.
21. Ibid., 151.
22. Czech, *Auschwitz Chronicle,* 55
23. Wagner, *IG Auschwitz,* 64.
24. Ibid., 78.
25. Czech, *Auschwitz Chronicle,* 75–76.
26. Wagner, *IG Auschwitz,* 93.
27. Czech, *Auschwitz Chronicle,* 261.
28. Wagner, *IG Auschwitz,* 97.
29. Zając ended up in the tents when he was transferred to Monowitz in July, 1943. "Life in the tents wasn't very happy. The [capos] tried to control and punish the incoming prisoners with cudgels." Zając, *Powrót Niepożądany,* 140.
30. Czech, *Auschwitz Chronicle,* 327.
31. Ibid., 343.
32. Czech, *Auschwitz Chronicle,* 355 and 355n.
33. Piotr Setkiewicz, "Häftlingsarbeit im KZ Auschwitz III-Monowitz. Die Frage nach der Wirttschaftlichkeit der Arbeit," in *Die nationalsozialistischen Konzentrationslager,* edited by Ulrich Herbert, Karin Orth, and Christopher Dieckmann, vol. 2 (Frankfurt am Main: Fischer Verlag, 2002), 594.
34. Setkiewicz, "Häftlingsarbeit," 595.
35. Wagner, *IG Auschwitz,* 163.
36. Ibid., 158.

37. Ibid., 150–51.
38. Ibid., 165.
39. Setkiewicz, "Häftlingsarbeit," 593.
40. Langbein, *People in Auschwitz,* 362.
41. Setkiewicz, *Z dziejów obozów*, 150.
42. Wagner, *IG Auschwitz*, 166. Wagner states incorrectly that Fischer brought Stefan to Monowitz. Wagner did not have access to Stefan's 1974 statement.

7

THE BUNA-MONOWITZ HKB, THE PRISONERS' HOSPITAL

Life while you wait.
Performance without rehearsal.

Życie na poczekaniu
Przedstawienie bez próby.[1]

ROLE OF THE SS

Stefan's appointment as the senior prisoner in the hospital barracks meant that he was now in a position to leverage the SS for the benefit of the HKB, the prisoner hospital. SS Dr. Wirths and SS Dr. Fischer cooperated with Stefan and the organization he developed since it was to their benefit. The first effort was to expand the hospital to provide more services for the prisoners. The demand by the SS and IG Farben was for more prisoners available to work at Buna. The net result for the prisoners was greater safety and protection, thus giving them better survival chances. It took Stefan a little longer to understand the political situation that developed when he cleaned house and ousted the nonmedical personnel running the HKB. They had powerful political connections over in the main camp, men such as Hermann Langbein. The political left prisoners considered losing control of the hospital's senior prisoner position a setback and distrusted Stefan.

Wagner writes informatively about the political battles being waged among factions of prisoners who were organized by political affiliation or nationality. Long-term political prisoners from Dachau, like Hermann Langbein and Ludwig Wörl, formed networks which helped their friends. They were able as camp secretaries to control good functionary positions like those at the prisoners' hospital, which enabled them to protect and hide, among others, their communist colleagues.

> Their attitude towards [Stefan] was confrontational from the beginning. Even before he arrived in Monowitz, they managed to plant an informer to spy on the new *Lagerälteste.* In order to get information directly about [Stefan], the Jewish prisoner Lindenbaum got the position of [Stefan's] personal *Kalfaktor.*[2] Already in the first week, [Stefan] had penetrated this ruse and took him to task. It can be assumed that sharp words were exchanged. Actually nothing more than shouting and a change in position in the HKB happened to Lindenbaum. In comparison with what happened to other discovered informers, [Stefan] was quite restrained. But [Stefan] had earned an enemy whose bitterness lasted long into the postwar period. Lindenbaum saw the verbal assaults as clear evidence that [Stefan] had to have been a convinced anti-Semite.[3]

Stefan, a political prisoner, a nationalist Pole, singled out by the SS, was a threat to the experienced, left-wing, often Jewish long term "prominent" prisoners. The battle in the camp for life-saving positions brought Stefan into an unwelcome confrontation. Going back to Marci Shore's phrase "the teleological deception of retrospect," these camp conflicts were reified as a "racial" confrontation after the war. Hindsight obscures the ambiguities of the past.

Stefan was forced to engage in balancing the expectations of the SS for better worker health, the niggardly attitude of the IG Farbenindustrie management toward paying for a larger hospital, the welfare of thousands of prisoners, the pressure of monstrous demands by the SS physicians for selections to the gas chambers, the dreadful reality of starvation and disease, and the political gamesmanship among prisoners themselves. Stefan recruited dozens of qualified medical personnel from among incoming prisoners. He more than tripled the size of the hospital, and gave thousands of men at least a chance at long-term survival. The history of the nineteen-month existence of this reorganized prisoner hospital (June 1943–January 1945) reveals the agency of prisoners during the last phase of Auschwitz III's existence. Stefan and his coworkers exploited the limited degrees of action available to them while changes took place which were altering the nature of the whole Auschwitz system.

With the constant expansion of the complex of camps called "Auschwitz" and the constant push for more income, the SS decided to reorganize the administration. It is likely that part of the reorganization was to end the reign of Rudolf Höss in an attempt to end the high level of SS corruption at the camps. The camp Gestapo chief, Maximilian Grabner, was found to have a large quantity of gold and money in his quarters. This was symptomatic of the looting going on. Grabner was dismissed and arrested in October 1943.[4] In Berlin, the SS administration felt that they were losing too much of the confiscated Jewish property in the camp to the black market. More than 700 SS men in various camps were arrested and some sent to the front in attempt to halt the losses.[5]

Historian Michael Thad Allen summarizes the change in the SS culture as the conflict between a newer SS management culture oriented toward business enterprises either owned or managed by the SS, and the older camp culture which was based on a policing model with a strong strain of brutality. The reign of Höss and the brutal criminal kapos was supposed to end. For example Phillipp Grimm, a graduate of the *Nüremberger Handelsschule* (business school), was sent to the Buchenwald concentration camp by the SS to promote the efficiency of the labor being sold there to local companies. He came into intense conflict with Commandant Karl-Otto Koch, who paid little attention to profits, since he saw forced labor primarily as a means of torture.[6] A notoriously corrupt and brutal man, Koch ended up arrested and executed by the SS itself. "As a rule, the camp SS continued to act upon the primacy of policing: they either hindered production by brutalizing prisoners or, at best, remained indifferent to factory operations."[7] Commandants such as Höss belonged to the old-school SS and were unresponsive to the business practices being pushed by SS Berlin. The context of the reorganization of the Monowitz HKB lies in these changes being fostered by Berlin.

The man sent to clean house at Auschwitz was Artur Liebehenschel. Before his transfer to Auschwitz, Liebehenschel had been responsible for all political matters in the entire concentration camp system (camp security, sentry duty, weapons, and training in the camps) as part of the SS WVHA, the Economic and Administration office of the SS in Berlin. The huge Auschwitz reorganization took place ten days after Liebehenschel replaced Höss on November 10, 1943 (this was about five months after Stefan arrived at Monowitz). The concentration camp was now administratively divided into KL Auschwitz I, the main camp whose commandant was Liebehenschel; Auschwitz II-Birkenau, the extermination center, whose commandant was Friedrich Hartjenstein; and Auschwitz III-Monowitz, the IG Farben labor camp, whose commandant until the end in January 1945 was Heinrich Schwartz.[8] While the new head of Auschwitz I, Liebehenschel, did not or could not stop the policy of gassing prisoners, life for the long-term prisoners improved as he prohibited the "shot trying to escape" excuse for random murder in camp and finally ended the beating of prisoners.[9]

Danuta Czech reports that on November 16, 1943, "Commandant Liebehenschel admonishe[d] the members of the SS garrison that the prisoners' property, whether clothing, gold, valuables, food, or personal belongings, no matter where it was found, is inviolable. The state determines the use of this property, since in special cases it is the property of the state. Whoever misappropriates state property is committing a criminal offense and excludes himself from the ranks of the SS."[10] Liebehenschel halted the weekly shooting of Polish political prisoners in block 11. The order read that the death penalty for escape and suspicion of escape was abolished. The bunker of block 11 was only for serving punishments and not as an interrogation prison. "This is a completely new era in the camp which is clearly perceived. The freeing of the prisoners from the bunker of Block 11 caused a quarrel between the Political Department and the Commandant, Liebehenschel."[11]

The culture clash between old and new SS objectives was not over. Liebehenschel was in the camps only six months before the tougher Höss was brought back on May 8, 1944, to prepare Auschwitz for the colossal influx of the Hungarian Jewish community.[12] Efficient and brutal, Höss returned to "aid" the relatively humane Liebehenschel during the desperate endgames of the war. From the perspective of the old school Höss, Liebehenschel was a desk-bound bureaucrat who had neither the experience nor the stamina to run a real death camp: "[Liebehenschel] thought he would just come in and play camp commandant. In his opinion, I had done everything absolutely wrong, and he proceeded to change everything from the way it had been done."[13] Four hundred thousand Hungarian Jews were sent to their death in Auschwitz in 1944. The new "business model" for Auschwitz did not impact the relentless death machine in Birkenau.

Liebehenschel's arrival and the new camp organization, however, did manage to open opportunities for long-term prisoner functionaries. Stefan's relative freedom to rapidly expand the prisoners' hospital was a product of this period of more lenient camp administration as well as of the unusual character of the SS Dr. Eduard Wirths. Stefan's experiences in Auschwitz to this date resembled those of other functionary prisoners who managed to find safer niches in the camps. Stefan now applied himself to creating a functioning medical facility in Buna-Monowitz. At last he could exert some agency.

A rudimentary prisoner hospital unit in three of the wooden barracks set up in October 1942 served the prisoners. Dr. Antoni Makowski, one of the prisoner doctors who later served in the restructured hospital, reports that "Until April 1943, the Austrian Heinrich Schuster was the *Lagerälteste* who just like Wörl was not a physician which stopped neither of them from performing physician's duties at the outpatient clinic."[14] Stefan arrived in July 1943 and according to Dr. Makowski, "[was] a man of great energy, ambitions and organizational ability."[15]

In his 1974 testimony, Stefan is clearly aware of some of the institutional changes which had taken place. He confirms Dr. Makowski's opinion of the laymen trying to fill the role of health care professionals.

> At this time the *Lagerälteste* in Monowitz was a German or Austrian prisoner, Schuster, a nurse, who nonetheless made all the decisions. He walked around in a white apron and used a stethoscope on the patients—in a word, he posed as a doctor. Naturally this didn't worry the SS involved in health care. Schuster was transferred to the Birkenau hospital a couple of days after I arrived.
>
> I was transferred to KL Auschwitz III-Monowitz around June 18, 1943—I don't remember the exact date. The camp was being expanded. Half of the camp was designated for prisoners—on the western side, the other half of the camp was separated by a fence with barbed wire. The gate was located about in the center of what was later the main street of the camp. That section had the barracks housing the SS men, the camp kitchen, and, separated out, for *Erziehunghäftlinge*, that is to say, for the re-education of prisoners. I don't remember all the details. The health services were limited to only three wooden barracks located in the western corner of the camp. Wirths's car[16] stopped by the gate where I had to leave the car, as the *Standortartz* informed the SS day guard that he had delivered the new *Lagerälteste* to the prisoner hospital. The SS men standing at the gate looked at me with some curiosity—indeed it was an unusual sight to see a senior SS man personally deliver a prisoner by car—but they called the SDG, the medical orderly, right away and then I got back in the car and we drove to the camp hospital.[17]

As early as January 1943 the director of the Buna Factory, Walther Dürrfeld, had complained to Höss of the many sick prisoners, a circumstance that impeded work at the factory site.[18] Dürrfeld also complained more effectively to the SS in Berlin. The WVHA office of the SS, now in business mode and looking at actual work output and income figures, was unpleasantly surprised when they realized that fully 50% of the workers in the Buna camp had died since the camp had opened. While the fate of Auschwitz prisoners per se was of little interest to either the SS or the Buna factory, the reliability of slave labor interested them a great deal.[19] Improving the hospital for prisoners working at the plant was an essential step to stabilizing the quality and quantity of slave labor. In retrospect, Stefan put these facts together as well.

In passing, Stefan used the term *Erziehunghäftlinge.* This was a group of young men in a small area of the Buna-Monowitz camp who had separate status. They were civilian workers who were deemed loafers or shirkers. The first camps to "educate" lazy or uncooperative workers were for German workers in 1939, but expanded quickly to include Polish forced labor workers in Germany who were essential to the war economy. By August 1940, an "education camp" for loafers opened up near Düsseldorf. Polish workers who didn't fulfill their work quotas were sentenced to six-week terms. This type of training course was paid for by the mine or factory that identified unproductive or uncooperative workers, but the camp itself was supervised by the SS.[20] When Stefan says, "for the re-education of prisoners," he is not referring to prisoners in Buna-Monowitz, but short-term inmates from surrounding factories using forced labor. One might speculate what a six-week course in re-education actually taught. Just being in a slave labor camp run by the SS for a brief stint might well have been enough to motivate these men to work harder without any retraining at all.

> I really want to say a few words about my transfer to KL Auschwitz III. I learned about some of the details from other prisoner doctors and other relevant prisoner functionaries—Władysław Dering[21] (who was named *Lagerälteste* of the KL Auschwitz I hospital after demotion of Hans Bock), Diem, and Langbein—as well as in conversations with SS health workers. It turns out that in 1943 a sharp conflict developed between the SS and Dürrfeld, the director of the Oświęcim branch of IG Farbenindustrie. The head of the factory

> apparently complained to the central SS authorities in Oranienburg that no sooner was a group of prisoners trained in various positions than these prisoners disappeared and in their place untrained ones appeared who had to be trained all over again. The reason for this heavy turnover was the prisoner hospital in Monowitz. One has to understand that in this time period all the important jobs at the Monowitz hospital were in the hands of long-term prisoners who had come through KL Buchenwald. The actual director of the hospital was Stefan Heymann, a German Jew, who was—he himself said—a journalist whose official position was that of a clerk in the hospital record office.

Stefan Heymann (1896–1967) was wounded in World War I and returned to Weimar Germany a committed communist. Politically active, he served a three-year jail sentence (1924–1927) for illegal political action. He was an early victim of racist and right-wing Nazi policy. His arrest in 1933 started him on his thirteen-year journey in the concentration camps of Buchenwald, Dachau, and in 1942, Auschwitz. Heymann remained in the prisoner hospital record office even though his influence was diminished when he lost the title of director. He was, however, the head of the communist resistance group.[22] His presence in the hospital, and his affiliation with compatriots like Langbein, is palpable for the duration of the prisoner hospital and even after the war. His stint in the Weimar prisons and Nazi concentration camps were part of a single long-term political battle with the ideologies of capitalism and fascism.

> The hospital barracks were run by men who had nothing to do with medicine—cabinet makers, carpenters, etc.—who had been in KL Buchenwald and Dachau.[23] At the very beginning, an x-ray technician, Ludwig Wörl, acted as *Lagerälteste* of the hospital. A couple of prisoner doctors, among them the surgeon Bronisław Rutkowski from Warsaw, an able and decent man, Prof. Epstein, and Dr. Silber, were actually afraid of these old prison hands and thus had no influence.

Stefan, recounting his arrival at the Monowitz prisoner hospital, is clearly outraged, even offended by the organizational chaos facing him. He understands that the SS Dr. Wirths is looking for improvements. However, no prisoner could accomplish the restructuring of this failed enterprise without the tacit cooperation of the SS. There is a fine line between cooperation and collusion. This gray zone (discussed below) is the subtext of all of Stefan's work in the HKB.

> The camp was reorganizing, the food was inadequate, and too little effort was expended, which led to a rapid depletion of the body, producing a general weakness, described as *allgemeine Körperschwäche*. These prisoners suffered edema and the slightest cuts led to the formation of abscesses (phlegmons). The patients would come to the outpatient clinic (the ambulatorium), but instead of getting treatments, they were sent to the hospital in the main camp. Trying to get into the ambulatorium, they ran to it as soon as they returned from work—missing their supper. Hungry, they were transferred in cars to the main camp, where once again they missed breakfast and even lunch. They stood for hours in front of the ambulatorium, which also exhausted them physically. But then in the main camp ambulatorium there were immediate selections and more than half of the sick received lethal injections of phenol.[24] The prisoner functionaries in Monowitz had to have known this but they were indifferent to the fate of average prisoners. In the first instance they protected their own colleagues with whom they had survived the camps in Buchenwald, Dachau, and Sachsenhausen. It is this system that caused the fluctuation of workers. A veritable brawl erupted among the camp's directors as a result of the IG Farbenindustrie complaint and that is why Wirths was forced to find a prisoner who could improve the prisoner hospital. The choice fell on me—as Langbein told me later—when camp Jawischowitz and its clinical service was first rate in providing sanitary conditions.

REORGANIZING THE PRISONER HOSPITAL (HKB): RECRUITMENT

The explosive typhus epidemics of the previous year represented a danger to prisoners and guards alike, but the prisoners alone faced the consequences of their brutal living and working conditions. Inadequate food rations combined with strenuous labor led to exhaustion. Workplace accidents resulted in broken bones or crushed limbs. Unchecked SS guard beatings injured prisoners. But there was one aspect of camp life that produced a specific and debilitating, therefore deadly, consequence: ill-fitting shoes. Friedrich Entress, the SS physician who specialized in phenol injections at Auschwitz I and was transferred to Buna-Monowitz by SS Dr. Wirths, testified at the Nüremberg trial that the prisoners often had to walk 8 to 10 kilometers daily on the extensive terrain of the IG Farben factory. "One could say that wearing wooden shoes often proved a death sentence for prisoners."[25] Camp inmate and novelist Imre Kertész presents a graphic picture of the problem and its impact on the worker: "Now, one thing that has become clear about the clogs is that the heels wear down over time. When that happens, one has to go around on a thick sole that at a certain point suddenly thins . . . [and] a gap, widening day by day, opens up . . . so that now cold mud, not to speak of tiny pebbles and sharp bits of debris of all kinds, can stream in unobstructedly at every step. Meanwhile those stiff uppers have long been chafing one's ankles and abraded countless sores on the softer tissues below them. Now, those sores by their very nature suppurate, and that pus is definitely sticky, with the result that it becomes impossible to free oneself from the clogs: they become stuck to the feet, veritably fused to them, rather like new body parts as it were."[26] Prisoners were caught in a life-threatening gauntlet: if they were not capable of work, they were consigned to death from the barracks, but if they sought help from the prisoner hospital, they were also subject to selections and a death sentence in Birkenau.[27] One solution to this ubiquitous problem was to get competent medical staff into the prisoner hospital and effective treatment regimes in place to heal these abscesses. The obvious solution of getting better fitting shoes for the workers is not mentioned anywhere.

Stefan, isolated for half a year in Jawischowitz, did not belong to any recognizable camp network other than that of former colleagues from the medical school and, generally, nationalist Poles. Historian Wagner notes: "Among the Polish nationalist resistance groups, political orientation is dominant."[28] The most effective of the prisoner groups, however, were not the bourgeois Polish resisters, let alone Polish Catholic groups, but the socialist and communist prisoners. By pulling Stefan in from Jawischowitz, SS Dr. Wirths counteracted the influence of men like Langbein in the Auschwitz I camp. Wagner, in his close analysis of the Monowitz camp, concludes, "One group of prisoners experienced the reorganization of the hospital as an at least temporary worsening of their position. [Stefan's] intervention in the personnel structure of the HKB was accompanied by a complete change in doctors and nurses. . . . From their point of view it looked like [Stefan's] actions were directed against the communist dominated prisoner self-government, even though the reorganized hospital benefited most of the prisoners."[29]

Stefan's view of this transition is striking. He is speaking with authority. He has discretionary power; Stefan hires and fires at will. He makes sure to explain (in 1974) that the displaced, untrained staff suffered no deadly consequences. He is defending himself here from what would be postwar recriminations. But Stefan had a level of discretionary power, what Oswald calls "room to maneuver," that was out of the ordinary. If he indeed acquired power and agency, it was only within a realm allowed by the needs of SS Dr. Wirths. Stefan exploited this opportunity to the hilt. But he also had a learning curve. The experiences of terror in Montelupich, the transition to Auschwitz, and his ability to pull together a working clinic in Jawischowitz now culminated in the Buna-Monowitz hospital. He had learned how to function in a prison.

> After I was moved to the hospital in Monowitz, I observed the conditions there for some time. I concluded that the prisoners who held functionary positions in the hospital barracks, *Blockälteste*, as well as some of the medical orderlies, having no appropriate training, got involved in the treatment of the sick and even operated on the phlegmons. Some of them abused narcotics and in a word made decisions about everything relating to the hospital without appropriate training. I could not tolerate the prevailing atmosphere and conditions. To begin to restore order to the hospital, I removed all the current prisoner functionaries and put prisoner doctors in their place. One must add that the former hospital functionaries did not suffer any consequences, simply being moved to other positions in the camp. At the same time I turned to my superiors to have doctors (prisoners) working in other units reassigned to the health services. I was of the opinion that the welfare of all prisoners would be best served by taking advantage of professionally trained prisoners. I also asked that all new transports direct arriving doctors to the hospital. In this way I managed to employ 15 to 20 highly qualified prisoner doctors—almost exclusively Jews—and they became the basis of our effectiveness. At any rate, with their help I began organizing a "real" hospital (if one can even talk about a "normal hospital" in the camps).

The chemistry student from Krakow, Zając, encountered Stefan's recruitment methods for the prisoner hospital his first day in Buna. It shows the straightforward system. "A group of prisoners in white hospital kit approached the new arrivals. One of them, a young, handsome brown haired man, had on his left sleeve a black band with '*KL Lagerälteste*' [i.e., Stefan]. He was the head of the hospital. He said out loud in Polish: 'If there are any doctors among you, step forward.'"[30] Stefan recruited skilled prisoners to work in the hospital and then he connived, borrowed, and repurposed equipment to outfit it. Fundamentally, Stefan and his coworkers were able to accomplish their task because of the tacit commitment of the SS officers to the goal of maintaining prisoners' capacity to produce labor.

However, the ordinary barrack SS guards did not necessarily share these goals. Stefan mentions Wilhelm Stolten, whose job it was to provide daily workers for the factory. He was a hard and brutal man and was actually killed in 1945 by prisoners in the Meckelburg camp.[31] The beatings were systemic until the Liebehenschel regime supported men like Stefan who argued strenuously against the brutality. Dr. Makowski, the chronicler of the Buna prisoner hospital, reports that "the hospital managed to minimize, if not fully eliminate, beatings prisoners got . . . The SS administration issued an order forbidding beatings and an SS physician requirement that all beatings discovered by the hospital be reported."[32] That was the theory. In practice, beatings were never fully eradicated.

To make changes in the hospital required the cooperation of the SS men who controlled all aspects of the concentration camp. It was possible to influence the SS officials and SS hospital orderlies by supplying them with gifts as well as services. Dr. Makowski relates that "for example, *Krankenbauälteste* [Stefan] Budziaszek managed to medically treat Vincenz Schöttl [*Lagerführer* of Buna-Monowitz] for a time."[33] Makowski explains that these relationships allowed greater independence and freedom of action for the hospital by narrowing the gap between SS men and the prisoners.

This logical strategy was opened to serious challenge after the war. Wagner states: "After the war only a few survivors dared to speak of their personal contacts with SS men. But there is no evidence that the behaviors of Hermann Langbein and Stefan Buthner [Budziaszek] were exceptional. Both, Langbein as clerk for the head physician in the main camp [SS Dr. Wirths] and Buthner [Budziaszek] as camp elder of the HKB in Monowitz, exerted noticeable influence on their SS superiors."[34] The tension between Langbein and Stefan was a struggle for control for the Buna-Monowitz prisoner hospital. Langbein quotes Zenon Drohocki, a physician from Krakow who worked in the prisoner hospital: "[Stefan] managed to turn Monowitz HKB into a model for the other infirmaries." Drohocki also called Stefan "a very capable physician and 'organizer,' a very good, helpful and tireless comrade."[35] Langbein then tries to present a picture of Stefan as an antisemite who had a bad reputation in the camp for working with the SS. Langbein, however, then contradicts his negative description with another quote from Drohocki: "Without the collaboration of the SS nothing whatever could be done, and certainly nothing good."[36]

Stefan managed to get the crucial agreement from the SS to recruit workers for the hospital. Once injured or ailing prisoners got help, fewer prisoners were killed. In 1943, about 4,500 hospitalized workers were transferred to Birkenau; in 1944, 2,500.[37] The prisoner hospital was the site of rescue for the vulnerable prisoner population. The political infighting needed for this result was unending: between the SS and prisoners, between red triangle political prisoners and green triangle criminal prisoners, and between various national and political prisoners themselves.

Stefan understood the political tensions more clearly after he took over the prisoner hospital:

> In my efforts I exploited the position of *Lagerführer* Stolten as well as the commander of the camp involved in the dispute with the directors of IG Farbenindustrie, because they, too, were interested in improving conditions. They were not, of course, well intentioned towards the prisoners, but wanted to avoid further interventions from IG Farbenindustrie and the negative consequences ensuing. So, as soon as I found out about prisoner beating, for example, from the *Lagerälteste*, I used this event to present a formal protest to the commander of the camp. As a result, beatings were formally forbidden—though in fact it proved impossible to stop all beatings. As a consequence of my intervention the *Lagerälteste* got "angry" at me, ignored my person for three months, and didn't even want to talk to me. He was the prisoner Paul Kozwara.[38] The current Lagercapo sympathies were with the group of long-standing prisoners from KL Buchenwald. All these prisoner functionaries—as I perceived—were a little afraid of me because as I took on a project, I worked with a great deal of energy. My position was also strengthened in that I was

sometimes called to give medical treatment to SS men when the SS doctors were unavailable. This gave the impression that I had some influence. I want to emphasize that the correct relationship with the camp directors was not as a consequence of their sympathy. Rather, their attitude was a consequence of their conviction that I could improve the conditions in the prisoner hospital compared to the regime of my Buchenwald predecessors. Thanks to constant efforts I actually was able to improve a lot of things—but I couldn't change everything. It was impossible to prevent homesickness among the prisoners, or to eliminate the heavy labor, hunger, infectious diseases, and so forth. We medical professionals discussed these conditions among ourselves.

Simultaneously I attempted to have doctors I knew transferred to Monowitz. For instance, that was what happened with the previously mentioned Dr. Cuenko. Using the medical orderly SDG Neubert (more about him later) I got in contact with Dr. Cuenko, asking if he'd like to work with me. When he agreed, I went to the *Lagerarzt* and proposed opening a laryngological unit and suggested bringing Dr. Cuenko to KL Auschwitz III.[39] This proposal appealed to the *Lagerarzt*, who eased the formalities. I want to mention especially some doctors with whom I worked closely: Dr. Drohocki, a psychiatrist and neurologist who worked in Krakow before the war and later got a Rockefeller fellowship, and Dr. Silber from Metz. Some of the prisoner doctors I simply "pulled" out of the newly arrived transports—I had that right. That's how I engaged Dr. Waitz from Strasbourg—he was a very shy man and I was able to protect him from the beastliness which faced all incoming prisoners. Unfortunately after the war Dr. Waitz wasn't grateful, but repaid me with resentment.[40]

I paid a lot of attention to the organization of the outpatient clinic (ambulatorium) of the camp hospital. We organized separate surgical, internist, skin, ophthalmic and x-ray sections. Naturally this didn't happen overnight, but using specialists, when possible excellent physicians, I provided the best chance

> of appropriate treatment for each prisoner. The surgical unit was run by Dr. Rutkowski, and Dr. Lengyel worked there, too. Drs. Makowski, Silber, and Waitz worked in the internist unit. The latter was offended that I didn't name him as the director of the ambulatorium, given his prewar prominence. I didn't do this maliciously, it's just that Dr. Waitz had none of the essential experiences of a camp inmate.

Dr. Miklos Lengyel was a Hungarian physician whom Stefan recruited for the HKB from among the enormous Hungarian Jewish influx in the spring of 1944.[41] He and his wife, Olga, saw their sons and Miklos's father driven to the gas chambers upon their arrival in Auschwitz. Olga served as a medical worker in the women's unit in Birkenau. She was able to see her husband briefly in Monowitz and reported:

> At the sight of me, he grew pale. I stood there speechless. How feeble and aged he had become. His features were drawn and his hair was gray. Beneath his white doctor's blouse I saw the striped prisoner's trousers . . . We found ourselves in an operating room, in the midst of the bright metal instruments and an atmosphere saturated with ether and chloroform. There was no comparison between our miserable place in Birkenau and this well-equipped establishment."[42]

EXPANSION OF THE HOSPITAL: THE BENEFITS OF "ORGANIZING"

By the time Olga Lengyel saw the prisoner hospital in the summer of 1944, it had two surgical units and several surgical theaters, including one run by Dr. Miklos Lengyel, her husband. Three physicians provided anesthesia services. Several wards were organized for postsurgical cases. Dr. Silber and Dr. Makowski ran one department for internal medicine for seriously ill, long-term patients and there were two others for less serious cases.[43] Additionally, the hospital had a dental practice. Mieczysław Zając, the chemistry student from Krakow who first saw Stefan recruiting physicians, was admitted to the HKB with a temperature and sore throat, but then stayed on with a *kalefaktor* position in the dentist's office.[44] The hospital busiest unit was the outpatient clinic, the ambulatorium, which treated 500 to 700 patients daily with peak periods of 1250 patients daily.[45]

The prisoner hospital in Buna-Monowitz was the best equipped of any in the Auschwitz system. Stefan and his crew of prisoner doctors, with the collusion of SS orderlies and SS physicians, more than doubled the size of the original prisoner hospital. Yet Dürrfeld, the factory director, resisted these improvements even while he demanded that he needed a healthier workforce. Just as IG Farben managers refused to build solid brick barracks in favor of wooden barracks, they now felt that the hospital should be kept small.[46] One could speculate that the unusual SS cooperation with Stefan was in part a reflection of contentious relationship between the SS and the factory manager. Huge sums of money were at play. The leadership of the enormous factory could, and did, complain to Berlin about the use of slave labor, labor which was income for the SS and a cost to IG Farben.

Hospital equipment became essential to develop the HKB. But where could prisoners find the equipment necessary to outfit a functional hospital in a milieu of contested money and horrific deprivation? Like many transactions in the camp, building the hospital involved trades, subterfuge, and that form of theft referred to as "organizing." The major source was that huge but random accumulation of material confiscated from incoming prisoners, the Birkenau "Canada." This warehouse was also the source of enormous amounts of valuable jewels, currency, artwork, and other valuables which led to the SS corruption scandal and which doomed the Gestapo chief, Grabner. Workers in "Canada" constantly fed the well-developed black market in the camp. Olga Lengyel, a prisoner working in Birkenau, explained: "When employees of 'Canada' . . . stole warm clothing for their badly clothed comrades, that was not common theft; it was an act of social solidarity. The more one took from the Germans and sent into the barracks of the camp for the use of internees instead of letting it be dispatched to Germany, the more one helped the cause. Thus the words, 'steal' and 'organize' were not at all synonymous."[47] Langbein states that "organizing," the name given to the appropriation of institutional property that had not yet been distributed, was part of the tradition of Nazi concentration camps.[48] This form of theft or conniving is also a well understood norm in prisons. Inmates gain both material and psychological benefits from "organizing."[49] The prisoner hospital was equipped using these risky but accepted methods.

Stefan mastered the process:

> At the same time, as the outpatient clinics were enlarged, I worked to organize essential services whose lack was manifest. The following wards were organized: a ward for postoperative patients, a surgical ward, a ward for septic surgery, and wards for internal medicine and dermatology. Simultaneously I tried to build and equip an operating theater. When the question was equipment—for instance, getting the necessary instruments for the operating theater—it didn't happen along any official channels. We simply made do with what we could find. A significant source was the warehouses [Canada], located in Birkenau, holding the belongings of the victims of gassing. Many of the physicians deported to KL Auschwitz carried their own instruments and pharmaceuticals with them. All of these were brought to the central pharmacy in KL Auschwitz. Since I had prisoner colleagues there (such as pharmacist Hommé), I equipped the Monowitz camp hospital with needed equipment and medicines. I am certain that these efforts were made simpler by the attitude of the acting SDG of Auschwitz III, Neubert, who listened to my requests and brought needed equipment from KL Auschwitz. All of these activities took advantage of what camp jargon called "organization." Going the official route produced medicines and equipment in minimal amounts, much less than what we actually needed.

In its broadest outlines, the hierarchy of authority in the clinics and hospitals had at its top SS Dr. Wirths. He appointed SS

Dr. Fischer to Buna-Monowitz and placed the prisoner hospital under his jurisdiction. Nominally another, lower SS functionary, the medical orderly, would rank higher than the highest prisoner functionary. But in the prisoner hospital, that orderly, SDG Gerhard Neubert, was subservient to Stefan. Wagner states: "he was in every respect subject to Stefan's stronger personality."[50] Stefan's ability to manipulate Neubert benefited the expansion and development of the HKB. There was no question that Neubert would, for instance, prohibit the ingenious organizing schemes devised by the prisoners. Dr. Robert Waitz reported that Neubert could be bribed.[51] In that zone of ambiguity between prisoners and their guards, Neubert drifted towards complicity with the prisoners.

> We had to "organize" many building projects. When we had to build or rebuild something specific at the hospital barracks, the appropriate workers called in sick—for instance, carpenters, and the next time some other kind of workman—and in this fashion we got things done without official permission as well as without opposition from the SS. There really was no shortage of lumber for the barracks. If we needed bricks, we "organized" so that, let's say, 400 prisoners returned to the camp from some building site each carrying one brick. Naturally each brick had to be hidden under the worker's shirt.
>
> There was never a shortage of helpers. Each prisoner who did some work for the camp hospital received a portion of soup. This was possible because I had cooperating prisoners working in the kitchens who "organized" food for the hospital. Thanks to them we got more bread and margarine (more than the official rations). One must emphasize that this was not at the cost of other prisoners. We got extras direct from the warehouses, but each *Blockälteste* also had to receive a designated amount of food. It is another matter that not all the *Blockälteste* distributed the food fairly. We got help from the kitchen also because the prisoners working in the kitchen were mostly Poles who didn't mind taking chances.

A typical example of "organizing" was building washrooms and disinfection rooms next to the hospital barracks. We built these because we needed to provide the patients with the means to maintain elementary cleanliness. The camp distributed heating from a central location (*Fernheizung*), but because of poor insulation, little heat reached us, especially the hospital barracks, which were at the end of the heating system. With the loss of heat we could neither heat the barracks adequately nor disinfect clothing. With the quiet permission of the *Lagerführer* and a lot of help from SDG Neubert we "organized" a small boiler (*lokomobile*). Neubert spotted it on the grounds of the factory. Moving this kettle proved little trouble. I sent 20 nurses to the factory grounds and, accompanied by Neubert, they moved the boiler to the camp. None of the guards—neither the ones at the IG Farbenindustrie gate nor the camp guards—even suspected that something illegal was happening in front of them. We placed the boiler behind the hospital barracks, so it wouldn't be glaringly obvious, and the appropriate workers attached the boiler to the internal heating system of the hospital. From that moment we were independent. The *Lagerarzt* [SS Dr. Fischer] was very satisfied with this and supposedly also the camp commander. We stressed the usefulness of this system, that we'd be able to disinfect all the camp clothing. The battle with the insects was fundamental in order to contain the epidemic, especially typhus. For the benefit of the prisoners we checked carefully for lice (the so-called *Läuseappel*) and if a prisoner was louse-infected, he was sent to the disinfection unit where his body was smeared with cuprexem.[52] This was a preventative safer and less dangerous for prisoners than a bout of typhus, which had caused death for countless people.

I have to say that my actions were not supported by Heymann's[53] group, though some of them, such as Erich Markowitsch,[54] did value my efforts. He and a group of nurses (*pflegerami*) helped in the shifting of the boiler (*lokomobil*) to the camp.

The theft of the Buna boiler and its installation in the Monowitz HKB has become a famous story. Langbein, not an admirer of Stefan's, mentions the noticeable improvements at the HKB, without mentioning Stefan by name, but relates: "Even an old steam engine was (illegally) rolled from the IG plant into the camp and was used to heat and disinfect the infirmary. With its help the camp became 'recognized as epidemic-free,' as Felix Rausch proudly put it."[55] Dr. Makowski provides the details: "Early in 1943 a group of some twenty prisoners employed in the HKB left the camp under the leadership of a political prisoner, a German—George Lay, escorted by the SS man Neubert . . . The prisoners took a 'lokomobile' [the boiler] and pulled it back to the camp about 1.5 kilometers. Once it was already in the [HKB] camp, the factory manager realized that a piece of their equipment was missing. The SS men answered they knew nothing about it."[56] Dr. Jaworski also describes this episode.[57] Wagner makes the important point that the SS tolerated the theft of the boiler because they were fundamentally interested in improving the conditions in the Monowitz HKB.[58] But what does this say about the relationship between the management of the IG Farben Buna plant and the SS management of the camps? Prisoner ingenuity transferred that boiler to Monowitz. There was no cooperative relationship between camp and factory.

Adding hot water to the camp was a complex and, most probably, a dangerous enterprise. It was the quotidian changes that improved prisoners' lives. The photographs from Auschwitz I and Birkenau show primitive toilets and no washing facilities. This changed for the patients of the HKB as Dr. Makowski describes: "Primarily due to the initiative of the new hospital elder, Stefan Budziaszek, new bathing and washrooms were build early in 1943, as well as the expansion of the disinfection rooms. The essential changes were the seemingly small but critical alterations in blocks 20, 15, and 16 in which sinks and toilets were added. This was of great significance for the patients in these facilities since previously they had had to make do with simple buckets."[59] In the Buna-Monowitz camp, here in Auschwitz III, prisoners who had the misfortune of being hospitalized found a small oasis of normalcy in the brutal camp environment: hot water, sinks, toilets.

The expansion of the HKB increased the blocks devoted to patients from three to nine. This was accomplished by prisoners' efforts. Dr. Makowski reports: "All building and installation work was carried out by prisoners—sometimes too, the functionary prisoners of the HKB [physicians and nurses], often skilled workers who worked evenings after return from the work, but more often specialists who were taken up illegally as patients. The materials for the construction (roof tiles, wood, cement, wash basins, lavatories, pipes, etc.) were fetched by trucks from the factory grounds having been placed inside the empty midday soup kettles. Clearly many prisoners had to be involved in this activity. The camp administrators had to be aware of this since it would have been impossible to build so much without their knowledge."[60] The tailors, carpenters, shoemakers, electricians, and metal workers who were listed in the HKB as patients actually set up workshops on the hospital grounds. "Here they repaired clothing and shoes for the HKB workers, repaired electrical gear and repaired and improved surgical instruments."[61] It was imperative that the SS men be kept in a cooperative mood: "A not unimportant part of their work was the preparation of gifts for the SS doctors and orderlies such as uniforms, shoes, small electric motors, children's toys, etc."[62] Under Stefan's leadership and the willfully blind eyes of the SS, this hospital experienced a new organization, new facilities, and manifest improvement in the most important output: services for prisoners debilitated by injuries and diseases.

Primo Levi, an Italian Jewish prisoner working in the chemical laboratory in the Buna factory in late summer 1944, adds further details: "In this complex network of thefts and counterthefts, nourished by the silent hostility between the SS command and the civilian authorities of the Buna [factory], the Ka-Be [prisoner hospital] plays a part of prime importance. Ka-Be is the place of least resistance, where the regulations can most easily be avoided and the surveillance of the Kapos eluded . . . The Ka-Be is the main customer and receiver of thefts occurring in Buna."[63] The list of items pilfered from the factory grounds was prodigious: light bulbs, soaps, files, pliers, sacks, and nails, but also goods highly useful in the hospital: thin rubber tubing useful for enemas and stomach tubes, colored pencils and inks for the bookkeepers, thermometers, glass instruments, and chemicals. Primo Levi was especially proud of thinking to steal "rolls of graph paper from the thermographs in the Desiccation Department, and offer them to the Medical Chief of Ka-Be with the suggestion that they be used as paper for pulse-temperature charts."[64]

Stefan echoes Makowski's analysis:

> Sometimes the sick arrived with such complex issues that we were utterly helpless. For instance, a group of prisoners arrived with fungal gland infections. Had we left them to their fate, it could have exposed them to selections and subjected them to transfer to the gas chambers. The only help we could think to offer was to treat them with x-ray radiation. Unfortunately the hospital did not yet have x-ray machinery available. I was able to convince the SS camp doctor to transfer these patients to Birkenau for treatment at their radiological unit at the women's camp. I took them there personally. This was the only time that I personally saw Birkenau.
>
> The camp hospital in Monowitz had its own workshops. We never managed to get official permission to employ craftsmen, so we recruited them by calling them nurses. They made various improvements and renovations. The prisoners even built some quite complicated apparatuses. I'm thinking specifically of an x-ray machine, the lack of which was particularly noticeable. We decided to build one ourselves. All the necessary technical elements were designed by the graduate engineer Kaplan,[65] who was employed by Philips before the war as a radio station builder (and after the war became a director at Philips). Also involved in this project was a Polish electrician (whose name I can't recall) who died after the war.[66] We "organized" the acquisition of appropriate electrical wiring on the

grounds of the camp. All the equipment was assembled in the hospital barracks. The one piece which we couldn't build ourselves was the lamp itself. But even this problem was solved. The lamp we needed was purchased by a civilian official with money we provided him. The camp organizers gathered this sum. We got this radiology unit operating towards the end of the camp's existence, in 1944. During the evacuation of the camp, the apparatus was moved to Gliwice and loaded on one of the evacuation trains which were directed to KL Buchenwald. I don't know what happened to it after that.

In similar fashion, oscillators and generators were assembled to provide electroshock therapy for mentally ill prisoners. Dr. Drohocki, who was passionately interested in these cases, hoped to produce an anesthetic effect with this equipment.[67] He hoped that anesthesia would result if he could match the electrical output of the brain with an identical electrical pulse from the apparatus. There was never time to do these experiments. I heard after the war that these investigations did not produce useful results.

These activities were accepted by both the SS *Lagerarzt* and by both SDG's—that is, Neubert and Hantel.[68] The latter came to Monowitz from the subcamp Brünn (Brno) in Czechoslovakia; he was originally from the Sudeten district and spoke Czech. Both SS doctors and SS medical orderlies (SDGs) tolerated the existence of the hospital workshops and even used them themselves. SS doctor König[69] ordered a pair of pants and a pair of shoes from the workshops—other SDGs did the same. These instances led us prisoners to understand the there was a certain level of dependency between us and the SS, which we would then try to exploit. This was a form of "politics" poorly understood by prisoners who were uninvolved and frequently became the subject of hostile remarks.

The following SS doctors, known as *Lagerärzte*, as far as I can recall, were responsible at various times for the Monowitz hospital: Entress, Fischer, König. During their absences, a tall

> SS doctor name Kitt[70] acted as replacement. I did not meet Dr. Mengele in Monowitz.[71] I saw him in the main camp where I went from time to time to "organize" medicines and to talk to my colleagues Mężyk, Kłodzinski, Feikl,[72] Diem, and others. I would give them information about what was going on in Monowitz.

Finding carpenters, electricians, and builders among the prisoners produced the needed infrastructure, but greater ambitions developed: building an x-ray machine. Buna-HKB patients would not need to make the always dangerous trip to the available machine in Birkenau. This required far more specialized skills. Dr. Makowski is of the opinion that the intense efforts to produce an x-ray facility reflects the sense of helplessness that physicians felt in the face of obdurate or difficult medical cases for which these chance-met physicians had no resources. "They were in a certain sense an attempt to escape the reality [of helplessness] into useful, creative work."[73] One could wish that Stefan had explained just how "camp organizers" collected a sum of money to purchase an x-ray "lamp," let alone who the "civilian" was who purchased it in Berlin.

NOTES

1. Szymborska, *Seventy Poems*, 190–91.
2. "Kalfaktor" was a concentration camp term for something like a janitor or odds-body. The term derived from the "oven keeper," the servant who kept the heating stoves going in the barracks.
3. Wagner, *IG Auschwitz*, 195.
4. Langbein, *People in Auschwitz*, 40.
5. Dixon, *Commanders of Auschwitz*, 96.
6. Allen, *The Business of Genocide*, 121.
7. Ibid., 117.
8. Heinrich Schwartz (1906–1947, executed by a French firing squad) served as the Auschwitz main camp *Lagerführer* before his promotion. He gave the order that any prisoner incapable of walking in the evacuation of 1945 be shot (Dixon, *Commanders of Auschwitz*, 185).
9. Dixon, *Commanders of Auschwitz*, 138–40.

10. Czech, *Auschwitz Chronicle*, 527.
11. Ibid., 533.
12. Dixon, *Commanders of Auschwitz*, 138–40.
13. Höss, *Death Dealer*, 298.
14. Makowski, *Häftlingskrankenbau in Monowitz*, 122.
15. Ibid.
16. Langbein describes Wirths's car as being wide with light brown military paint (*People in Auschwitz*, 46). The SS physicians didn't live in the camps and had to travel in from the town of Auschwitz.
17. SDG, *Sanitätsgrad*, were SS men who had jobs in hospitals as caretakers but also performed disciplinary functions. They acquired great authority since they were always present in the hospitals while the SS doctors appeared only sporadically (Wagner, *IG Auschwitz*, 177)
18. Czech, *Auschwitz Chronicle*, 309.
19. Wagner, *IG Auschwitz*, 166.
20. Herbert, *Hitler's Foreign Workers*, 118–22.
21. Dr. Dehring was a Polish surgeon in Auschwitz since mid August 1940, who was frightened by and refused to administer phenol injections, but was a notorious and enthusiastic participant in the sterilization experiments in the main camp hospital (Langbein, *People in Auschwitz*, 221–22).
22. Wagner, *IG Auschwitz*, 144.
23. Makowski (*Häftlingskrankenbau in Monowitz*, 121) confirms the lack of medical training of much of the staff of the hospital before Stefan took it over. Dr. Rutkowski became active in the outpatient unit, the ambulatorium, of the reorganized HKB (150). Dr. Silber was an internist from France (150).
24. Makowski (*Häftlingskrankenbau in Monowitz*, 136) writes: "The fate of the prisoners [deemed incapable of work] was sealed. The prisoners were 'admitted' but soon transferred to the Auschwitz I prisoner hospital and then to the Birkenau (KL Auschwitz II) hospital barracks BIIf which was tantamount to death by phenol injection or gas."
25. Quoted in Makowski, *Häftlingskrankenbau in Monowitz*, 156.
26. Kertész, *Fatelessness*, 167.
27. Makowski, *Häftlingskrankenbau in Monowitz*, 136.
28. Wagner, *IG Auschwitz*, 136.
29. Ibid., 195.

30. Zając, *Powrót Niepożądany,* 143.
31. Wagner, *IG Auschwitz,* 107.
32. Makowski *Häftlingskrankenbau in Monowitz,* 173.
33. Ibid., 175.
34. Wagner, *IG Auschwitz,* 154.
35. Langbein, *People in Auschwitz,* 225.
36. Ibid.
37. Makowski, *Häftlingskrankenbau in Monowitz,* 139.
38. Paul Kozwara, referred to as P. K., was born in Upper Silesia in 1899, and Langbein reports that he was called a "relatively good" camp elder in that he whipped block elders if they did not distribute food fairly (Langbein, *People in Auschwitz,* 151). Wagner, however (*IG Auschwitz,* 117), presents a darker picture and states that Kozwara, a "green" from Breslau, greeted newcomers with the statement: "This is a concentration camp; here you'll be beaten even if you are innocent and don't deserve a beating. Here you'll either work or you'll die."
39. Makowski (*Häftlingskrankenbau in Monowitz,* 163) reports that Dr. Leo Cuenca [*sic*] expanded the ear, nose, and throat service to a 30-bed unit and performed successful surgeries in new facilities.
40. Dr. Robert Waitz was involved in a controversy at a 1964 photo exhibit for "Auschwitz awareness" among young people in Frankfurt. His invitation to speak was withdrawn because of suspicion that he and the International Auschwitz Committee represented a "communist threat" (Pendas, *The Frankfurt Auschwitz Trial, 1963–1965,* 185). Twenty years after the war the ideological battles were still in force.
41. Makowski, *Häftlingskrankenbau in Monowitz,* 177.
42. Olga Lengyel, *Five Chimneys: A Woman Survivor's True Story of Auschwitz* (New York: Granada, 1972), 200. Her husband was shot to death on the road by the SS during the January 1945 evacuation.
43. Makowski, *Häftlingskrankenbau in Monowitz,* 150–52.
44 Zając, *Powrót Niepożądany,* 145.
45. Makowski, *Häftlingskrankenbau in Monowitz,* 150.
46. Wagner, *IG Auschwitz,* 166–68.
47. Lengyel, *Five Chimneys,* 106.
48. Langbein, *People in Auschwitz,* 133.
49. Goffman, *Asylums,* 54–55.
50. Wager, *IG Auschwitz,* 194.

51. Langbein, *People in Auschwitz,* 115.
52. Makowski (*Häftlingskrankenbau in Monowitz,* 165) also describes the ceaseless fight against lice.
53. Stefan Heymann was one of the men displaced when Stefan reorganized the HKB. Heymann appears in Tibor Wohl's memoir as the man who hid Wohl during a selection at the hospital.
54. Erich Markowitz is described by Makowski (*Häftlingskrankenbau in Monowitz,* 151) as a nurse in the surgical ambulatorium.
55. Langbein, *People in Auschwitz,* 142.
56. Makowski, *Häftlingskrankenbau in Monowitz,* 120.
57. Jaworski, *Apel Skazanych,* 258.
58. Wagner, *IG Auschwitz,* 126n89.
59. Makowski, *Häftlingskrankenbau in Monowitz,* 118.
60. Ibid., 120.
61. Ibid., 125.
62. Ibid.
63. Levi, *Survival in Auschwitz,* 84–85.
64. Ibid., 85–86.
65. He is identified by Makowski (*Häftlingskrankenbau in Monowitz,* 126) as Serge Kaplan, an employee of Philips in Holland.
66. Makowski (*Häftlingskrankenbau in Monowitz,* 126) identifies him as Śliwiński.
67. Makowski (*Häftlingskrankenbau in Monowitz,* 126, 153, 164) describes Drohocki's work.
68. Makowski (*Häftlingskrankenbau in Monowitz,* 130) identifies one Emil Hantl, a SDG corporal as does Langbein (*People of Auschwitz,* 432).
69. Dr. Hans Alfred König (born 1912) was an SS physician like Drs. Fischer and Entress. Langbein reports that he came to the camps to gain more experience with amputations. His duties did not sit well with him: "when he had to make selections, he got drunk" (Langbein, *People in Auschwitz,* 354).
70. SS Dr. Bruno Kitt was at Monowitz probably until the end of 1943, when he was transferred to Neuengame camp. After the war he was sentenced to death by a British military tribunal (Langbein, *People in Auschwitz,* 361).

71. No medical experiments such as those of the notorious Dr. Mengele took place in KL Auschwitz III-Buna-Monowitz. The only source who reported seeing Mengele in Monowitz is Elie Wiesel (*Night,* 71).
72. Langbein (*People in Auschwitz,* 357) mentions Dr. Władyslaw Fejkiel. Danuta Czech mentions, on February 8, 1943 (*Chronicle of Auschwitz,* 325) the prisoner #5647, Dr. Władyslaw Fejkiel.
73. Makowski, *Häftlingskrankenbau in Monowitz,* 173.

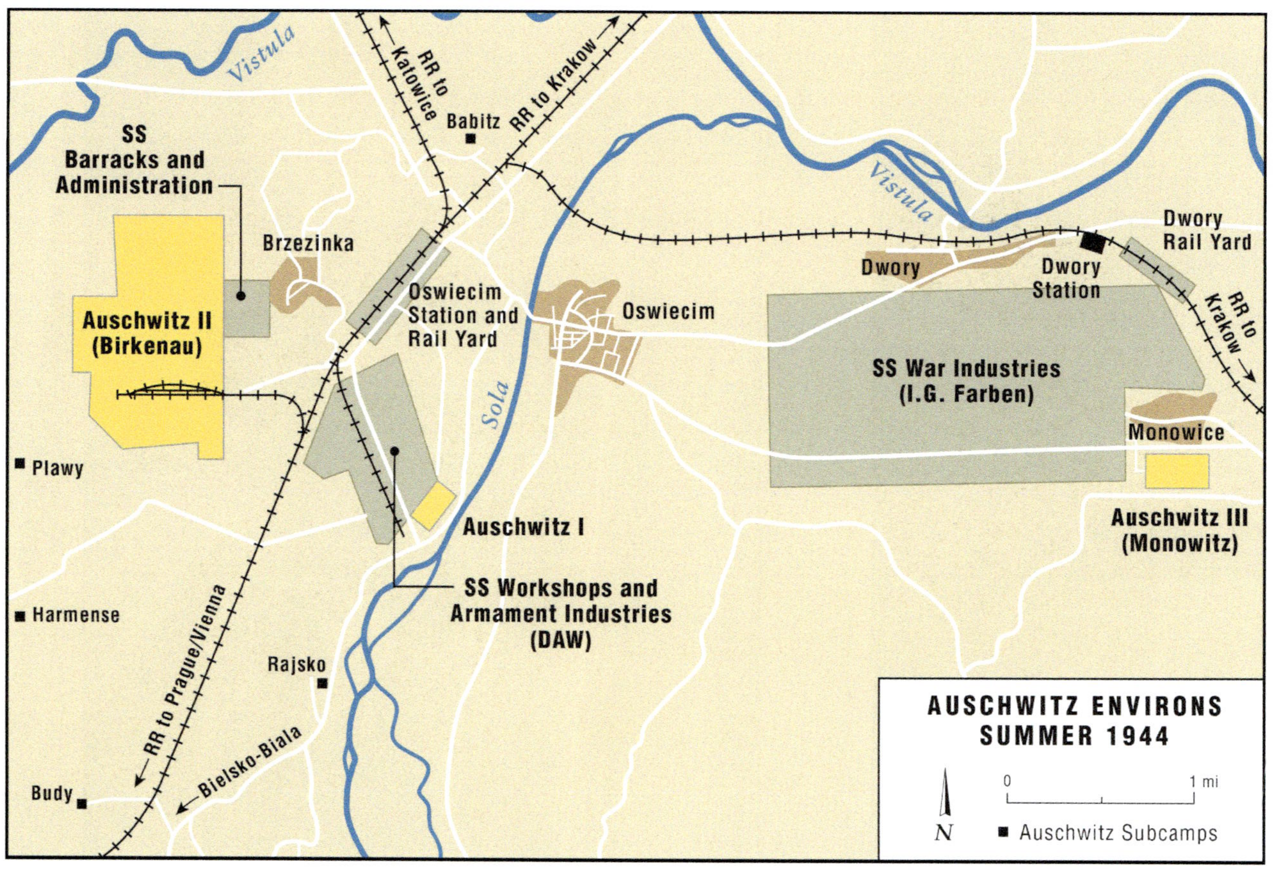

Main Auschwitz camps in 1944. Map adapted from the original, United States Holocaust Memorial Museum.

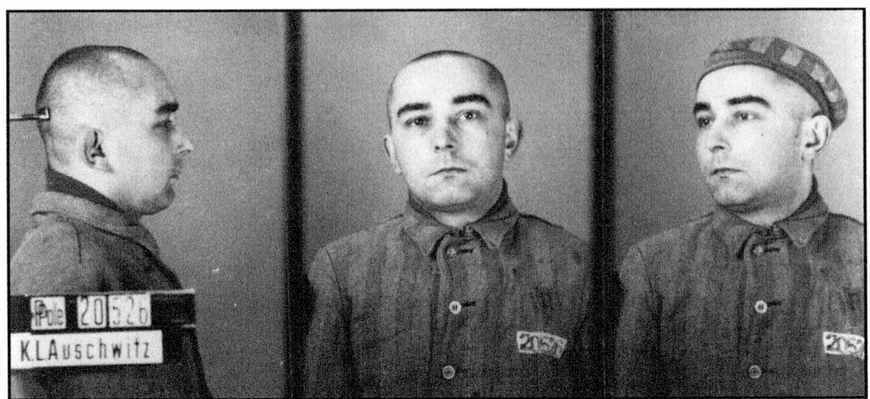

Stefan Budziaszek's arrest photograph, Auschwitz, February 1942.

SS Dr. Eduard Wirths with his wife and children on an outing near Auschwitz. Courtesy of United States Holocaust Memorial Museum.

IG Farben's Buna plant in Monowitz in late 1944. Courtesy of Oswiecim Museum.

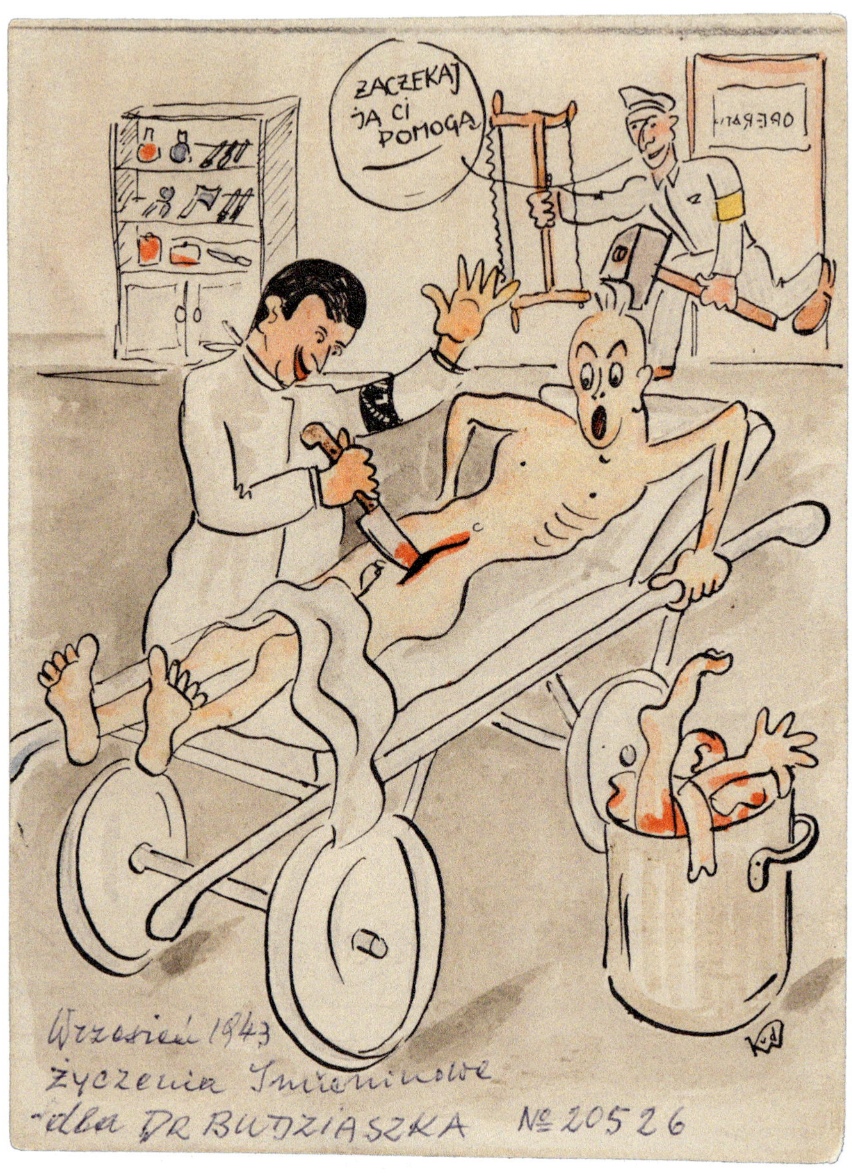

A fellow prisoner drew a name-day greeting card for the new prisoner-doctor. A close analysis of this example of black and gory prison humor reveals that prisoners formed communal ties and social networks that were essential for survival. The card has two sides: the cartoon on the front (above) and the greetings on the back (right). There is a small mark, a signature, that is perhaps the letters "KW" near the trashcan. In ink there is a note from Stefan: "September 1943, name-day wishes for Dr. Budziaszek, #20526." This note is written in Polish.

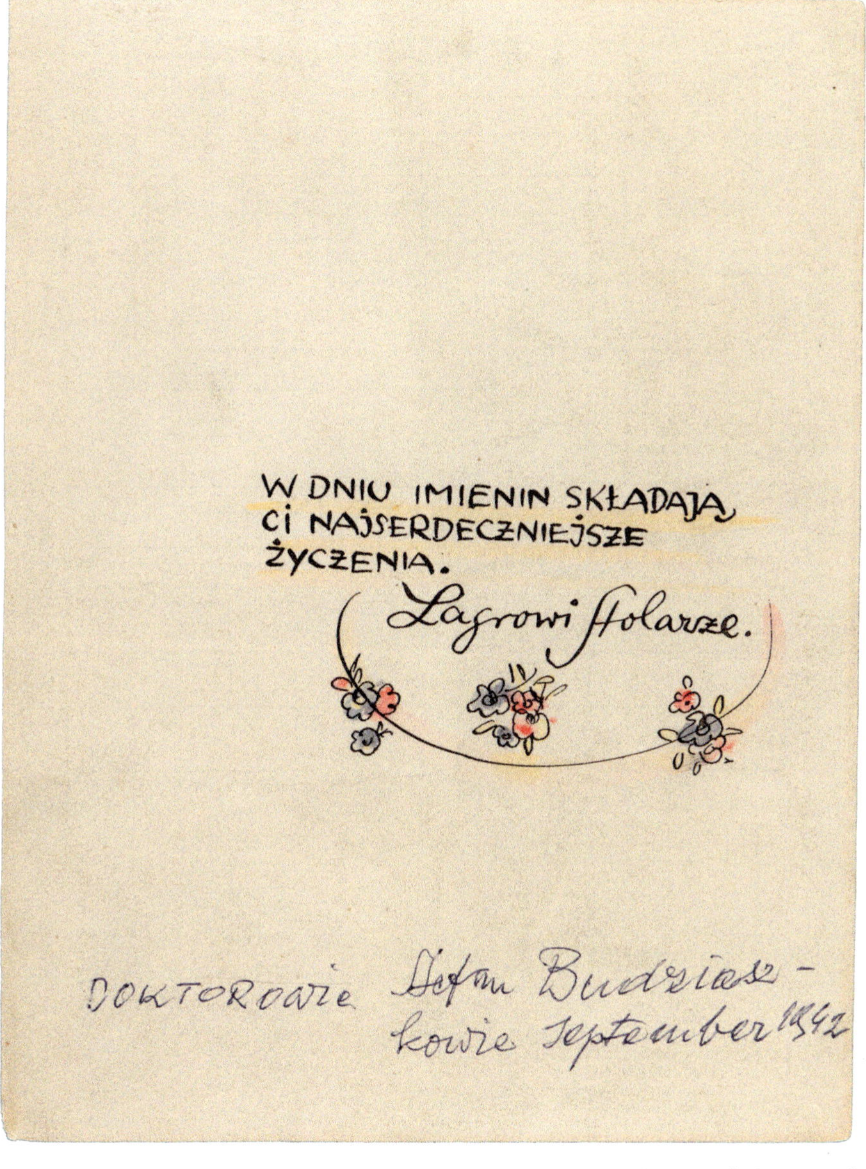

W DNIU IMIENIN SKŁADAJĄ
CI NAJSERDECZNIEJSZE
ŻYCZENIA.
Lagrowi Stolarze.

DOKTOROWIE Stefan Budziasz-
kowie September 1942

On the back, Stefan wrote: "For Doctor Stefan Budziaszek September 1942." This second note starts in Polish, with his name in the possessive case, but the date is written in German: "September" instead of "Wrzesien." He could not have received this card in 1942, as the scene is clearly an operating theater in the Monowitz prisoner hospital. I infer that the note on the back was added significantly later in that he uses a German term for the month, no longer references his prisoner number, and writes down the wrong year. The inscription reads, "On your name day, we send you our most heartfelt best wishes, The camp carpenters."

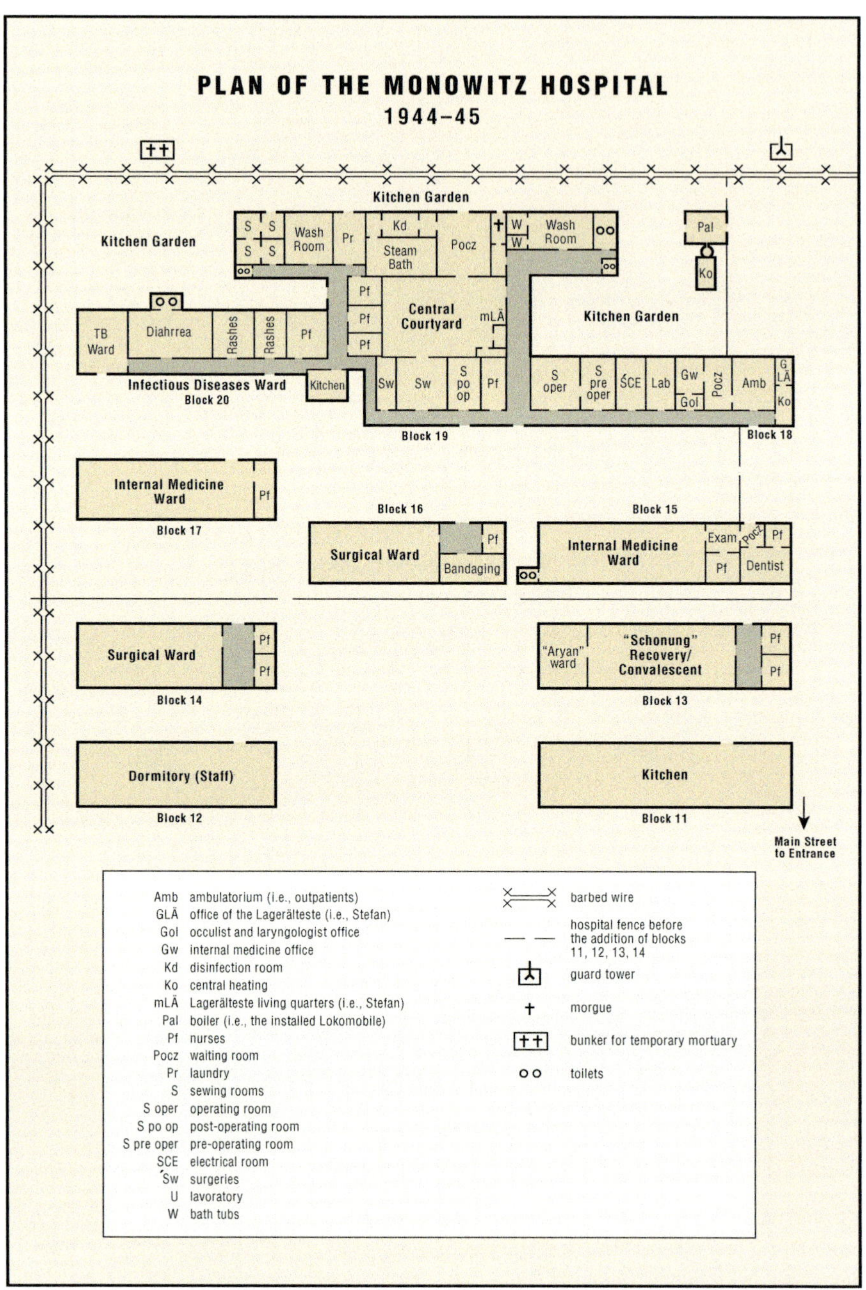

Map adapted from the original in *Apel Skazanych: Wspomnienia z Oświęcimia (Oświęcim, Brno, Monowice),* by Czesław Jaworski (Warsaw: Instytut Wydawniczy PAX, 1962).

Stefan's student photograph, 1933 (in his 20's), from his university transcript.

Stefan, circa 1980.

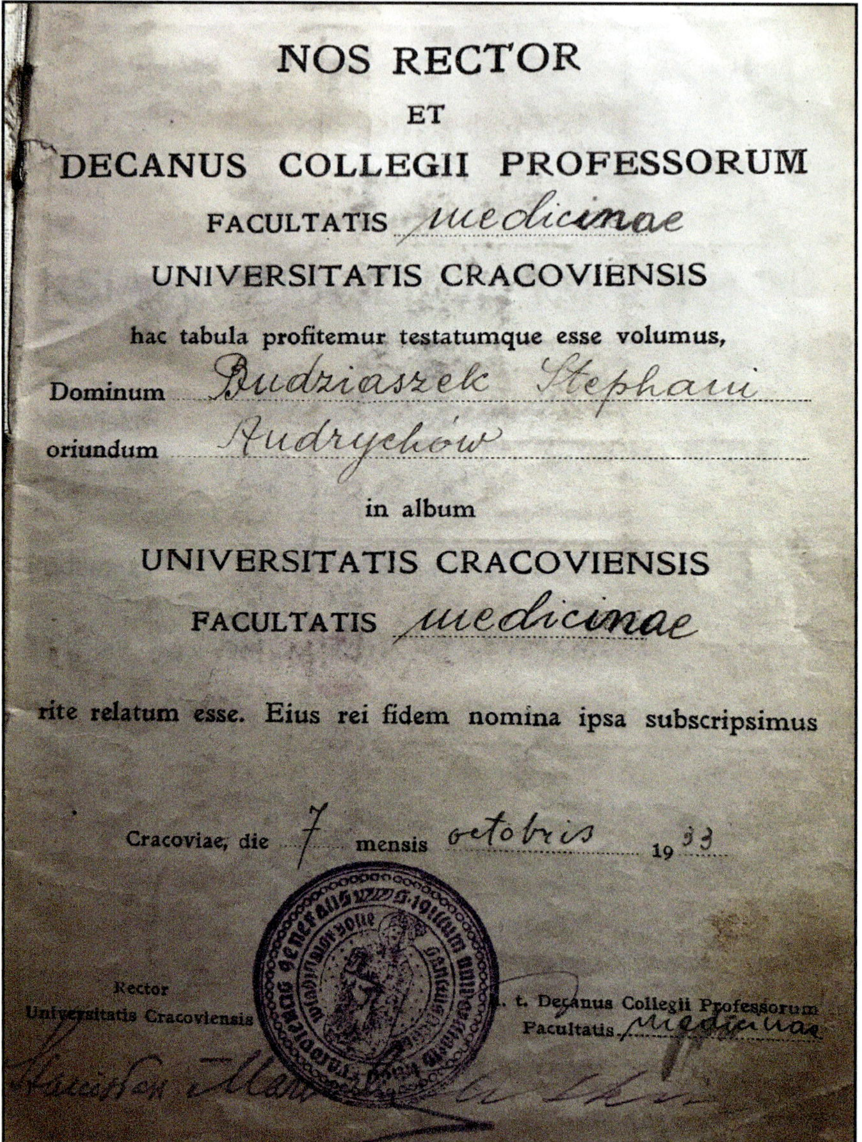

NOS RECTOR

ET

DECANUS COLLEGII PROFESSORUM

FACULTATIS medicinae

UNIVERSITATIS CRACOVIENSIS

hac tabula profitemur testatumque esse volumus,

Dominum Budziaszek Stephani

oriundum Andrychów

in album

UNIVERSITATIS CRACOVIENSIS

FACULTATIS medicinae

rite relatum esse. Eius rei fidem nomina ipsa subscripsimus

Cracoviae, die 7 mensis octobris 1933

Rector Universitatis Cracoviensis

h. t. Decanus Collegii Professorum Facultatis medicinae

Stefan's 1933 matriculation certificate.

8

SURVIVAL IN THE CAMP

In sealed box cars travel
Names across the land
And how far they will travel so,
And will they ever get out?

W zaplombowanych wagonach
jadą karzem iminone
a dokąd tak jechać będą
A czy kiedy wysędą?[1]

SELECTIONS

Concentration camps functioned as slave labor camps, but the annexation of western Poland into Germany also opened other opportunities, such as forced labor organizations. On October 15, 1940, Albrecht Schmelt was appointed by the SS to manage the Polish Jewish (but not Polish gentile) labor resources of Upper Silesia. With Schmelt's appointment, the SS controlled not only concentration camp labor, but also the labor of tens of thousands of Jews still living in the small communities in the annexed lands.[2] This SS-managed Schmelt labor system pioneered the policy of killing exhausted workers. "Since late fall 1941, the Schmelt office had performed first sporadic, then systematic selections in the forced labor camps. Persons unable to work [*arbeitsunfäig*] later were sent to Auschwitz and murdered there."[3] The Schmelt organization even stopped trains going to the Auschwitz camps to exchange healthy workers for disabled workers in the Schmelt camps.[4] The

SS accepted the concept of killing workers as a perverted system of efficiency. Workers in the Auschwitz system incapacitated by illness or injury who sought help from some medical unit faced an enormous dilemma: they might return to a healthier state with the help of the hospital staff or they might expose themselves to selections to the gas chambers during SS medical inspections. Prisoners, prisoner doctors, and SS doctors all understood the game: unfit workers died in the workplace, in the barracks, and in the hospitals.

There were distinct types of selections in the camps. The most feared selection affected the whole camp and was carried out on the roll call grounds. Any sign of weakness during the physically punishing routines could be deadly. Two kinds of selections took place in the barracks: one in which prisoners were forced to run naked past SS men in the barracks and another in which prisoners ran past the SS medical committee in front of barracks number 4. A particularly dangerous selection was organized by the Buna management, which took place at the camp gate on the ways to and from the Buna factory to eliminate weak or injured workers. But the most problematic selection took place in the hospital itself, after a prisoner's extended stay. If the prisoner was not capable of returning to work in two weeks, the SS doctors signed the order to move the prisoner to the Birkenau gas chambers.[5] Dr. Makowski adds: "The main interest of the SS doctors was to lower the number of prisoner patients in the camp . . . the SS doctors carried out systematic selections to eliminate the long-standing sick and the debilitated prisoners."[6] The prisoner physicians worked to frustrate this aim.

Prisoner patients and prisoner doctors used desperate methods to avoid the hospital selections. The easiest was to have oneself declared "healthy" and return to the camp, but this was only sensible and possible if one had sufficient health to return to work. If the prisoner was too weak for labor but had some kind of support network, he could find a kitchen or nursing position, a functional prisoner position. A patient's serious disease could be misrepresented by the prisoner doctors as less serious and the patient could be shuffled around the beds to hide him from the SS. Dr. Makowski mentions the maneuver of transferring a patient from one unit to another, then issuing a new chart with a more recent intake date, thus disguising how long the patient had been in the HKB.[7] Last, one could bribe the eminently bribable SS orderly Neubert and be hidden from the SS selection. Clearly, each of these strategies required that the hospital doctors and personnel were invested in that prisoner's survival.[8] Langbein confirms that prisoner physicians in the main camp and the Birkenau HKB also tried to protect patients from the lethal selection process.[9]

However, as soon as the SS doctors perceived the hospital as "crowded," prisoner doctors maneuvered to keep the hospital census as low as possible to limit selections and avoid SS doctor scrutiny. Wagner places the limit of the hospital at 5% of the camp inmates.[10] It is possible that the stated percentage of "permitted" patients in the hospital varied over time, since Makowski mentions both a 5% limit and a 10% limit.[11] Stefan mentions the 10% figure. In October 1943 (four months after Stefan was moved to Auschwitz III), the head of the SS economic office, the WVHA, Oswald Pohl, declared that system-wide, "I have made it our priority that we allow no more than 10% of all inmates to be unfit for work due to illness."[12] At the lower limit and with a Buna-Monowitz camp population pushing 10,000, the hospital capacity was 500 men; at the upper limit, 1,000 men. However, a great deal of the hospital activity took place in the ambulatorium, the out-patient barrack, which would not add to the bed count and was not subject to organized SS selections.

The process of selections in Buna-Monowitz is difficult to document. Danuta Czech chronicles of daily events in Auschwitz I but does not address Buna-Monowitz directly. Wagner's careful research links the last huge camp-wide selection, which also hit Buna-Monowitz, with the late fall 1944 destruction of the gas chambers in Birkenau.[13] The selections in the hospitals were also to decide who would have the best chances of long-term survival. Wagner summarizes: "To ask if it is more 'moral' to treat the young and intellectuals, the workers, or the members of a specific religion or nationality with the few resources available is not a questions that can be reasonably answered. The conditions for making such decisions in the camp did not give the physician true treatment alternative."[14] Robert Waitz, a prisoner physician in Buna-Monowitz, states: "Before selections [the physicians] concealed emaciated and ill inmates; they also forged medical records and hid unfortunate inmates who were destined for the gas chamber. This very necessary activity of the physicians repeatedly confronted them with a dilemma. Either do nothing, which would have been a solution dictated by cowardice, or act, which would have meant that they could save only a limited number of people and turned a physician into a judge. Only those could be helped who had chances of recovering physically and morally after receiving such help. Making a choice is one of the knottiest problems that a physician who is worthy of that title can face."[15] Wagner makes clear that Stefan had acquired some discretionary power. "His intervention on behalf of a patient could also save him from selection even if the patient appeared in a hopeless state. The SS had given him a lot of leeway to deal with medically interesting cases, which he used at least in part."[16] These were dangerous games being played with limited degrees of freedom.

Hermann Langbein reports on a conversation he had with Stefan after the war. Stefan explained the self-defeating strategy of prisoners: "Many inmates avoided going to the infirmary for as long as they could, even if they were sick, because they had heard about the selections. The SS camp leader noticed one time that numerous inmates on the labor details could hardly stay on their feet and dragged along the paper bandages that had opened as they marched out of camp . . . and thus he ordered that those unfit for work be identified in all blocks. No one had any doubt what awaited these men. [Stefan] received this order as camp elder, and he passed it on to the physicians who served under him. These physicians named only three of the several thousand inmates. [Stefan] asserted that 'the physicians would come to me with this low figure, but I could not take it to the SS medic.' A subsequent selection claimed 150 to 200 weak victims."[17] Langbein reviews stories of other prisoner functionaries and reached the conclusion "that condemnations of leading functionaries in the infirmary must be considered with caution"[18] and quotes a woman physician in Birkenau who warns against rash judgments and self-righteous condemnations of medical personnel.[19]

Getting an infection, suffering from a work injury, contracting an epidemic disease, or simply collapsing from malnutrition—all of these and more meant danger for a prisoner. He had to seek help. But—from whom? Prisoners understood quickly that they could only survive if they could work. Many prisoners—hundreds each day—sought help in the Buna-Monowitz ambulatorium, the walk-in clinic. But others had to be admitted to the hospital, for better or worse. The "worse" was clear: SS physicians would select debilitated workers and move them to Birkenau to be killed.

Standing between the patients and the SS men were several layers of protection. You could get a week or two of recuperation and rest enough to return to work. The doctors or the nurses—fellow prisoners—could hide you by producing falsified records to extend the hospitalization. This was not an uncommon strategy. Prisoner Dr. Romould Sztaba, writing about his experience in the Gross-Rosen concentration camp, reported protecting inmates in this fashion. He adds: "This required great diplomacy and understanding of the psychology of the [Nazi] superiors."[20] The Gross-Rosen prisoner hospital—like the one in Buna-Monowitz—got overcrowded. Dr. Sztaba reports that the SS physicians made a selection of the most seriously ill patients because they suspected that that the prisoner doctors were falsifying the hospital census. He also remarked that there were usually one or two highly energetic prisoners who were able to influence their SS superiors and to some extend able to create an atmosphere of cooperation between prisoners and their captors.

Primo Levi, a worker in the Buna facility and eventually a patient in the prisoner hospital, calls this narrow cooperative space the "gray zone." He defines it as the amorphous area of cooperation between inmate and guard. How extensive is this intersection?

"It is a gray zone, poorly defined, where the two camps of masters and servants both diverge and converge. This gray zone possesses an incredibly complicated internal structure and contains within itself enough to confuse our need to judge."[21] As the leader of the Buna-Monowitz prisoner hospital, Stefan stood in the gray zone. The ambiguity inherent in a prisoner working with his SS jailers exposed Stefan to accusations of collaboration with the SS after the war.

The distinguished psychiatrist Robert Jay Lifton interviewed Stefan in the early 1980s (after both the museum oral history deposition and the end of the German Frankfurt trials in 1974), for Lifton's book, *The Nazi Doctors*. He relegates Stefan to the chapter "Prison Doctors: Collaboration with Nazi Doctors." As many other commentators writing about Stefan have noted, Stefan had changed his name.[22] In 1955, at the behest of his second wife, Ursula Terner, Stefan changed his surname from the orthographical difficult "Budziaszek" to "Buthner," thus combining sounds from both their surnames. Stefan had now lived in Germany for a decade and had started a new family. In Lifton's opprobrious view this was seen as "having even Germanized his name."[23] Stefan's marriage and his other contacts with the Hanover German Jewish community after the war are dismissed with sarcasm. From Lifton's Freudian perspective, this "collaborating" doctor had crossed the ambiguities of a gray zone and behaved like a Nazi. He paints a picture of Stefan as "a rabid anti-Semitic Polish nationalist with an evil temper."[24] Lifton does not investigate the work of the Buna-Monowitz prisoner hospital or its expansion after Stefan arrived in 1943. In contrast, in Lifton's chapter on the SS Dr. Eduard Wirths, Wirths is praised for protecting prisoner doctors and even allowing Jewish prisoner doctors to work in the camps. These are the same physicians Stefan recruited from incoming prisoners. Lifton ascribes an "aura of moral scrupulousness" to Wirths.[25] Nonetheless, this more positive exemplar of SS physicians still succumbed to the Nazi imperative of selecting prisoners to death.[26] Neither the conflicted SS physician nor a prisoner doctor could avoid the death-dealing in Auschwitz.

Jan Oswald, a political scientist, invokes the term *Handlungsspielraum*, referring to a prisoner's space to maneuver, that narrow area Levi calls the gray zone. Oswald focuses on functionary prisoners: prisoner physicians like Stefan or camp secretaries like Langbein. A prisoner working as a dentist or doctor had a higher degree of freedom than a cook or a carpenter. In Oswald's view, the space in which functionary prisoners moved has not been well explored. He postulates that a social hierarchy developed among prisoners. Prisoners with low numbers (i.e., long-term prisoners) and likely to have a camp job had accrued social capital. Prisoners who provided personal services to SS men such as barbers, physicians, and even waiters could have favorable relations with the SS.[27] This is an area which has not been well-studied, according to Oswald, because of inadequate sources.[28]

Oswald does note, however, that a physician prisoner in a functionary position has something that the SS wants: a specific, needed skill. For instance, there is room to maneuver in the development of a hospital since the SS is looking for a specific outcome and needs specific prisoners. SS Dr. Wirths in Auschwitz I needed better facilities in Buna-Monowitz and obviously and publicly and even ostentatiously brought Stefan from Jawischowitz to Buna-Monowitz in his personal car. He publicly announced the special status of this prisoner. While Stefan and his cohort took pride in their energy, ingenuity, and effectiveness, the room for them to maneuver was supplied by Wirths.

After the war, Stephan Heymann, an active Jewish communist resistance organizer and hospital secretary, accused Stefan of being an antisemitic Pole who preferentially chose Jews during camp selections. Heymann's accusation was published in Eugen Kogon's *Der SS-Staat* (1946). Kogon was an important postwar author who was a strong anti-Nazi Christian and had been incarcerated in Buchenwald for six years. In a notarized letter (April 24, 1955) preserved among Stefan's papers, Kogon writes: "In the last six years I have received no corroboration to support Stephan Heymann's accusations. On the contrary, there are numerous testimonies to the contrary." Kogon goes on to apologize for his publication of Heymann's accusations and expresses the hope that "Dr. Stefan Budziaszek" does not suffer further consequences.

Stefan, however, was not at all absolved of accusations of favoring Poles and choosing Jews to die in hospital selections. Not until 1974, after the West German government undertook judicial processes to examine the activities of the concentration camps, was Stefan cleared of any wrongdoing. The courts could find no concrete evidence of preferential selections and dismissed what turned out to be hearsay statements. Wagner states that Heymann produced 1,500 pages of various documents for the courts which were not sufficient to convince the court of Stefan's culpability.[29] Oswald notes that the witnesses who supported Stefan during the Frankfurt trials described his improvements to the prison hospital. His accusers did not find this salient evidence.[30]

Stefan's oral testimony keeps circling back to the difficult and painful issue of selections. Thousands of prisoners cycled through the prisoner hospital, but not everyone survived. Death from diseases and injuries are not morally controversial, but selections for death are. The gray zone of ambiguity links the senior hospital prisoner with the SS physicians who had death-dealing powers.

Stefan here talks about selections:

> The SS doctors had various levels of interest in what was happening in the prisoner hospital.[31] The only one who was particularly interested was Fischer, who actually personally assisted a couple of times in our surgery. Occasionally the SS doctors demanded an inspection of all the patients to do a selection. Those selected were driven to Birkenau. The capacity of the hospital was of course limited, but the number of sick was always larger. We had to release a number of the sick. One has to remember that the SS looked over the state of the men marching off daily to work. This was done either by the *Lagerführer* or the *Rapportführer.* Ill-looking prisoners or ones with bandages were stopped and directed towards the hospital.

A vicious cycle formed and an overfilled hospital was always threatened with selections.

Regarding SS SDG Neubert: he was an older man, a carpenter by trade, who actually didn't bother prisoners. If we asked to do something for ourselves he tried to oblige, but he showed absolutely no initiative in the sense of, for instance, improving the prisoners' hospital. He was only concerned about himself and how to "organize" things for his own benefit. He didn't reveal any anger and he was probably the calmest SDG among those I encountered in the camps. It's thanks to this that we were able to accomplish such things as keeping patients longer or "organizing" medicines, which would not have been possible with a stricter SS man. Thankfully, the *Lagerführer* had no idea about our shenanigans. Those prisoners who manned the records office (*Schreibstube*) and the *Lagerälteste* Paul Kozwara, they knew.

On days when the SS *Lagerarzt* showed up, I myself had to present reports about the actual number of the sick in the hospital and if there were any unusual situations (*besondere Vorkomnisse*). This was a standard ritual. Next he'd go to the chancellery to exchange a few sentences with the SDG. Occasionally he'd look into the ambulatorium and observe the work of the prisoner doctors bandaging the injured—all this if he came in the morning. Sometimes he'd be present as the sick were being admitted. I'm making clear that one of my duties was to decide who could be admitted, from among those prisoners who had reported to the chancellery the night before. They'd been examined by colleagues and kept as candidates for hospital admission. The SS doctor never commented about my decisions. Dr. Silber often did this duty in my stead. The current SDG had to be present when someone was admitted and it was his job to police us prisoners to prevent any irregularities. Of course our "irregularities" were designed for the good of the prisoners. I can give the following example: once a prisoner was sentenced, for some violation, to one of the sub-

> camps near a mine. He was a Jewish prisoner by the name of Szleimo (I don't remember exactly). Such a transfer, followed by work under very difficult conditions, could have had tragic consequences for the prisoner. To prevent a transfer he got an appendectomy.[32]
>
> On one day, sadly I can't recall the actual date, the Monowitz hospital was visited by some SS dignitary, a physician, perhaps of the rank of Lieutenant General (SS *Gruppenführer*). Naturally he was accompanied by the SS *Standortarzt* and the *Lagerarzt*. Our own SDG commented and I learned that they had made positive remarks about the hospital.

Stefan next turns to the topic of music-making in the camp. But why would he segue to this unlikely topic? He is likely struggling with the memory of his most difficult task: prisoner physicians had to obey selection orders. So, he digresses. He describes activities he promoted to ameliorate the tensions and tedium of hospitalization. He organized musical events. The first camp orchestra, manned by prisoners, was organized in the main Auschwitz camp and was performing by January, 1941. Its function was entirely practical: the music helped maintain the cadence of the men marching in and out of camp. Both formal and informal concerts followed, and camp orchestras organized in the other camps. Langbein writes movingly about the comfort prisoners and prisoner performers derived from music-making.[33] Makowski remembers these concerts as well and stated that some lasted for hours and were a welcome event.[34] The patients in Buna-Monowitz heard concerts every other Saturday.[35]

> To relieve the monotony, I organized performances of the camp orchestra for the sick prisoners. They took place in an internal courtyard, which was created when we built connections between the barracks. The performers were soloists such as Stasiak, Wojszczyk, and others. This project was made easier since I was acquainted with many of the prisoners who cooperated with my requests. This type of concert by the camp orchestra was also put on for the other prisoners at Monow-

> itz; they even organized a kind of review. Famous singers appeared at these concerts, including a tenor with a booming voice. He had been brought to KL Auschwitz from the Compiegne camp and was then poisoned in the camp hospital by that prisoner group from Buchenwald I mentioned earlier. That prisoner had been accused of treason or denunciation. That all took place in 1944, I don't remember the exact date or the prisoner's name—he spoke Polish and was under Heymann's direction. I learned about this after the fact.

There is no other reference to the mysterious tenor with the booming voice. Stefan attributes this murder to the Buchenwald contingent. The relationships between Stefan and many of his coworkers and the cohort of older, ideologically opposed prisoners continued to be tense with mutual suspicion. Stefan's narrative returns again to the fraught issue of prisoner death rate and adds more details.

> I cannot recall ever getting any orders limiting the time a prisoner could spend in the hospital. On the other hand, the number of patients was not allowed to be more than 10% of the inmates of KL Auschwitz III. At the same time, the number of sick was markedly larger than the capacity of the hospital barracks. To somehow deal with the disparity I organized so-called "recovery" wards (*Schonungsblock*) to which less severe cases were moved and protected from selections. A lot depended on the psychological resistance of the sick. I remember, for instance, the tragedy of the Dutch Jews. Before their arrests and deportations they lived in optimal conditions. When they came to the concentration camp they weren't able to or couldn't come to terms with the grim conditions and regimes. Many of them broke down psychologically and sought the mercy of death by throwing themselves against the camp fence.

The "recovery wards" were part of the strategy to circumvent arbitrary and deadly SS rules. Cycling recovering patients out of the regular wards lowered the daily bed count. No such stratagem, however, could save new concentration camp arrivals who collapsed under the shock of depersonalization. As mentioned previously, Dębski and Kertesz described this collapse. Sociologist Goffman adds that total institutions have procedures for incomers: "photographing, weighing, finger printing, assigning numbers, searching, undressing, bathing, disinfecting, hair cutting, issuing institutional clothes, and assigning to quarters creates an 'object' to be fed into the system."[36] The shock to ill-prepared new prisoners was sufficient to create an irreversible withdrawal and—in the camps—led to death. After this brief digression, Stefan again returns to the salient issue of selections.

> During my incarceration in KL Auschwitz there were two—maybe three—large selections directed by the SS *Lagerarzt*. These selections took place only among the prisoners in the camp hospital. There was only one camp-wide selection. It began when the *Lagerführer* observed that a noticeable number of men marching off to their work units (*Kommandos*) were bandaged or looked ill—in a word, were on the verge of collapse from exhaustion and useless as workers. The camp commanders called for a selection (the order was given by Schöttl), with the concurrence of Commander Schwartz. Initially, the prisoner doctors from the camp hospital were supposed to do a first selection, but they only chose five prisoners. Then SS SDG Neubert stepped forward and did another exam of all the prisoners in the camp—this took place at the evening roll call. The "selected" prisoners were supposed to report to the camp hospital. I remember this exactly because I had to accompany Neubert going through the barracks, but unfortunately I don't remember the exact date of the selection. It could have been in the summer of 1944. The next day, when the prisoners selected by Neubert showed up at the hospital, SS *Lagerarzt* Fischer made yet another selection, keeping one-third in the camp (Monowitz) and sending the rest to Birkenau. I don't remember the exact number of prisoners that went

> to Birkenau then, but it was perhaps 100 or 120. Heymann was angry with me about this and wanted to know why I didn't influence Neubert to choose fewer prisoners. I explained that Neubert actually chose prisoners who were not all that sick to increase, paradoxically, the hope of saving those selected. I knew in fact that the second round of selections carried out the next day by the SS *Lagerarzt*—who immediately saw the obvious—would have to leave a lot of the selected in the camp. My calculations were borne out: as I said, *Lagerarzt* Fischer ordered two-thirds of the selected prisoners off the list. Only the remaining one-third were moved (*Verlegung*) to Birkenau. The selected prisoners were driven off in two or three trucks. We understood the tragic end which awaited these prisoners.

Langbein concluded his chapter on the camp hospitals with the following statement: "It is no accident that the resistance movement in Auschwitz gained a firm foothold among the personnel of the infirmaries, as it did in every other Nazi concentration camp. The infirmaries that the camp administrations had installed as 'waiting rooms for death' were frequently transformed into cells of rescue and aid, though never completely and certainly not easily. Because this was possible, one may say with a detachment born of experience, that it was proper to take positions in the infirmary. The moral burden that a person thereby shouldered for the rest of his life and the criticism from people who make judgments without knowledge of all the connections and backgrounds were the price that had to be paid. What weighs more heavily on the scale is the awareness of a physician that he remained a healer even in Auschwitz and that of a nurse that he did not lose his human face even in death's waiting room."[37] Though Langbein was upset that he had lost control over the cherished functionary prisoner positions in the hospital to Stefan, he nonetheless honored the role that prisoner hospital staff played in the dangerous and chaotic lives of Auschwitz prisoners.

FOOD AND MEDICINES

The nexus of talents, ingenuity, and audacity which formed in the prisoner hospital in Buna-Monowitz provided the agency needed to provide services for the patients. Hunger was the pervasive enemy, as debilitating in the long run as injuries and disease in the short run. The demands of heavy labor coupled with inadequate food ground prisoners down. Prisoners had no access to mirrors, but they could look at one another. The skeletal bodies, the grey flaccid skin, the sunken eyes, and prominent ribs were all manifestations of systematic starvation. The hospital food was unfortunately little better. Dr. Makowski estimated a daily 800 calories per day per patient, with a little more for postoperative patients.[38]

Prisoners who had family nearby were better off in general.[39] Prisoners who received food packages had better survival rates. De facto this meant Poles who received packages until the very end of the war, when the Polish postal system stopped operating. What wasn't consumed became camp currency. Dr. Jaworski's fragile heart made him especially vulnerable. It is likely he survived at Buna-Monowitz since he received food packages twice weekly from his wife and every other week from a cousin. He could avoid the camp food as well as distribute food to compatriots. This enormous benefit did not extend to prisoners who arrived from other countries, though apparently some Czech prisoners had access to food packages from home.[40]

Prisoners in other units of the colossal Auschwitz camp system claimed that the food in the Buna-Monowitz camp was special, better, more nourishing and superior: it was the so-called "Buna soup." Until the spring of 1943, the factory management actually provided soup for the prisoner workers in order to prevent contamination from the typhus outbreaks in the camps. This augmented soup, however, was far from legendary. It consisted of a thin watery liquid in which fragments of vegetables, occasionally potato peels, floated. Once the Buna-Monowitz camp kitchen was expanded in the spring of 1943, this concoction was prepared in the camp itself and carried in large thermos containers to the factory grounds. Evening meals in the barracks were more substantial with additions of beans and small measures of fat. One continual frustration for the prisoners was that there were so few implements for eating soup or brews. Prisoners had to fashion their own spoons and guarded them carefully.[41]

Stefan analyzed the diet and its impact on the prisoners and patients:

> The nourishment provided in KL Auschwitz III was a little bit better than that provided in the main camp, as I noticed when I was incarcerated there. But heavy labor and starvation led to physical exhaustion of the prisoners and brought about swelling, phlegmons (abscesses) and various infections. It's hard for me to accurately calculate the number of calories in the provided food. Assuming that prisoners received 150-200 grams of bread (1 gram of bread has an average of 4 calories), soup cooked with potatoes and meat remnants, and the meager additions of sausage (which tasted better and was perhaps richer in calories than that served in the main camp), a little bit of marmalade, and a poor grade of cheese or margarine, these combined to a daily calorie intake around 1600-2000. This could only be an average and could vary depending on how food was distributed in various barracks and if the prisoner got food parcels from his family or "organized" extra food in the camp. The physical state of the prisoners was also strongly influenced by their psychological predisposition. I remember how our colleague Dr. Drohocki suffered the death of his wife. When he received the news that she had died in Birkenau he came close to a complete breakdown. He got the news from some women prisoners who came by car from Birkenau to use the apparatus for electroshock therapy that Drohocki had set up. At that time it was one of the possible ways of contact with the women's camp.

Organizing and improving the conditions of the hospital barracks meant that postoperative patients had individual beds with bed linens.[42] In the rest of the barracks the patients slept

> in two-story beds.[43] These barracks had steam heat but it didn't become effective until we installed that "lokomobile" boiler. We also installed large showers next to the hospital barracks, where the patients could wash. This was very important because nowhere else in the entire camp did they have lavatories or baths with warm water (the barracks washrooms only had cold water). The washrooms were arranged so that a pipe with a row of spigots was suspended above a long stone washbasin. The toilets, if I remember correctly, were equipped with normal ceramic stools.
>
> I don't have much to say about the administration of the hospital. I only know that I had to produce a daily census of patients in the hospital and the number of employees working that day. The rest of the statistics were the duty of the SDG[44] and he was personally responsible for them. He also had to sign the orders to send prisoners to KL Birkenau. Naturally, the SDG didn't verify everything personally, but used prisoners employed in the hospital chancellery (*Schreibstube*), that is to say, prisoner Rausch and Heymann. I cannot describe the number of prisoners who were killed in KL Auschwitz III. I know that Heymann buried hospital records right next to the barracks during the evacuation. I heard that Heymann had ordered some statistical reports, which he also hid.
>
> At some time KL Auschwitz III became the center of all the subcamps.[45] However, only a small number of patients came from the subcamps and that only sporadically. On the other hand, a number of prisoner doctors were moved to subcamp hospitals. Dr. Wojciech Albert and surgeon Grossman (a Catholic of some kind of Jewish heritage) were transferred this way.[46] I met him and a couple of others after the war in Frankfurt am Main, where he died. If I remember correctly, patients from the subcamps were directed to the hospital in Birkenau.

Getting hold of medications was one of the challenges for the physicians in the prisoner hospital. The official list looked adequate, but medical supplies were always in short supply. Analgesics like aspirin, cough medicines, dermatological powders and ointments, bandages (often only paper bandages), disinfectants, plaster, and several anesthetics like ether and, occasionally, chloroform were available. Dr. Makowski lists numerous proprietary formulations: Prontosil, Cibasol, Eubasin, Solvochin, Kardiasol, Sepso, Ichtiol. However, a ward with 180 patients received only 20 aspirin tablets a day.[47] Procuring needed medicines was similar to equipping the hospital itself: the most direct method was scouring other parts of the camps for supplies.

Mieczysław Zając, working in the hospital as a nurse, was caring for a young man who had a streptococcus febrile infection. At the time, these infections were only curable with sulfides, which were not routinely available in the Buna-Monowitz hospital pharmacy. The camp-wide marketplace, however, depended on a barter system. Zając traded one sweater and a pair of gloves to an SS man working in the main camp pharmacy for the needed medication.[48] Yet this vital transaction paled compared to the suitcases full of medication Stefan procured from the main camp.

The ultimate source of large quantities of medications smuggled into Buna-Monowitz was that enormous warehouse of prisoner effects, "Canada." Incoming prisoners had been told to bring a suitcase, which was invariably filled with valuables. All property was confiscated when they entered the Auschwitz system. The SS was most interested in European currency and jewelry, but they also used "Canada" as a source for equipping the camp. Medications from "Canada" were used to supply medication to the Auschwitz I pharmacy. Fortunately, Stefan's boyhood friend, S. Hommé, worked in that pharmacy.[49] Stefan would claim he needed an urgent x-ray in the main camp. He then returned with large suitcases filled with medication, some of which proved useful in the hospital.[50]

"Canada" was not the only resource. The constant interchanges with men working at the Buna factory opened another channel for procuring medicines. The prisoner Roman Orzeł not only worked in the chemical laboratory at the factory, but he also had contact with Polish resistance units outside the camps. Stefan noted three occasions when Orzeł handed over medications to him. Orzeł was also able to liberate iodine and alcohol from the factory stores, which the hospital lab used to prepare iodine solutions, and disinfectants.[51]

Another highly unlikely source of medications was Stefan's father, Florian Budziaszek (1879–1948). The network of civilian and prisoner contacts in the Buna factory enabled Florian to send medications to Stefan. The exact nature of the Krakow underground, which kept in touch with events and needs inside the main camp as well as the Buna-Monowitz camp, is not clear. However, Stefan was able to communicate the needs of the hospital and received at least one clandestine shipment of antityphus medications. Langbein also made reference to another source: SS Dr. Wirths brought medicines with him when he was transferred to Auschwitz.[52] Dr. Jaworski also gave all of his accumulated medications and syringes from the clinic in the Brno camp to Stefan.[53]

As new prisoner doctors accumulated in the now vigorous and expanded unit, people with different skills went to work. This included Herbert Mohl, a Czech medical student. He and his parents were forced into Terezienstadt by the Nazis. The young Herbert was transported to Auschwitz and got a job in the hospital. Dr. Makowski wrote: "Finally we must not forget the medication produced by H. Mohl since his arrival in late 1943 to work in the laboratory."[54] Once again, the Buna factory was the clandestine source of the raw materials. The boiler earlier "organized" from the factory, lined graph paper for ersatz temperature charts, loads of construction material, and now chemicals and laboratory gear necessary to fabricate medication were all were unwittingly supplied by IG Farbenindustrie. In a letter dated December 11, 1945, Mohl recalls his work in Buna-Monowitz: "I had to get the appliances, chemicals, etc., without 'help' of the Storm Troopers or money. I succeeded, as I had hundreds of comrades, who 'brought' me the necessary glasses and chemicals from the IG Farben store, so that I was able to do all analysis and prepare more ointments, solutions, injections of glucose, and calcium for our sick comrades."[55]

As Stefan's testimony proceeds, there is no record of questions or prompts from Tadeusz Iwaszko. Stefan again changes topics according to some internal association. The narrative about medications brings up Stefan's surprising contacts with his father. Local prisoners from Krakow were apparently able to set up a very occasional meeting. Some prisoners had personal social contact not with family, but with the SS men who lived in the small town of Auschwitz. Hermann Langbein and some of his compatriots were actually able to leave the concentration camp for social occasions. These prisoners were hosted by SS Dr. Wirths, his wife, and their children.[56] In mid-1944, after Wirths's family had left to return to Germany, Langbein arranged a flower delivery to Wirths and presented him with a painted portrait of his absent family.[57]

Stefan's outside contacts were more circumspect:

> I mentioned that we got medicines for the prisoner hospital of KL Auschwitz. At any rate, the official amounts of medicines were meager, so I and my colleagues from the central pharmacy in the main camp tried to procure additional medications. I got in illegal contact with my father. A civilian worker (whose name I can't recall) working at IG Farbenindustrie was our go-between. The worker, as an electrician, had the right to enter the camp to check the electrical system. Thanks to this I got to see him occasionally. He visited my father, who then sent me antityphus vaccinations and others procured from the Weigl Institute in Krakow. Naturally there wasn't much of this. Unfortunately, I don't know all the details of my father's illegal activities, but he certainly had contacts with some underground groups in Krakow. My father died in 1948 and I had no opportunity to talk with him after the war. Besides, my father talked with no one at home, not even his wife, about these contacts. One thing I know for sure: he was able to get me things I asked for and he had many opportunities to get to Krakow. He was a railroad official (before the second World War he worked for the Krakow Railroad Administration and he was demoted by the Nazis for refusing to sign the *Volksliste* even after a lot of pressure).[58]

> My father had served in the Austrian army [in World War One] and knew how to speak German—though that made no one German. Father traveled on the Oświęcim-Kraków line two or three times a week. I do not believe that he had some other source for getting medicines, such as allied air drops, for instance. It is possible that such medical help reached the camps, but I knew nothing about them.
>
> Since I'm dealing with these issues, I'm eager to say that despite camp rules, we were able to contact significant sections of KL Auschwitz as well as KL Birkenau and the subcamps. When we needed information from a given camp, we pretended to have to transfer a prisoner to the given camp's hospital. Under similar conditions there were three or four trips made to us by women prisoners for electroshock. A Polish block functionary accompanied them—I don't recall her name. On the occasion of these trips to Monowitz the wives of other Jewish prisoner doctors were brought along. In this fashion they were able to meet—if only briefly—and to talk. It's thanks to these contacts that Dr. Drohocki learned of the death of his wife—she was killed in KL Birkenau.

The gray zone between the inmates and their jailers had many dimensions. Stefan's leadership role in the prisoner hospital depended on the willingness of the SS, particularly SS Dr. Wirths and SS Dr. Fischer, to tolerate Stefan's aggressive changes. Stefan's level of freedom included movement between various Auschwitz camps, the requisitioning of labor and material to build new wards, the outright theft of the lokomobile, his constant search and requisitioning of scarce medications, and the organization of both an outpatient unit and recovery ward. Critical for the successful functioning of the prisoner hospital was the recruitment of dozens of physicians from among camp newcomers. None of these activities was typical of a rote functionary prisoner. Jan Oswald explains that a prominent prisoner like Stefan had significant room to maneuver in the gray zone of Auschwitz. But Stefan had no influence over the major factors of prisoners' lives: he could not influence any capo work unit; he had no control at all over work demanded in the IG Farben worksite; and he could not avoid selections of moribund prisoners to an early death in Birkenau.

ESCAPES AND RESISTANCE

Reading Danuta Czech's chronicles of the daily activity in Auschwitz confirms the constant executions of prisoners trying to escape or organizing escapes. In the early years, when the main camp was almost exclusively Polish, ten or more prisoners were executed for every escapee. Fr. Maksymilian Rajmund Kolbe arrived from the Warsaw prison Pawiak on May 29, 1941. He was prisoner #16670. On July 19, he stepped forward and took the place of Franciszek Gajkowski, who was among 15 prisoners sentenced to death by starvation in retaliation for an escape. Fr. Kolbe and the others spent two weeks in the bunker of block 11. He was finally killed by a phonol injection by Hans Bock.[59] In late 1944, however, this form of terror had ceased and Zając reports constant escapes, especially at the Buna plant. A few people went missing daily and the camp experienced more and more roll calls.[60] Tadeusz Iwaszko, the Polish researcher who interviewed Stefan in 1974, documented 667 escapes from the Auschwitz camps. Only 16 were women. 270 of them were recaptured. Of all the escapees, 481 had known nationalities: 8% were Poles, 19% were Russian, 16% were Jewish Poles or Slovaks, and 6% were gypsies. It is possible that as many as 300 escapees survived their flight.[61]

Escaping the camps was a method of resistance, but prisoners also organized within the camps. As the concentration camps developed in Germany after 1933, Nazi opponents like Socialist and Communist Party members were prominent inmates. The Nazis and their far-right wing paramilitary units, the "Freikorps," battled ferociously with leftists in Berlin and Munich in the early years of the Weimar Republic. This hostility did not abate. After 1933, the new Nazi regime intensified the terror against the left. Mass arrests of both liberal and left-wing Germans followed immediately after a fire destroyed the symbolic seat of power in Berlin, the Reichstag. In the days after February 27, 1933, some 5,000 men and women were arrested. These were those public intellectuals, writers, artists, and lawyers who had opposed the Nazis. Subsequently, mass detentions ensued during 1933: "Almost all were German nationals, with Communists in the great majority."[62]

The result of detentions, arrests, releases, and re-arrests created a chaotic situation. Thousands of detainees were housed haphazardly in prisons and workhouses. Only some 5% of these early arrests were Jews, but they faced special abuse and humiliation. Jews were relegated to the bottom of the prisoner hierarchy.[63] The early holding pens, numerous and provisional, were superseded by Heinrich Himmler's new camp, Dachau. This model SS concentration camp started operation in Bavaria in March 1933. By April is was run not by the police, but by the *Schutzstaffel*, the SS. It began as a camp for communists and left-wingers, often just held for months. By 1937, repeat communist offenders, now imprisoned permanently, started forming groups to protect themselves from brutal capos.[64]

The "left," however, was not a unified group. Communists were at odds with German socialists. The two parties had competed for influence in the Weimar period. The dominant mood was one of hostility and in the camps they never formed a united front.[65] And, indeed, this was the fate of Hermann Langbein. It was the social democratic faction which dominated the Dachau hospital. "Together with other communists, I was shunted off from Dachau to Auschwitz." [66] In Auschwitz, he moved to consolidate his groups on familiar grounds: he worked to place his compatriots into the prisoner hospital and safe work sites. The quarrels among the left-wingers, which had developed in Dachau, did not continue in Auschwitz. As an extermination camp, Auschwitz was a much harsher and demoralizing environment that limited serious internal political battles among what Langbein called "international organizations."[67] In contrast, he observed that there were political conflicts among various Polish groups within Auschwitz.

The Auschwitz I camp, established for Polish political prisoners and army officers, developed the most organized groups, along affinity lines developed before the war. Members of the Polish Socialist Party, center parties, and the right-wing Polish Peasant Party, which had been in opposition before the war, remained at odds in the camp. Members of the Polish Home Army (*Armia Krajowa*) were highly active saboteurs in occupied Poland and attempted to contact and aid Poles in the camps. Eventually, a left-wing People's Army (*Armia Ludowa*) formed, later co-opted by the Soviets, also engaged in offering support to camp inmates. Within the camps, however, these groups were rivals, seeking to protect like-minded prisoners first.[68] There were fewer distinct groups in Buna-Monowitz, but descriptions of prisoner activists often were expressed in political terms. For instance, Dr. Makowski identified Ludwig Wöhl, later removed by Dr. Wirths, as "*ein Deutscher Kommunist*," thus placing him within both a national and political context.[69] The critical role of support groups among the prisoners cannot be stressed too often.

It is in this context, the formation of prisoner support groups, that Stefan states (see below), "I did not know of the existence of any resistance movement"; he then qualifies this with "which might have had a definite plan and program of action." The clear implication is that Stefan himself was not part of any resistance activity. This is open to speculation. Stefan clearly participated in a Krakow resistance group. He had adopted a pseudonym and identified with Fr. Skarbka's group. He was arrested, and in the Montelupich prison he saw resistance activities. In his personal papers Stefan preserved a postwar letter from the prominent Polish resistance leader, Józef Cyrankiewicz. Writing on May 8, 1946, Cyrankiewicz, now in the postwar Polish communist government, states that Stefan had contact with secret prisoner organizations in Auschwitz. Further, in a September 18, 1973, letter of inquiry from the Oświęcim Museum, the director Kazimirz Smoleń states the following: "From the testimony of Auschwitz prisoners Drs. Antoni Makowski, Roman Orzeł, Tadeusz Petrykowski, Johan

Hüttner, and others, you were closely associated with the resistance movement in Auschwitz III-Monowitz." Yet Stefan's testimony is evasive on his own participation in any resistance. His reluctance may well stem from the trauma of his interrogation by the SS in Montelupich and seeing SS bestiality in the basement interrogation center. Some of his compatriots in Auschwitz I suffered. He saw the executions in block 11. To say that he "did not hear and did not know" is not credible, especially in view of his contact with Dr. Czesław Jaworski.

Dr. Jaworski (1896–1975) a seriously ill and debilitated Polish resistance leader, ended up in the Buna-Monowitz prisoner hospital under Stefan's care. An army physician, injured during the Nazi takeover of Poland, he started working in a number of the Polish resistance groups. He and Dr. Diem provided medical service for resistance fighters in Warsaw. They provided free medical care, collected medical supplies, and ran a clandestine pharmacy. They trained nurses and health care workers as well. He expanded his activities to providing false identity papers for men seeking to avoid arrests as well as fake medical files for men seized for Nazi forced labor brigades. But their work was discovered and Dr. Diem was arrested early in 1941; Jaworski was arrested in early 1942 and transferred to Auschwitz in April 1942. Once there, the two conspirators continued to organize resistance in Auschwitz, especially among Polish professional military officers. This small group was discovered and was executed in September 1943. As luck would have it, Jaworski had been sent to another camp for temporary duty and escaped execution. When he returned, he was placed in Buna-Monowitz and under Stefan's care. Jaworski had developed both heart problems and a tubercular knee.[70] It is not credible that Stefan was unaware of Jaworski's activities. It is clear that he wanted to distance himself not only from participating, but also from even knowing about resistance. It is possible that Stefan believed that his precarious position in that gray zone between prisoners and their jailors was unsustainable if he participated in resistance.

After the war I heard and read about a resistance movement in KL Auschwitz. Some of the prisoners talked about the existence of organized resistance which had carbines, mines, and so forth. In my opinion, it's necessary to more strictly define what a resistance movement is. I can testify to one thing: while I was in KL Auschwitz III I did not hear and I did not know of the existence of any resistance movement which might have a definite plan and program of action. The same thing applies to escapes: they were organized independently by the prisoners. I remember, for instance, some issues involving the escape of a group of prisoners. Among them was an acquaintance, Tomczyk, who worked in the camp kitchens, and a Polish Jew named Chaim.[71] The latter, either a capo or block leader, was the uncrowned king of the camp black market. By means only he knew, he had collected a considerable hoard of gold and valuables, which he carried in the escape. They didn't bring him luck as he was murdered by his fellow escapees. But even they had no luck, as they were arrested and sent to the camps. I remember that Tomczyk walked around the camp for a period of time and described the escape to me. However, it turned out that he lied, didn't tell the truth. After some time he was placed under arrest in the camp and executed along with a second man involved in the escape. He was hung. In his prison pants pocket they found a postcard addressed to me on which Tomczyk asked my forgiveness for everything. At any rate, the discovery of this card caused some prisoners to believe me to be someone who had participated or at least knew the score—which was not at all the case.

No one in the camp spoke to me about any illegal organizations. Of course, in the intimacy of discussions with medical colleagues such as Dr. Jaworski and others, we discussed possible responses and actions should we be directly threatened. We feared that the SS leadership wanted to liquidate the camp and its inhabitants by some use of force. But this wasn't a conspiracy, in my opinion. I saw the consequences of getting involved while I was still in the main camp, where even the suspicion of belonging to illegal organizations caused the

> death of dozens, even hundreds, of prisoners. The SS had informers among the prisoners who identified and denounced suspects. From August 1944, only a handful of prisoners in the KL Auschwitz III were Polish and the Jewish prisoners didn't get involved in these issues. I also had not heard of threatening letters sent to some of the SS men. As concerns the Buchenwald prisoner group, they mostly acted to take care of their colleagues, that only they deserved to survive—the fate of the mass of prisoners was a matter of no importance to them.

Makowski reports, however, that a great deal of news had reached the prisoners about the worsening of the German position in the war. A group in the HKB, led by Heymann and Sylman, took action and wrote an anonymous letter in the summer of 1944. Stefan considered them part of the "Buchenwald" group. They addressed the letter to Vinzenz Schöttl, the *Lagerführer,* and Walter Dürrfeld, the Buna director. They warned the leader of the camp and the Buna director that they were known to the Allies and that they should handle the prisoners responsibly in view of the approaching end of the war.[72] Heymann was a significant leader of the communist resistance group, but national allegiances remained paramount. The young Polish resistance fighter, Zając, did not know of the resistance among the Czech Jews from Terezienstadt. Jews coming from different countries did not organize together. When groups formed, they were "fellow citizens, friendship groups, and ideological allies who knew each other when they were free or who had been in the camp system a long time and individual groups had to work very carefully. A fundamental rule was that each member only knew the men in his own group."[73]

> During my occasional trips to the main camp, I talked to my colleagues Mężyk, Hommé (while they were still in the camp), Cyrankiewícz, Kłodzinski, Pileck, and Fejkl. Naturally we talked about a lot of things. Personally, I got important information about camp issues from a group of young Polish prisoners who were employed by the *Lagerführer* as handymen (*kalifaktory*). I don't remember their names, unfortunately.

> Sometimes there was news about executions, for example. Using that civilian electrician at IG Farbenindustrie, I sent the information on to my father. Once I sent father the information on the killing of 300 prisoners in the main camp, and apparently three days later BBC Radio was already broadcasting these facts.
>
> In the camp hospital we had a secret radio receiver which was built in 1944 by the engineer Kaplan along with an electrician prisoner named Sliwowski or Sliwinski, I don't remember the exact name. When I met with Kaplan after the war, he said that he tried to visit Sliwowski in Poland, but he was no longer alive. Both of them listened to foreign radio broadcasts. Neubert knew about this but such things didn't interest him. The radio receiver was built while the electroshock and x-ray machinery was being assembled.

This activity was taking place in 1944. Langbein, working in the main camp, knew that the Polish resistance movement in Krakow had to be in touch with London. Occasionally the BBC was able to report on occurrences in Auschwitz within two days. It is not clear what these broadcasts reported specifically and whether they reported the Nazi activities in Birkenau.[74] Iwaszko, the interviewer, is clearly prompting Stefan to remember names. Thirty years after the event, Stefan is rarely able to oblige. Traumatic public events, however, are still accessible:

> In KL Auschwitz III the camp administrators had occasional public executions by hanging. I personally remember two or three such executions. One was the hanging of Tomczyk and his colleague; the victims of a second execution were three prisoners whose names I do not recall. These were young, very sympathetic Jewish prisoners, whom I had seen and spoken to in the hospital. I only learned about their escape attempt after their tragic end. On one day, I don't remember the date, officials from the Political Department came to the hospital and demanded that they come with them. In a corner of the disinfection barracks a hidden cache was opened in which

> tools were hidden which could cut the camp fence. All three were condemned for trying to escape the camp. For a certain time they were held in a bunker; later they were released to the hospital, where I even spoke with them. Unfortunately, soon thereafter the execution took place. I don't know who started the rumor that I had betrayed them. This was an even greater slander since I didn't know what they had done, nor was I informed about it by others, and I could not have known about their plans. I am certain that whoever betrayed them had to know the details, was well informed, and knew the hiding place of the tools. I was very surprised when the Political Department SS men found the hidden cache on hospital grounds. As a matter of fact, all the hospital workers were suspected—not only me.
>
> I don't remember the reason for the third execution: the victims were two prisoners. (The cause was probably an escape attempt or a work place sabotage.)

Jaworski, writing in 1946, remembers two executions. Five prisoners were hung for trying to escape. One of the condemned, Janek Grossfeld from Krakow, shouted out from the gallows: "Heads high, colleagues! We are the last ones." The other execution was of two escapees who had murdered their colleague.[75] Unfortunately, Danuta Czech's chronicle does not extend to events in Monowitz, so it is hard to establish a date other than late 1944.

Tibor Wohl, the young Czech, learned that the resistance movement, which had protected him in the camp, acutely feared that the SS guards would murder the Buna prisoners as the Soviets approached. A plan for a mass escape was made, which depended on toppling the tall chimney of the Buna hospital boiler. It was supposed to fall across the electrified fence to create a safe break. Hermann Schwarz[76] worked in the boiler installation and he had weakened the brick foundation by removing mortar and loosened and greased bolts which held the chimney upright. He had wire cutters, smuggled to him by colleagues working in the Buna factory, to use on the fence wires. Wohl himself received a pistol, which he carefully hid. The planning and scheming continued as tensions rose higher in the Buna camp. Since the resistance groups worked independently, Wohl did not hear of similar efforts by Polish resistance groups until after the war. These desperate plans by the inmates never came to fruition. The evacuation of the camps on January 18, 1945, took place without a mass escape as the resistance leaders deemed an escape too dangerous. Tibor Wohl's revolver remained concealed and unused. "However, during these last months the spirit of the resistance group gave us strength, courage and hope that we would survive," Wohl wrote.[77]

BUNA-MONOWITZ CAMP LIFE

From his vantage point as a prominent, long-time prisoner, Stefan had a unique view of the life in the Buna-Monowitz complex. The great Buna factory was nearing completion in late 1944. A vast structure covering several acres of ground, the Buna factory was supposed to bring critical fuel supplies to the German army. This never materialized, as events of the war overtook the production plans. The labor camp itself was no longer under construction and life had stabilized to some extent. The prisoners understood the Nazis running the camps. The major source of instability and finally chaos was the fact that the Germans were losing the war. A few bombing runs had hit the factory and the camp; eventually, the sound of artillery from the east signaled the end.

Stefan ruminates on various aspects of building the hospital and of camp life:

> During the time I was at KL Auschwitz III, two transports arrived directly from the ramp.[78] The prisoners had to strip in the hospital washroom. One of the transports, I think, came from Compiegne; the other also came from some western European country. At any rate, as soon as they arrived, I searched them for prisoner doctors (Dr. Waitz and Drohocki) and employed them in the prisoner hospital. Doing this, I spared them the ill treatment of arrival in the camp since

> it was so difficult to get accustomed to the conditions in the camp. Instead, in the camp hospital these physicians met people they knew—and that meant a great deal: additional portions of soup, the possibility of conversation. In a word, they weren't so very isolated. I know what that meant, as I myself experienced the well-being of collegial help when I arrived in the camp (my friends Mężyk, Hommé, and others showed me this). It was with their help that I was accepted at the hospital and no longer had to stand for hours in the cold during roll calls and avoided beatings and ill treatment.
>
> Every long-term prisoner of the camp yearned for open spaces, fields without barbed wire fences and the whole atmosphere of the camp. I, too, fell into this mood and decided to try my luck. I went directly to the *Lagerführer* requesting permission to go outside the camp perimeter, escorted by the SDG. As a reason I presented my many years in the camp. I caught the *Lagerführer* in a good humor and he agreed with my proposal. So on a beautiful, sunny Sunday I went out for a walk. I let my father know where we could meet using the electrician I mentioned earlier as a go-between. We met at Fr. Kmiecka's rectory in the village Poręba Wielka, not far from Monowitz. SDG Neubert was my escort. I also met Fr. Skarba's niece, whom I knew in the prewar period. A former prisoner—Ehrich—was recuperating at this place.

The *Lagerführer* was Vinzenz Schöttl, who had previously sought Stefan's professional services.[79] The notion that a prisoner could get parole to leave the camp appears unlikely in a stereotypical view of camp life, but it was possible (for example, Langbein's visits to SS Dr. Wirths's home). Zając, by no means a "prominent" prisoner like Stefan, also mentions an opportunity to visit with his family. He regretfully turned down this opportunity: "It would not have been a problem to see them, but I feared possible later reprisals against my family, but secondly, I dreaded having to return behind the fences after tasting freedom."[80] Wagner also stresses that the SS could not enforce the isolation of Buna-Monowitz. Prisoners just had too much contact with civilian workers to isolate them. The contact with Polish resistance groups also took place at the factory.[81]

> Through conversations and news which reached the camp, it became apparent that groups of partisans were active in the nearby hills and that escaping prisoners could count on getting help. Personally, I harbored no escape plans. I felt that I was more use to my colleagues in the camp than outside. The same belief convinced me to join the evacuation march.
>
> A section of the Monowitz camp was set apart for prisoners needing education (*Erziehungshäftlinge*)—these were young people of various nationalities.[82] They lived in three barracks on the main street—on the left-hand side, coming from the entrance. Occasionally some of them came to the prisoner hospital, but they were not subject to selections. An attendant named Halbreich was responsible for their health.[83] When an EH prisoner wasn't able to work for some reason, he spent time in a separate room of one of the barracks designated for prisoners of this category. When the need arose, Halbreich escorted the sick prisoner to the prisoner hospital. I can't recall that a single EH prisoner was liquidated in the camp, with the exception of a civilian miner who worked in a mine with prisoners whom he abused.

SS Dr. Wirths's deputy, SS Dr. Horst Fischer (1913–1966) was the main SS physician in the Buna-Monowitz prisoner hospital from November 1943 until September 1944. A near contemporary of Stefan's, Fischer saw his Auschwitz duties in terms of career development in the SS. Fischer offered testimony at the Frankfurt trials in which he assessed the varied prisoner physicians in the HKB as competent and as more experienced than he.[84] Oswald claims further that Fischer depended on Stefan for medical technical knowledge and on the SDG Neubert for organization and record keeping.[85] SS Dr. Fischer came to the hospital and scrubbed up for surgeries with a prisoner physician whom he had assigned to the

Buna-Monowitz. On another occasion, related by Robert Jay Lifton, he came to a demonstration of electroshock therapy. This was a new venture and the apparatus was constructed in the hospital (as Stefan confirms). The physician was the Polish Dr. Drohocki. "While collaborative efforts like these were unusual, the kind of medical bond they suggested was common enough. And however these bonds were tainted by the existence of selections, they meant a great deal to prisoner doctors and served a purpose for Nazi doctors as well."[86]

> I had frequent dealings with SS men in my work. SS *Lagerarzt* Dr. Fischer was a disciplined man and polite to me. Occasionally he'd walk through the prisoner hospital but showed no initiative in matters of organization. In essence, his attitude was to agree to my proposals for change and improvement in the situation of the HKB (*Häftlingskrankenbau*), the prisoner hospital. Nonetheless he ordered selections and carried them out himself.[87] In comparison, SS *Lagerarzt* Dr. Entress was very standoffish towards the prisoners and even avoided touching "*Häftlinge*," [prisoners] as if they represented some inferior form of humanity.
>
> SS *Lagerarzt* Dr. König was both unpleasant and unpredictable in his behavior. He hated the prisoners—you could feel this at every step. Unfortunately, as far as I know, there is no evidence as to what happened to him after the war. I was asked many times about him at the Frankfurt trial. According to prevailing rumors, he may have hidden in Sweden.
>
> SS *Lagerarzt* Kitt gave the impression of a high school teacher. I remember him still from my time in the main camp, when he would put a white handkerchief over his face during an execution. Quiet and unexcitable, he only came to Monowitz a couple of times during my time there.
>
> I've already mentioned Neubert's behavior. He was a carpenter by profession, and from remarks he made, he didn't quite know how he had ended up in the SS. He was chiefly concerned with organizing things for his own benefit. He performed no

> independent selections. Knowing his weaknesses, we were able to take advantage of him in various matters that only an SS man could take care of. He always tried to do what was possible under the circumstances. I remember that on the orders of *Lagerführer* Schöttl, he made preselections in the camp—I mentioned this earlier. (Neubert told the prisoner doctors to do it—and they only produced five candidates. This provoked a fit of fury in *Lagerführer* Schöttl, who then demanded that Neubert himself take over the job.) Equally quiet and harmless was SDG Hantl.
>
> The camp commandant Schwarz was an angry type with unpredictable reactions. At the sight of him, all of us felt our hearts beat faster. I felt it, especially at the beginning. I calmed down a bit as I became accustomed to his demeanor. It wasn't unusual to see the gates open and to hear the cry "*Lagerälteste HKB nach Vorne*!" ["Barracks eldest to the front!"]. That's how I was called to the SS men hospital if there was a crisis and the SS *Lagerarzt* was unavailable. *Lagerführer* Schöttl had a similar personality. Stolten was a typical conformist to all rules. We were all afraid of Rackers because of his vile character and his frequent ill use of prisoners.

Bernhard Rakers was an SS Master sergeant (*Hauptscharführer*) and the roll call leader in Monowitz. Langbein reported that he blackmailed prisoners and forced them to steal for him and his numerous mistresses. "In the whole factory there was no article that he could not use—from pins and padlocks, electric appliances, beds, bicycles, furniture . . . he made inmates, who had no other choice . . . steal everything for him."[88] A notorious character, Rakers also blackmailed his SS colleagues.[89] He was in charge of the SS men who guarded a column of men from Buna-Monowitz on their forced march in January 1945 to the railhead in Gleiwitz, on their way to other, western, concentration camps. Camp inmates called him the "Buna lion."[90] But Stefan makes the point that the criminal prisoners (green triangles), did not dominate the Buna-Monowitz camp, which made it less dangerous than Auschwitz I.

SS man Wieczorka[91] belonged to the Political Department in Monowitz and we considered him an idiot, but we were afraid of Taute—he was very dangerous to prisoners. Taute had the use of two prisoners. One of them was named Unikover[92]—he currently lives in Frankfurt am Main.

At the beginning of my time in the Monowitz camp, prisoners were frequently beaten. The capos mistreated prisoners beneath them and, having responsibility for certain work, they tried to impress their superiors so they beat prisoners to force them to work harder. Those were beaten who really could not work. You were actually beaten for anything: asking for a second bowl of soup, mispronouncing the name of the barracks leader, stealing bread, and so on.

Beatings were always very painful, resulting in large bloody bruises on the body, and many had to be named unfit for work. Understanding this, we decided to "calm down" those who abused the prisoners. Direct actions or interventions didn't have a chance so we decided to go an indirect route. Whenever we could we made systematic reports about prisoners incapacitated for work by beatings to the SS *Lagerarzt*. Well-timed remarks about the reduced labor force actually did produce results. Not much later an order was issued prohibiting the beating of prisoners. The order stated, among other things, that "after all, the prisoners are people, too." It was even funny to now hear the SS men stating "*Häftling ist auch ein Mensch, soll mann ihn nicht schlagen*" ["The prisoner is also a person, one should not beat him"]. I already mentioned that this order didn't stop the beatings, but at least it limited them. This took place in 1944, though I don't remember the exact date.[93]

The camp elder (*Lagerälteste*) in the Monowitz camp was a massively built man named Paul Kozwara, who wore a green triangle. He came from Lower Silesia and spoke a little Polish. He wasn't the worst but he beat prisoners and on this issue we came to a disagreement. The direct cause of our fight was a painful beating he and another functionary administered to

> a prisoner whom I tried to protect. Kozwara ordered me not to get involved in his business. After that he avoided me for a couple of months.
>
> Another unpleasant type was the Lagercapo Emil Worgul, who was prone to beating prisoners. Nonetheless, both of these men behaved better compared to the functionaries of the main camp (in the period when I was there). One of the characteristics of the camp was that most of the prisoner functionaries—capo and barracks functionaries—were being recruited among Jews. The criminal prisoners did not dominate this camp as they did others, which was important for conditions in the camp.

By 1944, 90% of the Monowitz prisoners were Jews and in Monowitz, Jews were permitted to hold positions from which they were barred in the main camp. Nazi ideology deemed no Jew capable of holding a position of power. In the camps this meant that in theory Jews were barred from all functionary positions, including that of barracks senior prisoners.[94] This was not a sustainable policy as the camps changed. Wagner goes even further and states: "Even more so than in the other concentration camps, in 'Lager Buna' the SS was dependent on the help of the prisoners to establish and maintain camp discipline."[95] Langbein, sitting over in the main camp, remarked that camp prisoners exercised a large measure of independence even before the war was winding down: "The prisoners' self-government was balanced in such a way that there was a permanent rivalry between political and criminal elements."[96]

Stefan continues:

> The camp chancellery (*Schreibstube*) was run by Jews and the most important among them was Gustav Herzog. On the other hand, Polish prisoners held important positions in the camp kitchen and the *Effecktenkammer.* A number of Poles, especially long-term prisoners, were active in the self-government of the prisoners. The same was true of

> Jewish prisoners. However, one could observe that the Polish intelligentsia had greater psychological resources for dealing with camp conditions than did the Jewish intelligentsia.
>
> KL Auschwitz III-Monowitz had a number of activities that could be labeled recreational. Among them were soccer matches, boxing, and artistic performances.[97] Some of these took place in a tent erected on the roll call grounds. The camp orchestra also gave performances featuring, among others, soloists like Wojszczyk and Stasiak. I have already mentioned a French artist who was liquidated by a group of prisoners from KL Buchenwald. His performances were first-rate and he sang, among other things, Italian songs. The song "Kammeraden" [*sic*] was known in the camp but I do not recall anyone singing the "Buna-lied." I also recall that the librettist Lehara (I can only recall his first name) was in the prisoner hospital. He died, if I remember correctly, of pneumonia. The prisoner Rausch reminded me of him.
>
> There was really no time to develop any kind of social life in the camp. There was only a short period of free time between the last evening rounds and nightfall during which a prisoner could meet friends. Sunday afternoons were free, too. Prisoners could meet and talk a little. I can't tell you more about this from my own experience, as I'm relying on my observations in the hospital. Hospital personnel were never numerous, but nonetheless formed a group. The French prisoner doctors held themselves apart—somehow all knew German or Polish.

The popular notion that the Allies didn't bomb Auschwitz is not correct. The illusion that a well-placed bomb could well have destroyed the gas chambers is just that: an illusion. A bomb would not have ended or even seriously interfered with the Holocaust. As a military target, Birkenau had little significance. Interfering with the production of war material was far more appealing. However, the difficulty of bombing even such an obvious target as the large Buna plant, easily ten times larger than the prison camp, is manifest. The 1944 bombings by the Allies barely had an impact on the plant but severely injured the prisoners.[98] The August 20 attack was followed by one other, on September 13.[99] Dr. Jaworski was a patient in the prisoner hospital at this time and reports that SS Dr. Fischer was sending injured prisoners for "treatment" to Birkenau, that is, to the gas chambers. Stefan, however, was able to conceal Dr. Woss and Alfred Ehrlich, a Czech, both of whom had been targeted for transfer.[100]

> Among other events I remember the first bombings in August 1944—many prisoners fell as victims. The hospital received more than 100 injured, whom we dealt with for two days. The situation was made worse by a lack of water. Unfortunately, our efforts came to naught when SS *Lagerarzt* Fischer ordered badly injured prisoners to be released from the hospital, who were then transported out of the camp—in our opinion, this was a death sentence. We were bombarded twice while I was there. During the second bombardment, a bomb hit the camp but didn't do much damage. We had thought that none of the buildings would survive an attack—but there they still stood. Naturally the bombs did cause damage, but not enough to actually stop the work. But the bombings had great significance for morale. Simply put, the prisoners were convinced that they were witnessing the approaching end of the Hitlerite curse.

Prisoners wearing a pink triangle were identified homosexuals. Nazi homophobia is notorious and Himmler himself was obsessively homophobic. Pink triangle prisoners were brutalized by guards as well as by other prisoners.[101] Homosexual guards were not exempt from the general opprobrium. A 14-year-old prisoner in Buna-Monowitz was brought to the hospital. The boy had rejected a German capo's sexual advances and was then beaten badly. The offending capo was found and his fellow capos beat him to death.[102]

> One could meet homosexual prisoners in KL Auschwitz III. Most often they were long-term inmates of Hitler's concentration camps, such as groups from Buchenwald or prisoners used as barracks functionaries. The SS authorities punished homosexuals

> brutally, and practicing homosexuals, if caught, were subject to special brutality. These took place in the main camp. There were also morphine addicts in the camp. One of these was the prisoner Bock (he had previously been the *Lagerälteste* in the KL Auschwitz I prisoner hospital), whom I met in Monowitz, and who was then transferred to one of the subcamps. He either committed suicide or overdosed on narcotics.[103]
>
> In the KL Monowitz hospital one of the barracks eldest (whose name I cannot recall) intoxicated himself with ether.[104] He was a German prisoner. A more common habit was cigarette smoking—cigarettes were also considered a good currency. I, too, smoked. I heard that some smokers even exchanged their food rations, craving something to smoke. Of course the consequences were tragic and hastened death.

The role of cigarettes in camps—concentration camps and POW camps—was something more than soothing an addiction to nicotine. Cigarettes were more than a commodity. Cigarettes became a currency, a unit of account, and a measure of value as well as a store of value. Unlike food stuffs, which could spoil, or items of clothing, which might not be useful, cigarettes enjoyed special characteristics: "they were homogeneous, reasonably durable, and of convenient size for the smallest or, in packets, for the largest transactions."[105]

> There was also a camp black market. Anything the prisoner had was subject to trade—as, for instance, food for cigarettes or tailoring services. I know about this because patients traded stolen bread through the fence which separated the hospital barracks from the rest of the camp. Our attitude—I'm talking here about work prisoners did in the hospital—was that we too engaged in trade: food for actual work such as painting or construction.

The construction work was formidable. The men who carried individual bricks for hospital use, the carpenters who built equipment, and the plumbers who provided the sanitation facilities on the wards were of course inmates who received food in their barracks, but they could augment it with extra food from the hospital kitchens. The Buna-Monowitz carpenters, for instance, presented Stefan with a hand-drawn name day card featuring a satirical cartoon of Stefan in the surgery and signing it "camp carpenters." Interest alliances formed and social niceties were preserved even within a Nazi labor camp.

The very notion of a camp brothel seems antithetical to the harsh environment of concentration camps, but the creation of camp brothels came by order of Himmler with the intent of combating homosexuality and creating a reward system. Himmler, responding to the push for more labor output, envisioned an incentive program. He wanted a graded system of privileges for especially productive workers. It was referred to as the "FFF system" for *Frauen, Fressen und Freiheit*, that is, women, food, and freedom.[106] The regulations for an incentive system (May 15, 1943) to reward effective workers included the right to send more frequent letters and to longer hair, more food, more script for the camp canteen, and cigarettes. There was no question that the "freedom" incentive was feasible. Concentration camp inmates in the east during wartime had no expectations of ever leaving the camps. But the right to visit the new camp brothel had some possibilities. This had been tried earlier (June 1942) in Mauthausen.

Working in the brothel was to be on a "voluntary basis," but the incentives given to women and girls were enormous: their own room, clothes, food, and privileges. Most of the women were German but there were also a few Poles and Russians.[107] These forced sex workers were themselves prisoners. Stefan mentioned the demoralizing sight of debilitated women prisoners going to work in the farm fields. While women did not face the heavy labor demands of carrying sacks of concrete, they faced danger from brutal SS women guards. An inmate in the Ravensbrück women's camp worked as a hospital nurse there. She was appalled to realize that the steady trickle of badly injured women she had to treat had been mauled by guard dogs. The SS women guards carried whips and guns, but also effectively used attack dogs to control and punish female inmates working in the agricultural fields.[108] At the very least, a berth in a brothel provided protection from the guards.

Fewer than 200 women were in brothels across the whole concentration camp system. The Buna-Monowitz facility was a single fenced-off barrack and housed ten women.[109] It was similar in size to the brothel established in the Sachsenhausen concentration camp in mid-August 1944: ten women from the Ravensbrück concentration were used there.[110] In Buna-Monowitz, most were labeled with the black triangle of asocials, meaning they had been prostitutes. In the camps, very few prisoners had the means or interest to visit a brothel. The payment was 2 RM, of which 45 pfennig was kept by the woman, 5 pfennig went to the camp for upkeep, and 1.50 RM went into the coffers of the Berlin SS management.[111] Some prisoners were barred outright (Jews and Soviet POWs), but realistically, most prisoners were too debilitated by work or hunger to engage in sex. Regular users were senior capos. For the women, "sexual exploitation proved a strategy for survival."[112]

Olga Lengyel reports, in her chapter 23, "Love in the Shadow of the Crematoria," not only about the prostitution forced on women by the SS, but also about the homoerotic relationships that developed among inmates.[113] Primo Levi described block 29, the bordello: "It always has its windows closed as it is the *Frauenblock,* the camp brothel, served by Polish *Häftling* [prisoner] girls, and reserved for the *Reichsdeutsche* [Germans from the Reich]."[114] Zając states that the new block for the bordello was surrounded by a taller than usual fence and was reserved for "Aryan" prisoners and staffed by women from Birkenau, prisoners from Germany, Russia, and Poland. They worked in the evening and were paid one "mark," a camp currency (thus perhaps the official 45 pfennig payment existed only on the books).[115]

> The camp brothel was staffed by volunteers from the women prisoners from KL Birkenau. I learned about this by talking to the women in the brothel. Jewish prisoners were not allowed to use the brothel. The personnel of the HKB were obligated

> to examine the women prisoners of the brothel. Once a week the women were brought to the HKB for closer inspection. While I'm on this topic I want to emphasize that many prisoner functionaries working in factories were able to establish sexual contacts with civilian workers—as did the SS men as well. Certain prisoners were interested in the creating of the camp brothel. The "young ladies" had their steady beaus, who supplied them with food or even valuables. Those were things I heard from steady brothel customers, among whom, for instance, were the prison orchestra members.

One of the strategies that prisoners used to get some medical attention without declaring themselves sufficiently ill to require hospitalization was to get help at the outpatient clinic, the ambulatorium. This was a critical site for health care. In a sense it was a triage site in which decisions had to be made about hospitalization. As explained above, prisoners knew that they ran a high risk of selections as patients, but they also ran a risk of barracks selections and even selections on their way to or from the worksites if they were ill or injured.

> Returning to issues related to the prisoner hospital, I want to emphasize that after its reorganization and the creation of specialized outpatient clinics we were able to help about 300 prisoners in one-and-a-half hours. When the prisoners arrived at the clinic, they removed their shoes and registered with the clerk (*Schreiber*), Leon Stasiak. He was most adept and handled this well. In such a crowd various conflicts developed between the prisoner patients and the prisoner doctors. With limited available space in the hospital barracks, one had to decide which person in the clinic should get admitted to the hospital. My colleagues, such as Drs. Silber, Rutkowski, and Makowskí, and I made this decision.

The ambulatorium served more functions than Stefan realized. Dr. Makowski, who did service there, was more attuned to the psychological dimension of prisoners' lives. Stefan paid attention to the dilemma of admissions in a hospital with limited space, but

Dr. Makowski had a more nuanced understanding of the prisoners: "Sometimes the prisoners came with the smallest complaints and sometimes only with the wish to complain to the physicians, to get help with questions about their daily life. In the eyes of the prisoners, the physician was often the only friendly soul to be found in the camp."[116] However, some cases were simply too acute to be handled quickly.

> Thanks to the construction of an operating theater and lighting, we performed surgeries under almost normal conditions. In acute cases we operated immediately. There were two operating rooms; nonsterile operations were performed in another barracks. I personally did many surgeries, as did Dr. Grossmann.[117]
>
> The most common illnesses were infectious diseases (influenza and typhus) and "*durchfall.*" *Durchfall* refers to that terminal state of starvation in which the body is poisoned by consuming its own cells, which produced the effect of metabolic collapse and swelling. In the majority of cases we could not help an acute case of *durchfall.* For instance, we had no way of infusing glucose, vitamins, or electrolytes. The worst plague, however, were the subcutaneous abscesses referred to as phlegmons. They formed under swellings. The smallest injury to this site became infected and abscessed. Some prisoners had these abscesses over much of their bodies, which led to their decline. In a word, the most common illnesses in KL Auschwitz III were these phlegmons.

"WAIT! I'LL HELP YOU"

When Stefan was transferred from the main Auschwitz camp to the Jawischowitz subcamp, he had no personal property, not even a handkerchief. When he was marched out of Buna-Monowitz in January 1945 to end up in Buchenwald, he was once again stripped of possessions. Despite this, he managed to preserve one item from Auschwitz. Not a photograph. Not a letter. It was an unexpected personal communication preserved from his wartime ordeal. When I received his trove of personal papers in 2002, eight years after his death, I found those items which he most valued. There were his university transcripts from before the war, his postwar accomplishments, and the large typescript from his 1974 oral testimony to the Oświęcim Museum. There was but a single item in this large collection, however, from his long years of imprisonment. The essential Auschwitz item is small, only about 5 by 8 inches. It is a hand-drawn cartoon on a stiff piece of paper. I laughed out loud when I understood what it was—just a funny, crude cartoon. When I considered it further, however, I was astonished. How could this be? Humor? In Auschwitz? A greeting card from hell? It was clearly deeply meaningful to my father. It reflected some aspect of the camp so important that it was the only evidence that he kept intact, so important that it was filed with diplomas, official letters, employment records, and citizenship papers.

The eminent anthropologist Clifford Geertz coined the term "thick description." For him the artifacts of the past cannot be understood in isolation. The shard of pottery or the fragment of fresco existed in a culture and a society and are more than just physical evidence. This piece of paper, preserved for decades by an ex-prisoner, is a complex piece of evidence. It reveals an entire aspect of the past, of Auschwitz, that has not been clearly captured in the thousands of words collected by diligent interviewers and historians. This personal greeting card reflects the existence of a community in the camp. The drawing is simultaneously coarse, rude, funny and horrifying. It is also thoughtful, sentimental, and perhaps calculating as well.

The card has two sides: the cartoon on front, the greetings on the back. It is a drawing in India ink, enhanced with some watercolor pigments. The artist, also an Auschwitz prisoner, had just a few colors available. A black wash forms the shadows. Red, yellow and blue are used. This is a palette one might find in a grade school watercolor set. The lettering on the card is careful. There is a small mark, a signature that is perhaps the letters "KW" near the trashcan. In ink there is a note from Stefan on the front: "September 1943, name-day wishes for Dr. Budziaszek, #20526." This note is written in Polish. On the back, he wrote: "For Doctor Stefan Budziaszek September 1942." This second note starts in Polish, with his name in the possessive case, but the date is written in German: "September" instead of "Wrzesien." He could not have received this card in 1942, as the scene is clearly an operating theater in the Monowitz prisoner hospital. I infer that the note on the back was added significantly later in that he uses a German term for the month, no longer references his prisoner number, and writes down the wrong year.

What is a name day? In the Polish Catholic tradition, each day of the year is associated with a number of saintly names. The celebration of a birthday is not on the actual birth date. Stefan was born on January 25; however, he celebrated his birthday on the day of St. Stefan, September 2. This note was sent to him on or about September 2, 1943, which would have been about ten weeks after he started reorganizing the prisoner hospital in Buna-Monowitz. Building and maintaining social networks was a critical component of camp survival. In the card, Stefan was recognized and acknowledged as a fellow Pole who had achieved a position of influence in the camp. The senders of this greeting were the carpenters in the camp. In the very dangerous and hostile environment of the Nazi concentration camp, the carpenters were building or enhancing a social network. Stefan apparently seemed to them like a valuable ally in camp life.

The black humor of the vignette on the card consists of the preposterous proposition that a carpenter can help a surgeon in an operating room. The carpenter bursts in carrying a bandsaw and hammer (surgical instrument and anesthesia?) shouting: "Wait! I'll help you." A pertinent detail of his cry is not visible in the translation. The carpenter is shouting using the informal voice. There are very few scenarios in Polish prewar society in which an ordinary worker would address a professional man in the informal voice. But these were not at all ordinary times. In this place the social niceties of polite language and status were suspended. In the few months that Stefan was working in Buna-Monowitz, he established critical personal relationships with fellow inmates and avoided pulling rank in favor of informality. In the card, the carpenters speak to him in the language of intimacy and fellowship.

There is still another text hidden in the joke: "Wait! I'll help you." And here we are not talking about surgery, but about the ongoing process of building a prisoner hospital in a Nazi labor camp controlled by the SS and ruthlessly used by a major German company, IG Farbenindustrie. The cooperation that Stefan was able to elicit from inmates to construct the new facilities in the HKB can be interpreted as a form of resistance to the Nazis. The carpenters' saw and hammer were for building new facilities. Stefan claimed he did not participate in any organized effort to resist. But there are different forms of resistance. Building a working hospital for injured, ill, and demoralized prisoners was one.

Scholarly narratives about the fantastic speed and extent of the buildup of the forced labor camps across Germany and the occupied territories emphasize that the Nazi regime was overextended. The war had absorbed working-age German men who were replaced by forced labor from across Europe. Once IG Farbenindustrie decided to erect an enormous factory next to Auschwitz and signed contracts with the SS to provide labor, the local competition for workers became intense. The lack of cooperation between the SS and IG Farbenindustrie management has been chronicled above. When the decision was made to build a separate camp (Auschwitz III), the labor situation was exacerbated. Where would the workers come from? The factory needed brute labor and the physical infrastructure of the camp and its barracks needed construction workers, carpenters, plumbers, and electricians. All projects were running into delays. Once Stefan arrived in June 1943 to restructure the prisoner hospital, he, too, experienced the chronic cycle of labor delays. Except that Stefan had the Polish carpenters on his side: "Wait. I'll help you."

The augmentations of the barracks of the HKB were performed clandestinely. Stefan and others describe the process of smuggling in bricks and of declaring needed workers as "sick" so that they could work inside the hospital. Workers themselves exhibited solidarity. The signature on the back of the name-day card is "*Lagrowi Stolarze*"—the camp carpenters. This group of prisoners expressed the sentiment: "Sincerest best wishes on your name day." The little flourish of three flower bouquets, tinted blue and red, give an almost Victorian formality to this little greeting card, a certain air of bourgeois propriety. This was happening amidst the terror and brutality of the most iconic and reviled concentration camp of the Nazi regime. But not all corners of Auschwitz were equal. The relentless wagon loads of incoming victims shunted along railroad sidings in Birkenau to their deaths existed in a reality that was running parallel to the work camp and its hospital.

When the Polish political prisoner Zając transferred to the Buna-Monowitz camp, he saw a young Polish doctor with black hair, and wearing an armband, recruiting workers for the hospital. There is no mistaking the image on the card. Stefan is caricatured accurately. His hospital whites are tied at the back, he is wearing his identifying armband as his *pass partout,* his signet of authority. Mind you, he is not operating in any normal sense but is rather wielding a kitchen knife in a bloody incision. A bucket of bloody spare body parts stands next to the gurney. The carpenter-artist had a vivid and rude imagination. However, there are other aspects to note about the three men. Stefan has black hair. This means he benefited from the Himmler order that prominent prisoners were not required to have their hair shaved. The nude "patient" on the gurney has a bare tuft of hair. The vigorous and helpful carpenter is wearing a billed hat and not the standard cloth cap of the camps. He, too, is wearing an armband (yellow), and good quality shoes. No one is dressed in the standard striped cotton uniform of prisoners. The small piece of reality that was the hospital was not operating under standard rules.

The little name-day card, carefully preserved for decades, is a symbol of the unusual moment in time when Stefan and his cohorts pulled together to form a functioning hospital. This demanded help and cooperation from a diverse set of ordinary prisoners, from kitchen cooks and helpers, to craftsmen, to prisoners "organizing" medicines and equipment. There is a sense that these prisoners were not utterly helpless victims, isolated and atomized, at the mercy of a murderous regime. Instead, they build coalitions. They shared crude and rude humor. They also continued to engage in social niceties, such as greeting cards that would seem completely out of place in that time and in that place. This card stands as testimony to the paucity of our scholarly and popular imagination. The life and tempo, the events of quotidian reality in this camp, confound stereotypes. Stefan's name-day card enriches our understanding of this moment in history.

NOTES

1. Szymborska, *Seventy Poems*, 22–23.
2. Lehnstaedt, "Coercion and Incentives: Jewish Ghetto Labor in East Upper Silesia," 407.
3. Gruner, *Jewish Forced Labor*, 254.
4. Höss, *Death Dealer*, 230.
5. Wagner, *IG Auschwitz*, 178–80.
6. Makowski, *Häftlingskrankenbau in Monowitz*, 130.
7. Ibid., 145.
8. Wagner, *IG Auschwitz*, 188.
9. Langbein, *People in Auschwitz*, 210–18.
10. Wagner, *IG Auschwitz*, 170.
11. Makowski, *Häftlingskrankenbau in Monowitz*, 144, 152.
12. Quoted in Marc Buggeln, *Slave Labor in Nazi Concentration Camps* (Oxford: Oxford University Press, 2014), 37.
13. Wagner, *IG Auschwitz*, 191.
14. Ibid., 197.
15. Langbein, *People in Auschwitz*, 212.
16. Wagner, *IG Auschwitz*, 194.
17. Langbein, *People in Auschwitz*, 226.
18. Ibid., 226.
19. Ibid., 231.
20. Romuald Sztaba, "Ze wspomnień lekarza oboszu w Gross-Rosen" in *Okupacja i medycyna*, 4th selection from "Przegląda

lekarskiego-Oświęcim" from 1963–1978 (Warsaw: Książka I Wiedza, 1979), 40.

21. Primo Levi, *The Drowned and the Saved* (New York: Vintage International, 1989), 42.
22. Most recently: Jan Oswald whose dissertation title actually calls "Buthner" an alias.
23. Robert Jay Lifton, *The Nazi Doctors: Medical Killing and the Psychology of Genocide* (New York: Basic Books, 1986), 242.
24. Ibid.
25. Lifton, *The Nazi Doctors*, 388.
26. Ibid., 395.
27. Oswald, *Die Ermittlungen im Fall "4 Js 798/64,"* 50.
28. In Oswald's short biography of Stefan, it is obvious that Oswald is also relying on inadequate sources. Stefan's first marriage in 1945 to Ewa Irena Balcerska and my existence, Stefan's daughter, are missing.
29. Wagner, *IG Auschwitz,* 322.
30. Oswald, *Die Ermittlung im Fall "4 Js 798/64,"* 62.
31. Wagner states: "The SS physicians responsible for Monowitz weren't present daily. They lived in the city of Auschwitz and visited the camp HKB only once or twice a week" (*IG Auschwitz*, 190).
32. Langbein relates a conversation he had with one Jan Trajster: "He remembers that [Stefan] once performed stomach surgery without having made a diagnosis simply to practice this procedure" (*People in Auschwitz,* 361). Robert Jay Lifton in *The Nazi Doctors* (244) claims: "[Stefan] came to resemble Nazi doctors in performing surgery on Jewish prisoners 'just to learn the operation.' While insisting that an experienced surgeon assist him; otherwise, he had little concern for patients 'as though they were nonexistent.'" Lifton uses pseudonyms and only identifies the man he is quoting as "Jacob R." Alternate explanations for "unnecessary surgeries" are not considered.
33. Langbein, *People in Auschwitz,* 125–30.
34. Makowski, *Häftlingskrankenbau*, 172.
35. Jaworski, *Apel Skazanych,* 259.
36. Goffman, *Asylum*, 16.
37. Langbein, *People in Auschwitz,* 232.
38. Makowski, *Häftlingskrankenbau in Monowitz*, 127.
39. Langbein, *People in Auschwitz,* 26.

40. Jaworski, *Apel Skazanych,* 186.
41. Wagner, *IG Auschwitz,* 129–31.
42. "They put me into a bed with white sheets. I had forgotten that people slept in sheets" (Wiesel, *Night,* 74).
43. Makowski (*Häftlingskrankenbau in Monowitz,* 153) points out that the two wards for less severely ill patients had three level bunks.
44. This low-level SS man was Gerhard Neubert. While Stefan did not deal with hospital statistics, Dr. Makowski kept meticulous track.
45. The administration of the major Auschwitz units was reconfigured when Liebehenschel arrived in November, 1943.
46. Zając (*Powrót Niepożądany,* 165) worked for Dr. Franz Grossman in the HKB.
47. Makowski, *Häftlingskrankenbau in Monowitz,* 148.
48. Zając, *Powrót Niepożądany,* 188.
49. In a conversation I had with Stefan Hommé in the early 1990s, he remembered that as they were sorting medical supplies sent over from "Canada," he found a large diamond hidden in a small tin of aspirin.
50. Makowski, *Häftlingskrankenbau in Monowitz,* 149.
51. Ibid.
52. Langbein, *People in Auschwitz,* 371.
53. Jaworski, *Apel Skazanych,* 256.
54. Makowski, *Häftlingskrankenbau in Monowitz,* 149.
55. Unpublished letter, December 11, 1945. Supplied (December 16, 2012) by courtesy of his daughter, Dr. Monika Freyer-Mohl, Basel, Switzerland.
56. Lifton, *The Nazi Doctors,* 388.
57. Ibid., 390.
58. Poles considered those who signed the *Volksliste* as collaborators.
59. Czech, *Auschwitz Chronicle,* 65, 76, 80. St. Maximilian Kolbe, a Franciscan friar, was canonized as a saint by Pope John Paul II in 1982 as a martyr for charity.
60. Zając, *Powrót Niepożądany,* 222.
61. Langbein, *People in Auschwitz,* 262.
62. Wachsmann, *KL,* 31.
63. Ibid., 44.
64. Ibid., 129.

65. Ibid., 131.
66. Langbein, *People in Auschwitz,* 248.
67. Ibid., 240.
68. Len Crome, *Unbroken: Resistance and Survival in the Concentration Camps* (New York: Schocken Books, 1988), 85. Len Crome used the personal experiences of Buna-Monowitz prisoner Jonny Hüttner, a member of a communist agitprop theater group. Hüttner perceived the accession of Stefan to the HKB as a setback (87). Hüttner is not mentioned in Langbein's *People in Auschwitz.*
69. Makowski, *Häftlingskrankenbau,* 116.
70. Stanisław Kłodzinski and Eugeniusz Niedojadło, "Płk. Dr. med. Czesław Wincenty Jaworski," in *Przegłąd Lekarski* 34, no. 1 (1977): 217–18. Eugeniusz Niedojadło appears on Makowski's list (see appendix) as a nurse and barracks elder.
71. Mieczysław Zając also tells the story of this notorious escape. Chaim apparently carried valuables he had gotten while he worked in "Canada." He was killed by his compatriots in Krakow. The murderers were caught and executed.
72. Makowski, *Häftlingskrankenbau in Monowitz,* 176.
73. Wohl, *Arbeit macht tot,* 158.
74. Langbein, *People in Auschwitz,* 255.
75. Jaworski, *Apel Skazanych,* 266.
76. Makowski, *Häftlingskrankenbau,* 179, identifies Hermann Schwarz as a disinfector, #71224.
77. Wohl, *Arbeit macht tot,* 160.
78. Wagner confirms that direct transports to KL Auschwitz III took place very seldom (*IG Auschwitz,* 105).
79. Makowski, *Häftlingskrankenbau in Monowitz,* 175.
80. Zając, *Powrót Niepożądany,* 220.
81. Wagner, *IG Auschwitz,* 205.
82. Herbert, *Hitler's Foreign Workers,* 118–22. These were civilian forced laborers and only "prisoners" in the sense that they were deemed poor workers, slackers, in need of remediation for around six weeks.
83. Langbein refers to Siegfried Halbreich as a camp elder in the Indoctrination Section of Monowitz (Langbein, *People in Auschwitz,* 418).

84. Horst Fischer practiced medicine in East Germany for two decades after the war. In 1966, however, he was put on trial, convicted, and then executed.
85. Oswald, *Die Ermitttlungen in Fall "4 Js 798/64,"* 75.
86. Lifton, *The Nazi Doctors*, 228.
87. Zając (*Powrót Niepożądany*, 154) states that everyone in the hospital felt threatened by the selection process and while everyone tried to look vigorous, those who were too weak to stand were doomed. Poles who had food packages from home were usually more able to recover from illnesses and had a better chance to avoid a selection.
88. Langbein, *People in Auschwitz*, 298–99.
89. Wagner, *IG Auschwitz*, 108.
90. Wachsmann, *KL*, 346.
91. Gustav Wieczorek was the SS Technical Sergeant in the Political Department and was Siegfried Halbreich's friend—they both came from Tarnowitz in Upper Silesia (Langbein, *People in Auschwitz*, 418).
92. Franz Unikower was an inmate working in the Political Department (Langbein, *People in Auschwitz*, 265).
93. It is likely that Stefan is reporting the combined influence of Liebehenschel and Wirths, both of whom attempted to ameliorate prisoner conditions so as to provide a more reliable work force.
94. Wagner, *IG Auschwitz*, 196.
95. Ibid., 111.
96. Langbein, *People in Auschwitz*, 14.
97. When Zając arrived in Buna, one of the first questions he is asked was "Do you play soccer?" (Zając, *Powrót Niepożądany*, 139).
98. Czech, *Auschwitz Chronicle*, 692. The attack took place on Sunday, August 20, 1944.
99. Ibid., 708.
100. Jaworski, *Apel Skazanych*, 263.
101. Wachsmann, *KL*, 127–28.
102. Jaworski, *Apel Skazanych*, 263.
103. Jaworski confirms this story (*Apel Skazanych*, 189).
104. Zając (*Powót Niepożądany*, 189) encountered an ether addict in the prisoner hospital.

105. Radford, *Economica*, vol. 12, 1945, http://albany.edu/~mirer/eco 110/pow.html.
106. Setkiewicz, "Häftlingsarbeit," 597.
107. Langbein, *People in Auschwitz,* 405.
108. Schwarz, "Frauen in Konzentrationslager," 813.
109. Setkiewicz, "Häftlingsarbeit," 598.
110. Odd Nansen, *From Day to Day* (Nashville: Vanderbilt University Press, 2016), 409.
111. Setkiewicz, "Häftlingsarbeit," 598.
112. Wachsmann, *KL*, 414.
113. Lengyel, *Five Chimneys,* 189–97.
114. Levi, *Surviving Auschwitz*, 32.
115. Zając, *Powrót Niepożądany*, 182.
116. Makowski, *Häftlingskrankenbau in Monowitz*, 150.
117. Until mid-1943, that is, until Stefan expanded the Monowitz hospital, sterile surgical conditions could only be met in the main camp hospital (Makowski, *Häftlingskrankenbau in Monowitz,* 153).

9

PATIENTS PRIMO LEVI, ELIE WIESEL, AND OTHERS

They knew the value of the moment,
Oh, if but a single moment

Oni wiedzli, co to takiego jest chwila
och bodaj jedna jakakolwiek[1]

Hundreds of men worked in the prisoner hospital. Carpenters, electricians, painters, and bricklayers were there temporarily. Orderlies, nurses, dentists, and physicians spent months or years working on the wards. Tens of thousands prisoners used the prisoner hospital either for medical treatments, surgeries, or recuperation periods. However, only a few patients wrote in any detail about their hospitalization in the HKB. While Stefan and his fellow physicians struggled with logistics, administration, and politics, it is the patients who can deliver a view of the hospital in action. These five men came from radically different backgrounds and had very distinct experiences in the Buna-Monowitz camp, but they all end up in the hospital and wrote about them after the war. These patients and concentration camp survivors provide the evidence of what it felt like and what it meant to stay in the prisoner hospital.

Primo Levi (1919–1987) was one of the latecomers to Buna-Monowitz, arriving in the 1944 roundup of Jewish Italians. His experiences translated into books with acute and detailed depictions of the fate of prisoners in the concentration camps. A trained chemist, he found safe work at the Buna factory. Levi resumed his career as a chemist after the war and began publishing on the subject of the camps in 1947.

Elie Wiesel (1928–2016), winner of the Nobel Peace Prize in 1986, was a Jewish teenager in 1944 when he and his family were seized by the Nazis and sent to Auschwitz. His trajectory in the Buna camp, however, was that of an ordinary laborer. His prodigious literary output battles with the issue of theodicity, the existence of evil in the world created by a loving God. His teaching and books have produced one of the strongest moral condemnations of the Holocaust and its perpetrators.

Mieczysław Zając, a young Catholic Pole, was deeply engaged in the resistance movement against the Nazis. After his arrest in 1942, he was consigned first to the Krakow Montelupich Prison and finally to Auschwitz. He was sent to the Buna-Monowitz camp and finagled a position in the prisoner hospital, but also sought treatment in the HKB. Tibor Wohl, a young Czech Jew from Terezienstadt, consigned to Buna-Monowitz as a laborer in 1942, ended up in the hospital both as a patient and a worker. These four young men each wrote about their experiences, which intersected at the hospital, though none of them was aware of any of the others. As a trained physician, the Polish resistance fighter Dr. Jaworski was a different kind of observer of the hospital and its routines. Each of these men reflects an aspect of the prisoner hospital.

PRIMO LEVI

In 1944, Primo Levi was 25 years old, an educated man, an Italian Jew, a chemist, and prisoner #174517 in Buna-Monowitz. Of more than 500 men, women, and children in his transport, unloaded from railroad cars in Auschwitz in February 1944, 96 men and 26 women were selected for work. The remainder died that day. The selected women were sent to Birkenau; the men to Buna-Monowitz. Primo Levi wrote *Survival in Auschwitz* in 1947.[2] It is the report of an eyewitness, educated, astute, and ironic.

Primo Levi had to learn the camp lingo and the insane routines of the camp from the bottom up. He started out as one of the brute laborers, a beast of burden in the massive construction of the Buna factory. A clumsy coworker tripped, and an iron support beam fell and cut Primo Levi's heel. The injury was painful and debilitating. That evening he decided to go to the Ka-Be, the *Krankenbau,* the prisoner hospital.[3]

His first encounter with the Ka-Be was in the ambulatorium, the active outpatient unit. The routine was the same for all men: strip off all clothing, carry your precious food bowl and spoon, queue for a fever check, and get a medical decision. No fever was found: good, which meant no typhus. "I have a good wound, it does not seem dangerous, but it should be enough to guarantee me a discreet period of rest."[4] On a busy day, the ambulatorium handled a thousand men. Most of them returned to the barracks and to work, but the next morning Primo Levi was sent to the hospital instead.

He was settled into hospital block number 13, which he referred to as a "dormitory." The entire hospital complex now consisted of blocks 11 through 20. Dr. Jaworski provided a sketch of the various buildings and their functions in an appendix to his book *Apel Skazanych.* Blocks 11 and 12 were the kitchens and a residential barrack for hospital workers. Number 13 was the most recent development: a *Schonungsblock*, a dormitory for recuperation. This hospital building had the conventional three-decker bunks of the rest of the camp. And it was overcrowded. There were 150 bunks for 250 patients. Primo Levi had good luck: "I am assigned bunk number 10—a miracle! It is empty! I stretch myself out with delight; it is the first time since I entered the camp [three months] that I have a bunk to myself. Despite my hunger, within ten minutes, I'm asleep."[5]

The hospital in late spring 1944 was at its full development. Other buildings served as specialized wards: numbers 14–17 were designated for surgical patients and internal medicine. Each had a separate room for the nursing staff. Additionally, block 15 had a dental service. The remaining buildings had been rebuilt to serve as a hospital. What had been three separate buildings were now interconnected. The carpenters, electricians, bricklayers, and painters recruited by Stefan, the *Blockälteste,* had constructed a unit for infectious diseases (separate wards for TB, *Durchfall,* and scarlet fever), a series of operating theaters with pre-op and post-op rooms, a laryngological office, an ophthalmology office, waiting rooms, and a laboratory. The outermost buildings housed a bathing room, a steam room, a disinfection room, and a laundry, all supplied with heated water from the boiler "organized" from Buna, now proudly installed and functional. The ambulatorium was one end of block 18. Gardeners maintained three separate vegetable plots abutting the barbed wire fences and the watch towers which formed the outer perimeter of Buna-Monowitz and the hospital.

Primo Levi's routine in the *Schonungsblock* consisted of a 4 a.m. camp wide reveille, but rather than going off to soul-numbing labor, patients were left in peace to eat bread at 5:30 a.m. and soup at midday, and then to continue resting until afternoon medicines and medical visits. The men ate evening rations in bed and lights went out at 9 p.m. Talking to fellow patients, Primo Levi learned about the danger of becoming *arbeitsunfähig,* what happens to laborers who can no longer work. "Everybody speaks about it indirectly, by allusions, and when I ask some questions they look at me and fall silent."[6] In this calmer, restful place, fellow patients explain to the naïve, newly arrived, ignorant Italian Jew what it meant to be selected, to be transferred to Birkenau for gassing and cremation. Selections in the hospital wards happened bed by bed. "The [SS] officer, followed by the doctors, walks around in silence, nonchalantly, between the bunks . . . he brings out the book, checks the number of the bed and the number of the tattoo . . . He has drawn a cross beside Schmulek's number . . . The next day Schmulek is part of the group transferred out of the Ka-Be. In this discreet and composed manner, without display or anger, massacre moves through the hut of the Ka-Be every day touching here and there."[7]

However, the tension and fear of selections were not the whole story. Primo Levi adds, "But life in the Ka-Be is not this. It is not the crucial moments of the selections, it is not the grotesque episodes of the diarrhea and lice control, it is not even the illness. Ka-Be is the *Lager* without its physical discomforts . . . In this Ka-Be, an enclosure of relative peace, we have learnt that our personality is fragile."[8] Primo Levi spent twenty days in the *Schonungsblock* until his foot healed. "I was discharged to my great displeasure."[9]

From the patient's perspective, the prisoner hospital represented both opportunity and threat. Primo Levi learned, that, yes, here was a site of respite, but, no, not safety. In better health and perhaps in a better frame of mind, Primo Levi was again exposed to the dangers of camp life as a brute laborer. The Italians had no support system in Buna-Monowitz, did not usually speak German (let alone Polish), and could receive little family support (one package reached Primo Levi from his sister), so how did he survive?

Primo Levi provides an outstanding picture of the Buna factory:

> The Buna is as large as a city; besides the managers and German technicians, forty thousand foreigners work there, and fifteen to twenty languages are spoken. All the foreigners live in different Lagers which surround the Buna: the Lager of the English prisoners of war, the Lager of the Ukrainian women, the Lager of the French volunteers and other we do not know. Our Lager (*Judenlager, Vernichtungslager, Kazett*) by itself provides ten thousand workers who come from all the nations of Europe. We are the slaves of the slaves, whom all can give orders to, and our name is the number which we carry tattooed on our arm and sewn on our jacket.[10]

The key to surviving this complex environment was to find a niche, a function. Doctors, tailors, shoemakers, musicians, and cooks had useful skills. Ordinary laborers would probably not survive. Primo Levi, a trained chemist, with a summa cum laude degree from Turin in 1941, became part of kommando 98, the chemical kommando.

The difference was dramatic. In the last months of his Auschwitz ordeal, Levi had found a refuge.

> In camp, in the evenings and the mornings, nothing distinguishes me from the flock, but during the day, at work, I am under shelter and warm, and nobody beats me; I steal and sell soap and petrol without risk, and perhaps I will be given a coupon for a pair of leather shoes. Even more, can this be called work? To work is to push wagons, carry sleepers, break stones, dig earth, press one's bare hands against the iciness of the freezing iron. But I sit all day, I have a notebook and a pencil and they have even given me a book to refresh my memory about analytical methods. I have a drawer where I can put my beret and gloves, and when I want to go out I only have to tell Herr Stawinoga, who never says no and asks no questions if I delay. He has the air of suffering in this flesh for the ruin which surrounds him.[11]

Primo Levi was working in a useful place which provided opportunities for "organizing" resources and he also understood the market, especially in the HKB. "I was hungry and on the lookout for something small and unusual (and therefore of high commercial value) to steal and exchange for bread."[12] He found the ideal objects: a drawer full of pipettes, small precisely graduated glass tubes, and he knew where they had value in the camp: the hospital laboratory. He made a deal and sold the pipettes for soup. It turned out to be a horrifically bad bargain. The soup was tainted. Primo Levi contracted scarlet fever and once again returned to the Ka-Be, but this time with a serious illness.

He was hospitalized in January 11, 1945, one week before the camp was evacuated and the Nazis fled west. This time he was placed in the block for infectious diseases, in the room for scarlet fever patients. It consisted of a clean room with ten bunks on two levels, a wardrobe, three stools, and a commode. He had a high fever but felt enormous relief at the thought that he would have isolation and rest. It was very cold outside, but this room was heated and he received appropriate medication: strong doses of sulfa drugs.[13] On the fifth day, still seriously ill, Levi heard the first excited rumors: the camp was going to be evacuated! As rumors went, this one had credence, since the camp and the factory had been subject for several months to very intermittent Allied bombing. But now the daily sound of Soviet artillery was audible in Auschwitz. For seriously ill prisoners, however, this news generated enormous fear. Evacuation meant marching through the January snow towards an unknown destination with a group of 20,000 prisoners from the various Auschwitz units guarded by highly nervous and stressed SS men. "We remained in our bunks, alone with our illnesses, and with our inertia stronger than fear. In the whole Ka-Be we numbered perhaps eight hundred . . . The rhythm of the great machine of the Lager was extinguished."[14]

ELIE WIESEL

Elie Wiesel was a pious, observant teenaged Jew from a small Romanian town, transferred into Hungary in 1940. On May 4, 1944, the Germans seized his small Jewish town and the families were shipped out in boxcars to an unknown destination. "Someone near a window read to us: 'Auschwitz.' Nobody had ever heard that name."[15]

Wiesel and his father Shlomo were immediately separated from the others in the family. His mother and youngest sister were killed that day; the two older sisters ended up as workers in Birkenau. Wiesel and his father faced an immediate selection: "All specialists—locksmiths, carpenters, electricians, watchmakers—one step forward."[16] No readers of the Talmud were required in the camp.

The Nazis had perfected the process of subjugation, dehumanization, and terror which faced these naïve Jews from Hungary. Wiesel lost his name to his tattoo identification: A-7713. He was reduced to a cipher and his function became that of a low-skilled laborer. After a brief stint of several weeks in the main camp, Wiesel and his father were transferred to Buna-Monowitz. A sliver of good fortune awaited them: they were assigned to a kommando which did not require exhausting labor. They were sent to work in an electrical warehouse counting inventory rather than outdoors hefting sacks of cement.[17] This was not enough, however, to protect either Wiesel or his father from inadequate food, poor clothing, or atrocious footwear. Wiesel fell victim to a common disaster: he injured a foot. "In the middle of January, my right foot began to swell from the cold. I could not stand on it. I went to the infirmary."[18]

He was met by a Jewish doctor, "a prisoner like ourselves," and heard the terrifying news: this was not swelling due to the cold weather, but rather an acute abcess, a phlemogen, that would require surgery. Elie Wiesel was admitted to the prisoner hospital in the last stressful month of its existence, yet it was still a place of refuge. Much like Primo Levi, who was at this juncture a patient in the infectious disease ward, Wiesel discovered that the prisoner hospital was outfitted in ways unimaginable in other camp barracks. "They put me in a bed with white sheets. I had forgotten that people slept in sheets. Actually, being in the infirmary was not bad at all: we were entitled to good bread, a thicker soup. No more bell, no more roll calls, no more work."[19]

But Wiesel was facing an operation the next morning. He had been taken to an operating room and was much relieved to find "his" doctor there, smiling at him and encouraging him. He received general anesthesia for a procedure that lasted about an hour. He was profoundly relieved when his smiling physician assured him that with two weeks of rest in the hospital, he would be just fine. One can infer from Wiesel's description of this crisis that the hospital was functioning normally, that an operating room was fully equipped, that anesthesia was available for prisoners, and that indeed this rather modest operation was fully routine for the doctors there. Additionally, the "great, Jewish doctor" had good bedside manners and brimmed with optimism to reassure his stressed patient.

It was not, however, to be an uneventful recuperation. Only two days after his surgery, Wiesel heard the exciting rumor that the Soviet battlefront was much closer. "The Red Army was racing toward Buna: it was only a matter of hours."[20] The doctors came to reassure the patients that while, yes, an evacuation was going to take place, those too sick or injured would remain in place in the hospital. This announcement amounted to a huge crisis for patients, since they were convinced that the SS had other plans for hospital. Prisoners suspected that the camp and the hospital were slated for destruction by the Germans and that staying in place was a death sentence. Wiesel limped out into the camp to find his father and left the decision up to him: stay in the hospital or march? Like a number of decisions father and son made in the months in Auschwitz, this one, too, is one he regretted in retrospect. They decided to join the exodus to Buchenwald. "After the war I learned the fate of those who had remained at the infirmary. They were, quite simply, liberated by the Russians, two days after the evacuation."[21] This is an oversimplification; however, the decision to march was the final exertion which would lead to his father's death.

MIECZYSŁAW ZAJĄC

Mieczysław Zając titled his memoir *No Return Required*, the post office designation for abandoned mail. It was also the SS term, *Rückkehr Unerwünscht*, for a death, similar to the code words *Nacht und Nebel* (Night and Fog) for prisoners destined to disappear. Intimidated by his lack of experience as a writer, he hesitated to write about his life under German occupation for forty years, until 1986. Zając chronicled the reaction of a young, educated Pole to the defeat of his country and the impact of the German takeover.

Surprised and dismayed by the rapid collapse of the Polish army in September, 1939, he and his compatriots at Jagiellonian University listened to clandestine radio broadcasts, in spite of the German demand that such radios be immediately surrendered. The students learned about the Soviet-Nazi pact and the loss of Eastern Poland and realized that Poland was isolated and surrounded. The news in the coming months and years continued to reveal the depressing success of the German armies: the fall of

Denmark, Sweden, Belgium, the Netherlands, France, and finally the air war against England. Though it was dangerous to listen to the radio (often hidden under blankets in darkened rooms), students continued to keep informed about the progress of the war. This very activity would finally trip up even an apolitical student like Stefan in the summer of 1941.

A chemistry major, Zając was immediately affected by the closing of Jagiellonian University in November 1939 after the wholesale arrest of professors and staff by the Germans. The students' hope that the university would serve as a locus of resistance collapsed. The source for an organization to bring politically active students together was actually the popular scouting movement in the Krakow region. He became an active resistance fighter. "We started hearing whispers that a concentration camp had been established in Oświęcim in which those arrested were dying and political prisoners were being shot."[22] In June 1942, Mieczysław Zając was betrayed by compatriots, arrested, and subsequently spent one year in the Montelupich prison. He arrived in Auschwitz I in a bus with blacked-out windows on June 23, 1943. He was tattooed with number 126825. Stefan's number on February 10, 1942, was number 20526: more than 100,000 men had arrived in Auschwitz in sixteen months. The SS doctors chose him to be a medical subject and he was injected with a "brown fluid" which made him violently ill with typhus.[23] As soon as he recovered, friends in Auschwitz I maneuvered to get him transferred to Auschwitz III: Buna.

His arrival in Buna was memorable. The first question he was asked was: "Do you play soccer?" The *Kleiderkommando Kapo*, Paulek, in charge of clothing and food, organized a pick-up game right there on the *Appelplatz* in front of the two enormous canvas tents that served as temporary housing for several hundred men each. But Zając stayed on the sidelines as a substitute, feeling that he could not sustain running after a year in prison and a bout of typhus. He encountered Stefan that day: Stefan was recruiting specialists. "There were no doctors. There were also no pharmacists or veterinarians. Finally he asked about chemists. I stepped forward.

Many would later be readmitted. As SS Dr. Fischer, SDG Gerhard Neubert, and Stefan walked through the wards, patients were forced to stand. Fischer gave them a cursory look and checked their paperwork. Fischer placed their chart in either one pile (saved) or another (doomed). Those too sick to stand or leave their beds were in the greatest danger.

There were strategies to circumvent selections. Medical charts were removed and patients hidden or moved to other rooms or barracks. In an effort to subvert the selection process, Dr. Grossmann once told Dr. Fischer with a straight face that one of his surgical patients, one of Zając's close friends, had such an unusual and special surgery that he should be allowed to stay in this hospital longer.[30] Zając is straightforward in pointing out that Polish prisoners were in an advantageous position in the camp and the hospital and more able to avoid selections. They received packages from home and had better food and thus sturdier health, they had contact with Polish civilians in the Buna factory who could supply food or medicines, and they often formed unofficial groups in the camp and hospital to protect their weakest compatriots. Zając estimates that in late 1943, Poles comprised only about 10% of the prisoners in Buna and cooperated with each other when possible.[31]

The lynchpin of the hospital, in Zając's opinion, was Stefan himself. He maintained control over the "green triangle" prisoners (criminals) and fostered a working relationship with the SS physicians. Zając, of course, was not privy to larger issues of the Buna director's demand for healthier workers. Jews with skill were employed rather than summarily worked to death or consigned to death on arrival. The staff was increasingly pulled from all over Europe and physicians, regardless of nationality or religion, were recruited as quickly as Stefan could identify them. In Zając's opinions, Poles saw Stefan as a protector of his Polish coworkers, doctors, and patients. However, he was noted for not tolerating slackers or incompetence regardless of their shared Polish nationality.[32]

The role of the SS medical orderly (SDG) Herbert Neubert was an important element of Stefan's success. Zając describes him as an atypical SS man. He was both passive and cooperative and he was under the sway of Stefan's stronger personality and drive. Stefan's presence and leadership was important to the hospital staff. There was general consternation among them when Stefan fell seriously ill. He developed double pneumonia and was absent for some weeks. Postwar, Stefan realized that he had also contracted tuberculosis.

Zając bemoaned the need to resort to paper bandages as they were inadequate and flimsy. No one in the hospital could prevent the impact of hunger, overwork, lack of vitamins, and the hopelessness that exhausted prisoners experienced in the months and years of imprisonment. Zając constantly consoled himself with the thoughts of returning to his family. This consolation was not possible for those like Elie Wiesel or Primo Levi, whose families and compatriots had already been murdered in Birkenau. Zając and his coworkers, Kujawa and Kowalski, did learn how to provide a modicum of preventative services so that exhausted and depressed prisoners did not succumb to serious illnesses. They learned that it was critical to deal with small, seemingly trivial issues when they appeared in the ambulatorium. Small injuries to hands or feet were treated seriously and early to prevent escalating problems. They developed a simple antiseptic of salt water and compresses to apply to wounds before they became septic.

Zając found that prisoners had very different responses to their hospitalization. Some were so demoralized by hunger and illness that they had very little resistance left. They gave up. They either died in the Buna hospital or were so debilitated and passive that they were doomed to selections for Birkenau. Still others were absolute fighters with a focus on survival by any means. These men increased their chances for survival by stealing bread and soup or food from mailed packages from fellow patients too weak to protect their food. If a thief was discovered, other less seriously ill patients and hospital workers turned on him in fury and beat him. But others, though ill themselves, fought for their health and came to help and to encourage their fellows. Zając particularly remembers a young French Jew named Jean, perhaps 17 years old, who despite his own chest surgery was of such a sunny and positive disposition that other patients worked to help him and shared their food packages with him. Many of the French, Belgian, and Greek prisoners who were now, in 1944, coming into the hospital knew little or no German, but the hospital workers tried to create a simple vocabulary to teach them. Apparently Jean had no problems communicating across this divide.[33]

Poles in the Buna camp were galvanized by the news that Poles had staged an uprising in Warsaw in August 1944. The news filtering into the camp about the advances of the Soviets from the east convinced them that the end stage of the war was approaching and that the Germans were losing. Unlike the patients like the debilitated Primo Levi or injured Elie Wiesel, healthy hospital workers as well as others in the camp were considering the option of escaping into civil society and joining the Polish uprising. Zając is emphatic in stating that Poles were escaping from the Buna worksite in small groups daily. The rumor was that a Polish organization, unspecified, had organized support and safe houses in the vicinity of Buna. He also claims that none of the escapees was captured and returned to the camp. The SS guards staged no draconian reprisal executions in camp: "The SS men realized that it would not have made any difference."[34]

The end stages of the Buna camp now involved food shortages as well as the disappearance of cigarettes on the camp black market. The news in mid-August was that a new list was being prepared, limited to the Poles in Buna. Twelve hundred men were on this new selection list. But selection for what? The young men were gathered on the central square in the camp and they whispered among one another that if they were being moved to Birkenau to be gassed, they would try to overwhelm their guards. Stefan calmed Zając with the news that their destination was not Birkenau, but some camp to the west, probably Buchenwald. No revolt materialized.

The young Poles were marched out of Buna, past the main Auschwitz camp, until they came to a railroad siding. They were loaded into boxcars with canvas tops, fifty men in each. Stefan's information had been correct: they arrived in Buchenwald where they were greeted with great suspicion and hostility. The "Auschwitz bandits" had arrived for processing. They only stayed a few weeks before they were sent on to yet another camp: Dora, the site of great underground facilities to produce the V-1 and V-2 rockets. Zając had to endure another eight months of danger before liberation day.

TIBOR WOHL

Hitler's Germany was a racist state with a clear hierarchy of humanity: Germans as the Aryan Übermenschen, Slavs as the inferior slave humans, and Jews an expendable population to be segregated, expelled, exploited, and finally exterminated. These were Jews of all social classes, pious or secular, practicing their faith or converted to other faiths, urban or rural. It didn't matter. Ghettoization, segregating Jews into barbed wire enclosed city sections, was the German policy developed to control the labor and lives of Jews in occupied territories.

The Czech Jews were sent to an unusual ghetto: the entire Czech city of Terezin. It was renamed Terezienstadt and became labor camp and concentration camp. Organized by the gestapo, the camp started filling with Jews on June 14, 1940. It became a closed ghetto on November 24, 1941 for Czech Jews and eventually other European Jews. They were put to work, transforming the old Terezin prison and barracks into what the Nazis touted as a model installation for older and prominent Jews. This Potemkin Village registered over 75,000 men, women, and children. For many it was just a transit station to other sites such as the labor camp Auschwitz and its extermination camp, Birkenau.

Among them were Tibor Wohl and his family. Tibor Wohl decided to write down his experiences and published *Arbeit Macht tot* (*Work Kills*) in 1990, just three years after Mieczysław Zając's *Powrót Niepożądany* (1987), more than forty years after the traumatic events of their youth. He wrote because he felt compelled to be a witness to history: "I wrote this book to shake off a burden of many years. The past keeps seizing my memory: I want to forget, but I cannot."[35]

Tibor Wohl was 18 years old when he and his parents and younger brother were seized in Prague and brought to Terezienstadt on December 10, 1941. Less than a year later, October 26, 1942, they were loaded into railroad cars and transported to Auschwitz. The young man was selected to work, tattooed number 71255, but his family was immediately sent to the gas chambers. Only seventeen other people from the 1,866 Czechs in this transport survived the Auschwitz "death factory."[36]

Wohl was sent to Buna as an ordinary laborer with no skill set to protect him. There was no cohort of knowledgeable prisoners available to guide him through the acclimatization months of prison life. He survived because he was young and strong and had sufficient luck and determination to navigate the dangers in life in a KZ. Wohl reported the constant beatings, kicks, and outright killings of ordinary workers at the Buna site. "The SS didn't care about the work. The prisoners were to be destroyed by overwork. There were plenty of people in the camp. The reserves were also plentiful."[37] As an ordinary brute laborer on the grounds of Buna, he heard nothing but vulgarity and saw constant scenes of horrific and senseless violence aimed with particular virulence towards Jews.

Wohl was highly conscious of the existence of layers of privilege among the prisoners and noted that both "Aryan" and Jewish prominent prisoners were able to avoid the extreme levels of overwork, violence, and hunger that he was subjected to. His first reference to the hospital unit in the Buna camp was in the context of loss. A fellow Czech had been beaten so badly for not making his bed properly that he was sent to the hospital—from which he never returned.[38] This occurred in October 1942 while the hospital was still under the control of men with little medical training.

By the time Wohl became a patient himself in mid-1943, the Buna prisoner hospital had just come under the new organization of the "*Lagerälteste* Budiaszek [*sic*]." Wohl was working at the Buna factory as a *Kabelkommando*, carrying heavy steel cables. A clumsy coworker dropped a heavy steel cable, which lacerated Wohl's heel. He was sent back to the camp on the truck which carried the midday soup and heard the camp guard call him "*arbeitsunfähig*" (unsuitable for work). The guard predicted Wohl would get a transfer to Birkenau and the gas chamber. A Czech nurse led Wohl to the hospital secretary, Heymann, who brought a sympathetic doctor into play. The physician noted a bacterial skin infection and reclassified Wohl from "injured worker" to "medical patient." Wohl was saved from transfer to Birkenau. Fellow patients advised him to keep on scratching to keep the infection going to enable him to stay in the hospital as long as possible.[39]

Why stay? The new barrack that had been designated as an infectious disease ward was a comparative paradise. The prospect of two weeks of rest felt like a happy eternity. "My comrades surrounded me. The quiet murmur of voices in the air: the situation felt unreal . . . I fell asleep. The soft shake of my comrades woke me. Food was shared. Everything took place without beatings. Everyone received their portion of soup and ate in peace and quiet and then lay down for an afternoon nap. Heavenly!"[40] The hospital had hot water and washrooms and also the first mirror he had encountered since his arrival in Buna. He was appalled by his dreadful appearance. His skin condition demanded the application of some kind of salve but more than that, he barely recognized his grey and skeletal features.

Once a week the doctors made a general inspection of each patient in the infectious disease ward. An SS doctor and Stefan examined the afflicted and determined how much longer they could stay on the ward. Each patient hoped to stay longer in this quiet haven, but feared that their sickness doomed them to transfer to Birkenau. After his second week, Wohl was approached by Dr. Silber (Dr. Jonas Silber, number 38968)[41] who quietly warned him that he would be released to the camp to protect him from a selection in the hospital. Tibor Wohl's return to a new set of barracks brought him back into the chaotic and violent reality of life in the Buna camp.

In June 1943 Wohl saw the erection of two giant tents on the Buna camp grounds. These were the tents that first housed Mieczysław Zając, who arrived that June. Two thousand men were using them: more men than the camp barracks could accommodate. The camp was crammed past its capacity. The solution that the SS men devised was a grand selection which would "remove" the excess. Mid-June the dreaded event took place. The great camp bell rang midday to announce a full camp assembly. The men stripped and lined up by number and each group of some 200 men was inspected by SS Dr. Fischer, SDG Neubert, and their block leader. This was a cursory visual inspection, which lasted only seconds and determined each man's fate. Thirty-nine men in Tibor Wohl's block were selected to move to Birkenau. In this fashion, the SS men reduced the camp by about 20%. The men were loaded on trucks. In a couple of hours their clothing returned to the disinfection station in Buna.[42]

Lice were endemic and with them came repeated epidemics. The summer 1943 infestations were severe and typhus struck the Buna camp. It was centered on block 7. For fear of contagion, the SS men isolated the block in an attempt to quarantine the infection. All 180 men in block 7 were sent to Birkenau. When Tibor Wohl started to feel ill with fever and severe headaches, he hoped he had a passing infection and refused to seek help. He avoided going to the prisoner hospital because he feared further selections. When, after four days, he finally showed up, he was seriously ill with a high temperature and the dreaded red spot lesions on his abdomen. Dr. Cuenca diagnosed him with typhus and his nurse was his *Landsman* Felix, who provided fresh clothing and a shower.

Though seriously ill, Tibor Wohl had been in the camp long enough to know trusted men in the hospital. Dr. Cuenca provided an injection which helped to pull Tibor through this crisis. It was not only a physical crisis: he also battled the hopelessness and despair engendered by his bestial existence. He remembered the deaths in Terezienstadt, but they were not to be compared to the systematic extermination routine in the Buna camp. How, he wondered, could the professional and highly qualified civilian managers of the Buna factory not notice the deaths of so many workers? How could they not protest the organized murder of men in the Auschwitz system?

His fever broke, his heart survived the assault, and his friends were cheered to see him regain both appetite and better spirits. Within days he was strong enough to sit with friends on the lawn outside of the ward. However, another selection was rumored. Men whispered to each other that the SS had stopped all transfers out of the hospital and planned a selection in the hospital for the next day. This time there would be no way to evade the SS doctors inspection by a quick return to his regular barracks.

The man who came to his rescue again was "Stefan Heimann," that is, Stephan Heymann, the politically active hospital secretary. He had a simple but not foolproof plan. He hid Wohl and another youngster under a bed in an adjoining ward and absconded with their medical records when SDG Neubert left their hospital charts in Heymann's care. Several truckloads of men were taken out of the hospital that day, but Tibor Wohl was not among them.[43]

Another year passed and in 1944 and the newly arrived Jews from Hungary, Italy, and other European states were integrated into the camp. Wohl, a secular Jew when he was growing up in Prague, now met with rabbis and prayed with other Jews. He noted that the camp had changed significantly since he had arrived: groups of Jews meeting to talk and pray were not beaten and driven apart by screaming SS men. The reports reaching Buna from Birkenau, however, spoke of the grim reality that Jews from all over Europe were being murdered there and incinerated in the great crematoria. These Jews were seldom given even the slim chance of survival as workers for the Nazi Reich. For instance, of the 70,000 Greek Jews brought to Auschwitz, only a couple of hundred remained alive. Columns of men, women, and children by the thousands were daily led to the gas chambers.[44]

In the spring of 1944 Tibor Wohl had managed to get work in the hospital's *Schonungsblock*, the recovery ward.[45] The barracks leader was a German political prisoner, Paul, a caring man who tried to make life bearable for the patients. He was scrupulous in dividing the bread, butter, and soup fairly. In some wonderment Wohl wrote: "There were Germans like this, too!"[46] Wohl had time and opportunity to talk more freely with fellow inmates. A fellow Czech, Arnost Tauber, an older prisoner arrested in 1939 and in Buna since October 1942, revealed to Tibor that there was a resistance movement in the camp and asked him to join. Tibor was transferred to the disinfection unit of the hospital through the further efforts of this network of resistance-minded prisoners. Tibor states: "This was not easy for them since the hospital senior prisoner Budziaszek only wanted to employ his fellow citizens, Poles, in the hospital."[47] On the register of physicians maintained by Dr. Makowski, eight out of 47 names are clearly Polish. On the register for helpers and administrators, 24 of 66 names are probably Polish (see appendix). Tibor Wohl was in a hospital setting that was operating under a Polish prisoner, Stefan, but he was not correct in assuming that the majority of workers, let alone doctors, were chosen because they were Poles.

The resistance movement that Wohl now joined had as its primary objective to make the life for prisoners bearable by providing extra food and safer jobs. Each political group tried to assure that their members had control over the functionary positions which impacted the ordinary prisoners: block leaders, kapos, block secretaries. Wohl states that by 1944 this had been mostly accomplished and that life in the camps was safer. He saw the trajectory of change from the murderous brutality to the much safer conditions in 1944 as a consequence of prisoner action. These efforts to improve quotidian existence, however, did not manage to affect the ongoing SS policy of selection and deaths.[48] While Wohl saw the situation from a specific point of view, he was not in a position to note that many others in the hospital unit itself also worked to improve prisoner survival and despaired at the continuing selection episodes.

The construction of the great Buna factory continued, but by the fall of 1944 there were clear indications that the war was turning against the Germans. Wohl was at the Buna factory on a Sunday in September when allied bombers, small silver slivers flying silently high above them, dropped bombs on the factory. The small building in which Tibor and fellow prisoners were working shattered under the impact of the bombs. Grey with dust and lacerated by debris, Wohl and others dug themselves out and saw to their wounded. In October, the news seeped into the Buna camp that the Germans had closed the gas chambers in Birkenau and by November that they had blown up the crematoria.

In December 1944 the SS men collected all "Aryan" German prisoners, thus excluding all German Jews. About three hundred men, political, criminal, asocial, Jehovah's Witnesses, and homosexual prisoners, were gathered on the *Appellplatz.* Auschwitz Kommandant Schwarz and the camp leader Schüttel, along with other prominent SS officers, faced them in full official regalia. The gathered prisoners then heard an address by the *Lagerälteste* Paul Kozwara. Wohl later learned the deal the SS were offering. German prisoners were told that through their excellent and willing work ethic they had proven they had true German blood and understood the need to sacrifice for the *Vaterland.* Manifestly the homeland was in danger from foes both from the east and west. German prisoners in Auschwitz were now declared true German citizens and no longer prisoners of the Reich. Insofar as they were healthy enough, they would now be allowed to join the Waffen SS. Though they were now "free men," they were not allowed to leave the camp quite yet. This was a different deal from what was offered to Polish prisoners in August. The Poles were shipped west to other labor camps.

The German political prisoners realized that they were given a deal which would put them on the front lines just as the Nazis were losing the war. This was an unattractive option. Some did not reject future military training, since it meant that they would get to hold weapons in their hands. Men who had been for years beaten, humiliated, demoralized, and starved by these same SS men were now asked to join their racist and murderous jailers. Wohl reports that some one hundred men, German "Aryan" concentration camp prisoners, were issued black uniforms and weapons to guard their camp mates during evacuation.[49]

DR. CZESŁAW JAWORSKI

Dr. Jaworski was a major in the Polish army, a physician, and a married man with a 12-year-old son, living in Warsaw in 1942 and working as a doctor but also heavily involved with the Polish resistance movement. SS men showed up in his Warsaw apartment the night of January 30, 1942, to arrest him. Buses with blacked out windows carried him and the other 160 men seized that night to the notorious Warsaw prison, Pawiak.[50] Jaworski became a functionary prisoner in Pawiak. In all subsequent imprisonments, Jaworski always managed to find a protected position, either because prisoners acknowledged his status in the Polish resistance or because of some ineffable personal characteristic of authority or privilege. The men in Pawiak maintained clandestine contacts with fellow Poles in Auschwitz.

The situation in the Pawiak facility changed for the worse for the prisoners in the spring of 1942. The relatively stable relationship that had developed in the prison between the SS officials and their Polish prisoners was severely disrupted when the German SS officials were pulled out of the prison into the war effort in the Soviet Union. The German SS men were now replaced by Ukrainian and Romanian guards. While the Germans were in charge they virtually always allowed their Polish underlings to organize the prison. However, the new guards and officials eliminated the Polish workers and introduced a far harsher regime. A move to Auschwitz seemed almost desirable. A German SS man assured Jaworski that a transfer would be an improvement: Auschwitz was no longer as dangerous as previously and it was, after all, just a labor camp and prisoners got to work in the healthy fresh outdoor air.[51]

On April 16, 1942, Jaworski and 475 other men, almost the entire Pawiak prison population, were loaded on buses and accompanied by SS guards on motorcycles were brought to the Warsaw railroad station. They were loaded into covered railroad cars, 60 per wagon, for a sixteen-hour journey south to the ramps of Auschwitz. He received the tattoo number 31070. His examining physician was his friend and fellow resistance fighter from Warsaw, Dr. Diem. Jaworski got essential advice: answer that you are in good health to all questions and do not bring up your heart problems.[52] During his first two months in Auschwitz I, he had been hospitalized twice and worked on three different job assignments when he finally got appropriate work as a nurse in the prisoner hospital of Auschwitz I due to the strenuous efforts of Dr. Diem.

Lagerarzt SS Dr. Friedrich Entress, an energetic and active racist, ran the Auschwitz I prisoner hospital. He refused to work with any Jewish prisoners and would not accept other prisoners as hospital workers until they had spent some time in the camp on other work assignments. Entress addressed Jaworski and the other new hospital workers and told them that they would experience many things working in the hospital, but "don't see anything, don't try to understand anything and tell no one anything of what happens here."[53] Entress was referring to the phenol injection murders (which were not used in the Buna-Monowitz camp). Jaworski was assigned to the ambulatorium and his task was bandaging injuries, especially those caused by ill-fitting shoes and hand injuries from handling construction bricks with bare hands. The Auschwitz I prisoner hospital had an x-ray machine.[54] Prisoners from other camps would be transported to Auschwitz I to use the machine.

On October 1, 1943, Dr. Jaworski was transferred to a new site in Czechoslovakia, *Kommando Brünn*, and escaped the execution of a group of Polish Army conspirators. He participated in a building project in Brno. Upon its completion he was assigned to the Buna-Monowitz camp on May 2, 1944. Dr. Jaworski found himself among friends here and was immediately incorporated into the network of physicians recruited into the hospital. With obvious pride, Stefan showed him the newly constructed facilities which now made the prisoner hospital a functioning organization: the ambulatorium, the surgery, the wards. Dr. Jaworski's sketch of the hospital as it existed mid-1944 identifies all of the buildings and also depicts the famous "organized" boiler which provided essential hot water for this part of the camp.

Dr. Jaworski's health, never robust, now deteriorated even further. His knee was failing with a tubercular infection and he was admitted to the hospital and put under the care of Dr. Makowski, the other significant chronicler of the Buna-Monowitz prisoner hospital. He was ordered to rest on a stretcher in the sun, augmented on cloudy days with a sun lamp. He ate vegetables from the hospital garden: lettuce, radishes, and onions supplied the vitamins he needed.[55] From this relatively secure location, Dr. Jaworski noted changes in the camp and the hospital. Stefan was recruiting heavily for physicians from the incoming Hungarian transports (such as Drs. Lengyel and Stern) as well as from Western Europe (such as Dr. Cremieux from France). The influx of these and other new physicians and patients created a Tower of Babel issue in the hospital. The doctors hoped to avoid confusion by organizing patients on the ward by language. Very few Polish physicians were now working at the prisoner hospital.

The news continued to be grim. There were huge losses in the uprising in Warsaw in August 1944. Some 250,000 Poles were killed in the city and many in the camps feared for families left behind. At the end of September, Stefan brought the news of the liquidation of the gypsy camp in the Birkenau gas chambers. Even though selections in the Buna prisoner hospital became less frequent, on October 9, 1944, Dr. Jaworski was threatened with death by the last selection at the hospital. Realizing the danger to the convalescing Dr. Jaworski, Stefan put him into the position of a bookkeeper.[56] Functionary prisoners, unlike the patients, were not subjected to selection and liquidation by the SS physicians. SS Dr. König was the leader of the last selection.

The war was creeping nearer: on August 15 an allied airstrike injured 300 men at the Buna factory. Those injured were gassed by the SS. There was no significant damage to either the factory or the camp, but tensions in the camp increased markedly. Yet Christmas, 1944, was celebrated regardless. The Germans lit candles on their evergreen *Tannenbaum*, and Stefan treated his staff to a dinner in his quarter, highlighted by coffee and cookies supplied by his parents.[57] The calculations for the end game were complex. Primo Levi, Elie Wiesel, Tibor Wohl, and Dr. Jaworski each had to make decisions as to their ability to survive. The order to abandon the Auschwitz camps came on January 18. The Buna camp was evacuated on January 19, 1945. Primo Levi and Dr. Jaworski stayed in the prisoner hospital, while Elie Wiesel, Tibor Wohl, and Stefan were among the marchers.

NOTES

1. Szymborska, *Seventy Poems*, 80–81.
2. *Survival in Auschwitz* is the revised title of *If This Is a Man (Se questo è un uomo),* translated from the Italian in 1958.
3. Levi, *Survival in Auschwitz,* 45.
4. Ibid., 47.
5. Ibid., 50.
6. Ibid., 52.
7. Ibid., 53.
8. Ibid., 55.
9. Ibid., 56.
10. Ibid., 72. In December 1944, 17,828 workers were employed at the Buna factory in Auschwitz. 40.3% were non-German men, 12.7% were non-German women, 2.1% were POWs, 18.3% were Germans, and 26.6% were prisoners from the Buna-Monowitz concentration camp (Wagner, *IG Auschwitz*, 332).
11. Levi, *Survival in Auschwitz,* 141.
12. Primo Levi, *Moments of Reprieve: A Memoir of Auschwitz* (New York: Penguin Books, 1987), 110.
13. Levi, *Survival in Auschwitz,* 151–52.
14. Ibid., 156.
15. Wiesel, *Night*, 27.
16. Ibid., 39.
17. Ibid., 50.
18. Ibid., 78.
19. Ibid.
20. Ibid., 80.

21. Ibid., 82.
22. Zając, *Powrót Niepożądany,* 42.
23. Ibid., 137.
24. Ibid., 143
25. Makowski, "Häftlingskrankenbau," 177.
26. Ibid.
27. Ibid.
28. Zając, 166.
29. Ibid., 153.
30. Ibid., 170.
31. Ibid., 155.
32. Ibid., 152.
33. Ibid., 166.
34. Ibid., 155.
35. Wohl, *Arbeit Macht tot,* 16.
36. Ibid., 15.
37. Ibid., 37.
38. Ibid., 33.
39. Ibid., 65.
40. Ibid., 67.
41. Makowski, "Häflingskrankenbau," 177.
42. Wohl, *Arbeit macht tot,* 82.
43. Ibid., 101.
44. Ibid., 153.
45. Makowski,"Häftlingskrankenbau," 179 notes Tibor Wohl, prisoner number 71255, *Desinfektor.*
46. Wohl, *Arbeit macht tot,* 157.
47. Ibid.
48. Ibid.
49. Ibid., 156.
50. Jaworski, *Apel Skazanych,* 22. Pawiak served as a political prison from 1863 until 1918 for the Russians, from 1919 to 1939 for the Polish regime, and from 1939 until 1944 for the Nazis. The Gestapo blew up Pawiak during the late 1944 uprising in Warsaw.
51. Ibid., 30.
52. Ibid., 42.
53. Ibid., 103.

54. Ibid., 112.
55. Ibid., 259.
56. Ibid., 265.
57. Ibid., 268.

10

THE EVACUATION

Cor-rect, cor-rect click the wheels.
Gladeless forest.
Cor-rect, cor-rect.
Through the forest a convoy of clamor.

Tak to, tak, stuka koło. Las bez polan.
Tak to, tak. Lasem jedzie transport wołań.[1]

THOSE WHO STAYED

In late 1944 the war in Europe was in its fifth year. The vastly bloated area of German hegemony was contracting. The conquest of the Soviet Union, begun in June 1941, suffered a decisive blow at Stalingrad in February 1943. The June 6, 1944, Allied offensive, D-Day, had turned the war into a two-front engagement. By July 1944, the Soviet troops were a mere 200 miles from Auschwitz and advancing on the General Gouvernament. The Polish resistance organization, the Home Army (AK), believed that their moment had come. The Warsaw Uprising began on August 1, 1944. Poles hoped to seize control of their capital from the Nazis before the Soviets arrived, but failed. Nazi plans for an expanded empire across Eastern Europe and the Soviet Union were disintegrating. The *Altreich*, Germany itself, now needed essential protection, as Hitler's house of cards was collapsing. The SS decided that they needed to shift laboring prisoners from the periphery into the heartland.

There were multiple objectives for clearing the labor camps. Foremost was the need to bring more workers into the German armament industry. Between August 1944 and January 1945, the SS effected a massive transfer of workers from concentration camps. In Auschwitz alone, 65,000 men and women were put on trains going West. (Zając was in the selection for healthy workers in August.) Another motive for moving inmates was the fear of uprisings in the concentration camps. With the August 1 explosion in Warsaw, the SS feared a contagion effect in the slave labor camps. There was also a pragmatic fear that the liberated prisoners would be armed by the Soviets to fight the German oppressors.[2]

Birkenau BIIe, formerly the Gypsy family camp, was designated as a transport center. Prisoners from across the Auschwitz complex were aggregated and examined for health and skills before being loaded into boxcars. More than 130 trainloads with 100 men per boxcar left Auschwitz between October and November 1944. The majority were sent to the Buchenwald camp and its subcamp Dora-Mittelbau, which produced essential war material. Ironically, even at the moment when workers were desperately needed, the racist brutality of the SS was still the dominant mindset. Critically needed workers were packed into trains with little food or water. They arrived at their destinations exhausted, debilitated, and in part useless.[3]

Quotidian shortages appeared in Auschwitz. Lightweight summer striped pants and shirts were not replaced by winter weight clothing.[4] Anticipating the end, the SS began the destruction of the evidence of their genocidal murders. The prisoners, the *Sonderkommando*, who were employed to deal with gas chamber remains, revolted on October 7 and damaged the number 4 crematorium. In November and December, two crematoria were dismantled and sent to Germany. The gas chambers closed. Historian Wachsmann quotes a letter from SS Dr. Wirths to his wife (November 29, 1944): "How nice it is for me that I don't have to do this horrible work anymore, and that it exists no more."[5]

The Nazis also wanted to blot out evidence of their thefts. "Canada" was emptied. Between December 1 and January 15, over 500,000 pieces of clothing were sent westward, 20% of it to other concentration camps.[6] They then torched the 30 barracks.[7] Boxcars left Auschwitz filled with bricks, roof tiles, cement, and sewer pipes packed by prisoners to be reused in Germany. This process of dismantling the camp was relatively orderly until January 1945. The German army was unable to slow, let alone halt, the Soviet advance and panic set in. A mass evacuation was hurriedly instituted. A tide of forced laborers, POWs, concentration camp prisoners, and civilian Germans became a tsunami in mid-January. The Soviets were advancing; the Germans were fleeing.[8]

The existence of the Buna-Monowitz prisoner hospital, the HKB, was coming to an end. As Auschwitz was abandoned men too weak to march were left behind. Some 70,000 prisoners marched out, but what about the patients who were left behind in the Buna-Monowitz prisoner hospital? Stefan urged Dr. Jaworski, still limping heavily, to remain in the hospital barracks to avoid the risk of death from an SS bullet on a march. Jaworski received the keys to Stefan's room and moved in. He put on the arm band of the *Lagerälteste,* an unenviable and now obsolete position. He was not the only physician to remain behind. Dr. Woss, a Hungarian, was convalescing in ward 14 and in all a total of 18 physicians, mostly Hungarians, were scattered around the hospital grounds.[9] Jaworski was reassured by Stefan's last comments that the Soviets were only two days away. In fact, the hospital was about to undergo a ten-day period of increasing misery and danger before Soviet help arrived.

The Buna-Monowitz camp had been abandoned, but the hospital had some 800 patients left. Jaworski and Dr. Woss (sharing a single cane), Dr. Ehrlich (walking with the help of two canes), and a French doctor, Heimrat (on crutches), attempted to visit all of the hospital buildings still occupied by patients. They had no food in the hospital, but Jaworski assured the patients that there was a large storehouse of potatoes, but not on the hospital grounds. There were still SS guards manning towers, so there was danger of shootings. All four physicians were urging calm and stressing the need for cooperation to maintain some sense of order and especially to find food.

Their optimistic hopes were dashed when they arrived at the building which served as the administrative center of the hospital and which also contained the pharmacy. The content of the building had been wrecked by the patients. They had scattered medications on the floor, crushed ampoules of drugs, and smashed and overturned tables, chairs, and cabinets. The floor was fouled with excrement. A frenzied search by ambulatory patients for food or hidden wealth had yielded nothing. Frustration and fear led to this dangerous act of vandalism. A young Hungarian patient identified himself as a pharmacist and, in return for access to some warm clothing, set to rescuing whatever medication was still usable from the chaos.[10] The Germans delivered loaves of bread and kettles of soup on January 19, even as Soviet airplanes could be seen above the camp. A Soviet bomb hit the camp and ignited a fire, and that night all electrical power ceased and the camp and its hospital descended into darkness. The hospital now had no access to water, electricity, or heat.[11]

In Dr. Jaworski's account, the next few days appeared calm, as he and his companions were able to find food at the factory site and bring it back to share with patients still in the hospital. He also stated that the SS man who had delivered food on the 19th returned two days later with the last truckload of food: 850 loaves of bread, sausages, and margarine. But how to distribute this windfall? Dr. Jaworski found that he really could not establish any fair system of distribution, as patients were wandering between hospital wards and even out into the camp itself.

An orderly military man, Dr. Jaworski was both repelled and helpless in the face of the chaos developing in the hospital. He controlled only of a few barracks around the surgical unit. Each day, the disorder, misery, cold, and random deaths of the more seriously ill patients in the hospital increased. The first Red Army soldiers finally entered the camp on January 27 and immediately handed out the food they carried. By mid-morning on January 27, Dr. Jaworski formally relinquished his position as the head of the prisoner hospital to a Soviet captain. This military doctor now organized civilians to come into the hospital to restore order and cleanliness.[12]

The Soviets dissolved the hospital and some 600 surviving patients were moved into Soviet army hospital units. The prisoner hospital formally ceased to exist on February 11, 1945.[13] Jaworski arrived at the Krakow Jagiellonian University Hospitals for treatment and was outfitted by the Polish Red Cross. He wrote his memoirs in Poręba Wielka, Krakow, and Zakopane between May and November of 1945.[14]

Dr. Jaworski's account of his attempts to maintain order and discipline in the face of prisoner patient anarchy stands in strong contrast with Primo Levi's account of the same ten-day period. Levi and his companions had no interaction with Dr. Jaworski and his compatriots. The storehouse of food from the grounds of the factory building accessed by Jaworski never reached Levi and the eleven men left behind in the infectious disease ward. Levi also noted the last two food deliveries by the SS men, but after that, the patients were on their own. The bomb which exploded on the grounds of the hospital had destroyed two empty huts. The concussion broke windows and a fire threatened occupied wards. Debilitated men were fleeing the conflagration. Levi and his companions barricaded the door to their ward so as not to be overrun. A more severe threat was the cold, as they not only had no central heat, but no intact windows after the bomb blast. The night time temperature was below freezing.

Levi describes the apocalypse:

> The Lager, hardly dead, had already begun to decompose. No more water, or electricity, broken windows and doors slamming to in the wind, loose iron sheets from the roofs screeching, ashes from the fire drifting high, afar. The work of the bombs had been completed by the work of man: ragged, decrepit, skeleton-like patients at all able to move dragged themselves everywhere on the frozen soil, like an invasion of worms. They had ransacked all the empty huts in search of food and wood; they had violated with senseless fury the grotesquely adorned rooms of the hated *Blockältester*, forbidden to the ordinary Häftlinge until the previous day; no longer in

> control of their own bowels, they had fouled everywhere, polluting the precious snow, the only source of water remaining in the whole camp.[15]

Levi and some of the healthier men in his hut went scavenging for food and heat. They found a heavy cast iron stove with a usable flue and with great effort got it on a wheelbarrow and brought it to their ward. The heat it produced was essential for their survival. But their survival was not just physical; it was also mental and moral. The eleven men decided to share what food stuffs they had among themselves. This was un-camp-like behavior. The rule of the Lager was not only to eat your own food, but also to steal from your neighbor. They laboriously melted snow for water and scavenged along with other patients for abandoned food (a pile of frozen turnips and potatoes) and potentially useful items. Primo Levi made it to the pharmacy on the third day and found the scene described by Jaworski: inexpert looters had trashed it. However, he did find a charged car battery. That night their ward had light.

On January 21 the camp was completely abandoned by the SS. The guard towers were unmanned, the Germans had fled: "Armoured cars, Tiger tanks camouflaged in white, Germans on horseback, Germans on bicycle, Germans on foot, armed and unarmed."[16] Levi and his compatriots from France, Holland, Hungary, and Slovakia were on their own in the abandoned hospital. They managed to cobble together a soup and used it to pay a Frenchman, an erstwhile tailor, to concoct some warm clothing of many colors from fabric scraps scavenged from the rooms of the guards.

On the January 22, the patients realized that they could now leave the hospital grounds and explore the abandoned camp: the electrified fence was down. Getting access to the larger Buna-Monowitz camp was essential. The hospital patients uncovered a treasure: a huge supply of potatoes in long ditches, layered with straw and soil for protection. The food issue was resolved. Levi and his compatriots were also able to find potentially interesting items such as newspapers, and excellent eiderdown quilts (which

Levi managed to hold onto until his return to Italy). However, the dreadful cold and the underlying weakness of the sick meant that the dead were accumulating in piles along the sides of the barracks or alone and abandoned on their bunks. Of the eleven men in Levi's hut, one died during these ten days. The Soviet army arrived on the 27th and started to assuage the chaos of Auschwitz. Five others from Levi's ward died in the following weeks in the Soviet hospital. The five others survived and made it home.[17] Of the 800 patients, some 200 died before the Soviet army arrived.

THOSE WHO MARCHED

After months of systematic evacuation of workers and material from the camp, the January 17–21 events were hurried and disorganized. Not only were tens of thousands of prisoners involved, but they had to be aggregated from various camps.[18] The best routes back to Germany involved areas north of the main Auschwitz units, but they were already threatened by the January 12 Soviet offensive.[19] It was midwinter, cold days and colder nights.

The roads leading directly west became infamous for the number of prisoners who died on the march. Historian Martin Gilbert explains that not only were there shootings by the SS guards, but "many died because, too weak to rise after they had fallen down, they froze to death in the snow."[20] Enormous traffic jams clogged the streets as German civilians joined the rout. Dead prisoners, dead horses, and wrecked vehicles compounded the disaster. Planned stops for food or night resting places were abandoned and the SS forced prisoners to march through the night.[21] Special SS groups followed the columns of prisoners and shot the weak, the stragglers, and those trying to escape. Since the strongest, ablest prisoners walked at the front, they didn't witness these murders—they only heard the shots, as Stefan attests. Graves dot the routes out of Auschwitz, most now obscure and lost. The estimate is that 25% of the prisoners died, some from exposure but most from the panicked and short-tempered SS men who shot prisoners at will.[22]

Various roads led west. The groups leaving Buna-Monowitz numbered about 9000 men and were joined by 3000 more from various subcamps.[23] About 100 were shot on their way from Monowitz toward the railroad head at Gliwice, a 50-kilometer trek.[24] The ultimate destination for this group was the Buchenwald concentration camp. Elie Wiesel, hospitalized for an infection which had been surgically drained, had made the decision to join his father in the march to the west. Wiesel contrasts the agony of the evacuation and his father's death of dysentery on January 28 in Buchenwald with what he believed to have been the far easier fate of the abandoned hospital.[25] It had not been simple or that easy for those who stayed back.

Stefan said the following about the evacuation and the march:

> At the end of 1944 and in the first days of January 1945, there was more and more talk in the camp about an evacuation. A day or two before the camp was abandoned, we were ordered to identify those prisoners who were unable to march or be transported. No one knew their own fate. Various rumors circulated that the SS authorities were going to destroy the whole camp and blow up the factory sites and so on. Camp records were destroyed. All of this increased our insecurity about the fate which awaited us. A portion of those patients who could march left the camp. Before we left, we got dry rations. The march started on January 19, 1945. We were escorted by SS men under the direction of the camp authorities. The SDG walked on foot with us. The column marched and, after the bridge, turned toward Bierun and Mikołow. We avoided these cities. The march continued all day and night. We could hear shots behind us. Some of the prisoners fled, taking advantage of the confusion. We had ambulances (*Sanki*) with us but this didn't make the march easier.[26] We slept along the way but I don't remember the place. The destination of the march was subcamp Gleiwitz II in Gliwice. There, SS *Lagerarzt* Fischer ordered SDG Neubert to separate out the sick prisoners who were unable to march. Neubert ordered the prisoner doctors to do this. The sick prisoners were to be moved by train. At

> any rate, a portion of them was loaded into open wagons and another group (as I heard later) was marched out of Gliwice to the west.

Tibor Wohl also made the difficult decision to march. Working at the hospital, Wohl knew that the Czech resistance movement had prepared a hiding place above the ceiling in the disinfection room on the hospital grounds. Should he use it? Wohl had a gun, but the guards in the towers had machine guns. He decided to join the evacuation. The morning of January 18, Tibor stood with others prisoners for their last roll call in the Buna-Monowitz camp. He realized that the hospital itself was not going to be cleared of the sickest patients. He witnesses the hospital being stripped of anything of imaginable value. "A lot of boxes were already stacked in front of the hospital grounds filled with equipment and material. I saw the x-ray machine loaded onto a wagon."[27] At midday the columns finally started marching westward with their guards, guns ready to fire, but Tibor Wohl's exultant only thought was that he had survived Buna. It is not clear which group Tibor joined. Nine days later Soviet troops overran this group of marchers and liberation had arrived. In May 1945, he returned to his homeland, alone: three generations of his family had been killed. He rebuilt his life; however, he could not escape the impact of the concentration camp experience. "The past still has me in its grip."[28]

Stefan and the physicians and patients from the Buna-Monowitz prisoner hospital made plans for some kind of action on the march but then discarded them. The SS guards remained alert, armed, and dangerous. Stefan reports from the evacuation:

> Hospital personnel, including me, and other prisoners were loaded into wagons. This train stopped in Prague. I had planned to escape there with Karol Minc (a Czech-Jewish prisoner, a very sympathetic man of a cheerful disposition). However we were unable to do so as a cordon of SS men surrounded our train. Some prisoners escaped by leaping off the moving train. The train route went through Egar and Jena to

> the Buchenwald concentration camp. Many prisoners died en route. The trip from Gliwice to Buchenwald lasted about a week. The corpses were thrown into a coal wagon at the end of the train, which had some 20 to 25 wagons total.

The Germans were fleeing back to the *Altreich*, Saxony, and the city of Weimar and one of the early concentration camps: Buchenwald. This camp was opened in July 1937 for political enemies of the Nazi regime such as German socialists and communists. Buchenwald became the administrative center of an enormous labor organization, encompassing over 80 subcamps all over Germany. They produced bombs, munitions, explosives, and aircraft components for, among others, BMW and IG Farben.

The Buchenwald camp census in December 1944 stood at 63,048. In January 1945, 24,197 men were added to the camp. Another 19,594 arrived by boxcars from other camps in February and March, pushing the number to over 80,000. More than 13,000 prisoners died between January and April 1945.[29]

Stefan was among the new arrivals in January. He now became Buchenwald prisoner number 122773:

> The evacuation and the transport totally destabilized the prisoners [from Buna-Monowitz]. When we arrived at KL Buchenwald, we were quartered in a large tent. They took away our striped prison clothes and gave us old and torn ones. In a word, we were treated like any other arriving transport (*Zugang*). Naturally those colleagues who had previously been in Buchenwald were in a completely different situation. They kept their clothes, were able to move freely in the whole camp, and got access to good work units or functions. They stayed in barracks for prominent people. The other prisoners found themselves in unbelievably difficult situations because of the overcrowding of the camp. Once again, a typhus epidemic broke out. The situation was made worse because not all the prisoners went out to work.

Stefan was no longer an influential *Funktionshäfling*, no longer a prominent prisoner. He was not just demoted, he was humiliated. He lost his clothing, his secure role in the HKB, and his authority and rank. He was now in one of the lowest ranking groups in Buchenwald: a Pole from Auschwitz. Buchenwald was overcrowded and epidemics raged. Stefan knew little about the social and political games that were played in Buchenwald. His naiveté was a dangerous problem.

Who had connections in Buchenwald? Who got the position of a "prominent" prisoner? Who controlled the "good" jobs? Buchenwald was one of the early camps in Germany and had evolved an idiosyncratic camp culture. By 1944, it was under the domination of communist red triangle prisoners. This was not a unique development. Writing in November 1943, Odd Nansen, a prominent Norwegian prisoner in Sachsenhausen noted: "It's extraordinary how the communists managed things here: they have all the power in the camp next to the SS, and they attract all other communists—from other countries—and place them in key positions."[30] However, the concentrations camps were highly fluid politically, as Stefan experienced in Buna-Monowitz where neither the communist red triangles nor the criminal green triangles prevailed or dominated the SS. Unlike Buchenwald, in Sachsenhausen, the SS reacted powerfully in April 1944 and decimated the communists' dominant functionary positions with executions and transfers.[31] The upshot of this derailment was that Nansen could report in May 1944 that the ongoing struggle for power among red and green prisoners in Sachsenhausen was now won by the criminal element: the green triangles.[32]

Imre Kertész, also now transferred to Buchenwald, described the "camp aristocracy" of high-ranking red triangle communist prisoners who strode about the camp, well-dressed and well-fed.[33] These influential prisoners dominated the SS and created a prisoner self-government. The strategy of this highly active political and social group was to control the key functionary positions:

Lagerälteste, the camp police, the camp secretary positions, and—most critically—the camp hospital.[34] An early report (April 14, 1945) from Buchenwald, days after liberation, describes "A communist dictatorship in a Nazi concentration center, a terror machine within a terror machine, a concentration camp within a concentration camp."[35] The SS guards controlled the camp with barbed wire and the use of force, but "more and more of the actual power in the camp—that is, its inner structure and driving forces—thus came into the prisoners' hands."[36]

When new prisoners from Auschwitz flooded Buchenwald in January, functionary prisoners, not the SS, interviewed the newcomers. Early on, the dominant communist prisoners had identified a critical area (*Schaltstelle*) of the camp: the prisoner hospital. Langbein, transferred to Auschwitz from Dachau, also understood this and had tried, unsuccessfully, to control the Buna-Monowitz prisoner hospital positions. Buchenwald went one step further: "The prisoner hospital was a safe place for one's comrades as well as a reliable place to liquidate one's opponents."[37] Opponents in the camp were the SS, but could also be inmates labeled as traitors or informers. The SS was complicit with this level of prisoner control since in Buchenwald the communist prisoners kept an orderly, well-managed camp.

However, the gray zone of prisoner-SS relations was fraught with borderline ethical decisions. How far would prisoners running the hospital go to support the racist, murderous SS agenda? Communist prisoner Helmut Thiemann recalls: "In order to maintain our party line we were forced to help the SS doctors, which was difficult for us. We communists were faced with the question: do we refuse their work [murdering prisoners] to remain clean and humane or do we abandon our [HKB] positions and thus cause the indirect death of comrades. Since we valued our comrades more than other prisoners, we had to cooperate with SS killing of the sick patients and of collaborators."[38]

The preferential treatment of political allies went as far as the organization of a special hospital ward for German and European communists, which was supplied with available medicines. Other prisoners were neglected. Political and social hierarchies, here as in other Nazi concentration camps, were critical for long-term survival. These "old hands" in the camp dealt with the administration of a profusion of Buchenwald subcamps, handled the Babel of European languages, and functioned like a professional bureaucracy with their own forms, stamps, and filing systems.[39]

Stefan, now stripped of all status, stereotyped as one of those lazy, dirty, ill-disciplined Poles, faced a critical interview. The outcome would decide his fate at Buchenwald: liquidation or work.

> After a couple of days a German prisoner approached me, claiming that the hospital capo wanted to see me. When I reported there I was kept in hospital as if I were sick—and so it began. Over the next couple of days the surgical barracks leader named Helmut (a German wearing a red triangle—I don't remember his last name) talked with me for many hours. He was particularly interested in the state of KL Monowitz. I was so naive that I talked to him totally candidly, not understanding that Helmut was an executioner who had orders to liquidate inconvenient prisoners. That fate met many KL Auschwitz prisoners whose names I knew but can't remember at this moment.
>
> As I mentioned, these "conversations" lasted a couple of days. Finally Dr. Ciepielowski came and talked to me. He represented a group of Polish communists in KL Buchenwald. This discussion resolved some questions, as I was now left alone and got work in the second operating theater, where I worked for two months until liberation on April 13, 1945 [*sic*]. The conditions in the hospital were typical for Buchenwaldian methods, that is, all the most important decisions about the patients were made by barracks elder Helmut, a bricklayer, and not by the prisoner doctors.

It is frustrating that Stefan does not elaborate on this resolution of "some questions" in his interview with Dr. Ciepielowski (possibly Dr. Marian Ciepielowski). One could speculate that

Stefan's Montelupich and Auschwitz contacts with the prominent Polish communist Cyrankiewicz now paid some dividends. Stefan's disgust with the conditions in the Buchenwald prisoner hospital is manifest. This is what the Buna-Monowitz situation had been before Stefan took over its development.

The liberation of Buchenwald by the US Third Army was the first American encounter with an active concentration camp. Though the SS tried to empty the camp, more than 20,000 prisoners were still in situ on April 11, 1945. The morning of April 11, prisoners who served as the camp police took control of Buchenwald and, cutting through the barbed wire, seized the gate and camp entrance as well as the guard towers. The Americans found Buchenwald under the control of the prisoners.[40] Stefan reports:

> During the liberation of KL Buchenwald, the most important communist conspirators covered themselves by spreading rumors that the SS authorities were planning to liquidate them. They showed themselves immediately after the American soldiers entered the camp. Enthusiastic prisoners broke through the camp barriers and fled into freedom. I have to say, I experienced a certain horror when I left the camp and saw the corpses of young Nazi boys who believed Nazi propaganda and stayed at their posts to the end, shooting at American troops. So even freed, I again had to see the needless victims of fanatical education.
>
> Once the camp was liberated, there was a public meeting of all the prisoner doctors. During this meeting the hospital capo suggested that the organization of the hospital remain unchanged. I couldn't stand it so I rose to answer that his suggestion was just his personal viewpoint. On the other hand, we physicians believe that thanks to our education and profession, we alone should decide the fate of the sick. My statement met with enormous applause by those present, who selected me as the head of the committee running the hospital. I didn't get the support or help of other prominent people of the camps, since immediately after liberation they abandoned the

> place, driving away in cars. We were left alone with an enormous number of sick and borderline exhausted. So I turned to the American authorities to transfer the sick to the now abandoned SS barracks.

Stefan and his fellow physicians were now in a position to create a functional hospital. The need was critical. Epidemics were raging. Prisoners suffering from years of starvation were unable to cope with abundant food now available. Their emaciated bodies could not handle the sudden influx of proteins, sugars and fats. Many fell ill and many died from too much food. There was little solidarity among the now liberated nationalities. For instance, in the Bergen-Belsen camp, the barracks divided into Polish, Russian, Czech, French, Italian, and Jewish inmates.[41] Under American leadership, Buchenwald became a displaced person's camp. Those remaining prisoners who were either unable or unwilling to return to their home countries faced an uncertain future and difficult recoveries from starvation and illness. Germany lay in ruins and the work of caring for the sick was overwhelming.

Stefan once again began to organize:

> They [the US military] agreed, and with the help of dozens of prisoners and around 2,000 local German civilians, I moved several thousand patients to new quarters. I then sent them on to their own countries or moved them into civilian hospitals. This lasted until May 8, 1945. On May 8, I received the news my youngest brother lay ill in Stössel/Wartburg in a former prisoner of war camp. I drove there immediately, but I wasn't able to find him. Shortly thereafter I got employment as a doctor for foreign refugees in a large facility near Dortmund. There were 15,000 people here and once again I started practically from the beginning to organize a hospital and clinic service. I also did surgery in the Dortmund municipal hospital. I exchanged a couple of words with General Montgomery, who visited my work place. There was a lot of work to do; there were not many willing to do it.

> For a year I ran a 450-bed hospital in Salzkotten near Paderborn. When this hospital was liquidated, I sent all of its equipment along with repatriated people to the city of Elbląg.

Stefan does not address the issue of why he chose not to return to Poland. He had spent four years in prison or in concentration camps. He was now 32 years old and searching for some kind of normal life. In May 1945 he met Ewa Irena Balcerska, a Polish nurse and POW shipped out of Warsaw after the August 1944 uprising. They married August 15, 1945, in Dortmund and he was soon anticipating the birth of a child in the following year. Perhaps the single most salient issue for this new couple was the reality that Poland was now in Soviet hands. He felt no loyalty towards that new state. His wartime experiences with communists had been on the whole, confrontational. There could also be the ambition to live and work in what, war devastation notwithstanding, was part of developed Europe. Working in Poland with its low socioeconomic status, mired in the problems of Eastern Europe, compared poorly with developing a career in Germany. To work in Germany, however, meant acquiring German credentials.

> I wanted to broaden my technical skills so I enrolled in the Göttingen University clinic. There I completed my degree, took all my exams, defended my doctorate, and did my specialty until 1951. In 1951 I moved to Hanover. Many years of incarceration in Nazi concentration camps had an impact on my health. In KL Monowitz I had pneumonia and spent a significant amount of time hospitalized. After liberation, it turned out that I had tuberculosis. I had my last hemorrhage ten years ago [1964].
>
> If there are any souvenirs like letters or birthday cards of the camp, I would suppose my sister, Maria Kissler, might have them. I have not written any memoirs since in my active life I've never had the time. (After I moved to Hanover, I built and equipped one of the largest private hospitals in Germany.)

Since I remained permanently in Germany I decided to change my name, difficult to spell and pronounce by non-Poles, to Buthner.[42]

NOTES

1. Szymborska, *Seventy Poems*, 22–23.
2. Andrzej Strzelecki, "Der Todesmarch der Häftlinge aus den KL Auschwitz," in *Die nationalsozialistischen Konzentrationslager*, edited by Ulrich Herbert, Karin Orth, Christopher Dieckmann, vol. 2 (Frankfurt am Main: Fischer Verlag, 2002), 1095.
3. Ibid., 1096.
4. Wagner, *IG Auschwitz*, 262.
5. Wachsmann, *KL*, 553.
6. Strzelecki, "Der Todesmarch," 1097.
7. Wachsmann, *KL*, 545.
8. Ibid., 546.
9. Wagner, *IG Auschwitz*, 279.
10. Jaworski, *Apel Skazanych*, 272–74.
11. Ibid., 276.
12. Ibid., 286.
13. Ibid., 291.
14. Ibid., 295.
15. Levi, *Survival in Auschwitz*, 158.
16. Ibid., 162.
17. Ibid., 173.
18. The estimates range substantially. Strzelecki estimates 60,000; Martin Gilbert estimates 98,000. The difference may be due to the confusion about which units of Auschwitz were considered among the 50-odd affiliated camps subject to evacuation.
19. Wachsmann, *KL*, 554.
20. Martin Gilbert, *The Routledge Atlas of the Holocaust*, 3rd ed. (New York: Routledge, 2002), 214.
21. Strzelecki, "Der Todesmarch," 1100; Wachsmann, *KL*, 554.
22. Wachsmann, *KL*, 556; Wagner, *IG Auschwitz*, 283. Olga Lengyel was evacuated from Birkenau. Her husband, evacuated from

Buna-Monowitz, was shot by SS guards on the march (Lengyel, *Five Chimneys*, 201).

23. Strezelecki, "Der Todesmarch," 1102.
24. Ibid., 1102; Gilbert, *Routledge Atlas*, 215; map 281.
25. Wiesel, *Night*, 82, 112.
26. There is no mention of these ambulances in the secondary literature.
27. Wohl, *Arbeit macht tot*, 163.
28. Ibid., 177.
29. David Hackett, editor, *The Buchenwald Report* (Boulder, CO: Westview Press, 1995), 114. This publication was prepared in April and May of 1945 by an intelligence team from the Psychological Warfare Division, SHAEF, assisted by a committee of long-term Buchenwald prisoners. David Hackett translated, edited, and introduces this pivotal report by the prisoners.
30. Nansen, *From Day to Day*, 418.
31. Ibid., 458.
32. Ibid., 455.
33. Kertész, *Fatelessness*, 169.
34. Karin Hartewig, "Wolf unter Wölfen? Die prekäre Macht der kommunistischen Kapos in Konzentrationslager Buchenwald," in *Die nationalsozialistischen Konzentrationslager*, edited by Ulrich Herbert, Karin Orth, and Christopher Dieckmann, vol. 2 (Frankfurt am Main: Fischer Verlag, 2002), 945.
35. Ibid., 944.
36. Hackett, *Buchenwald Report*, 84.
37. Hartewig, "Wolf unter Wölfen," 945.
38. Ibid., 946.
39. Ibid., 949.
40. Hackett, *Buchenwald Report*, 104.
41. Zajęc, *Powrót niepożądany*, 242.
42. The choice to simplify complex Polish names for ease of spelling and pronunciation was not uncommon. Chancellor Angela Merkel's grandfather was Ludwig Kazmierczak. He Germanized this complex name to "Kasner." (*The Economist*, June 28, 2014). Stefan Budziaszek made this decision in 1955 after the birth of his son Stevie (1955–1996) and his acquisition of German citizenship.

11

HINDSIGHT BIAS

> Homer holds down a job in the bureau of statistics.
> No one knows what he does at home.
>
> *Homer pracuje w biurze statstycznym.*
> *Nikt nie wie, co on robi w domu.*[1]

There was yet another eye witness who saw the Buna-Monowitz prisoner hospital and was qualified to assess its facilities and its functions. Dr. Leonardo De Benedetti (1898–1983) was on the same transport to Auschwitz as Primo Levi (1919–1987). They were both left behind in the January 1945 evacuation of the camps and after an arduous journey, returned to Italy together in October 1945. Primo Levi would go on to write the indelible *Survival in Auschwitz.* However, his first published report of his concentration camp experiences was unnoticed until 1993. The Italian historian Alberto Cavaglion discovered the report Levi wrote with Dr. De Benedetti in the November 1946 issue of a Turin based medical journal.[2] The English translation appeared in 2006.[3] Primo Levi provided some details about his friend. One salient fact was that De Benedetti spoke no German and was consequently consigned to brute labor. He did not become a functionary prisoner and his medical training was not used. Instead, Dr. De Benedetti was a patient in the prisoner hospital. An older man, worn out by heavy labor, Dr. De Benedetti was selected for transfer to Birkenau's gas chambers, but Primo Levy reported that "French or Polish prisoner doctors of the infirmary, intervened: four times they managed to have his name crossed off."[4]

Like Primo Levi and Elie Wiesel, Dr. De Benedetti arrived in the spring of 1944 and only saw the prisoner hospital fully developed and functioning. As a trained physician, he was able to provide detailed descriptions of the living and working conditions in the Buna-Monowitz camp. His descriptions of the meager diet, the ill-fitting shoes, the routines of washing, the fight against louse infections support the reports of many others.

Dr. De Benedetti provides rare data about the actual work of the prisoner hospital and its doctors. "Even major surgery was regularly performed, mostly abdominal, such as partial gastrectomy, and pyloroplasty for gastroduodenal ulcers, appendectomies, rib resections for emphysema, etcetera; as well as orthopaedic interventions for fractures and dislocation. If the general condition of the patient did not offer sufficient guarantee of resistance to the trauma of surgery, he would be given a blood transfusion before the operation; this was also done to combat secondary anaemia and serious haemorrhages caused by gastric ulcers or accidental trauma."[5] This report demonstrated the level of care that the prisoner doctors were able to provide as a matter of routine. His was also the first report to mention the availability of blood transfusions though I have found no other source which mentions this procedure. Dr. De Benedetti reported that newly arrived prisoners could become blood donors, paid with a week's rest in the hospital. Dr. De Benedetti stated firmly that "no operations for the purpose of scientific research were performed in the Monowitz hospital, as they were on a vast scale in other concentration camps."[6]

The labor of the doctors, their staff and various carpenters, electricians and other workmen over many months had finally produced a working hospital. Dr. De Benedetti described an operating theater, but was not able to appreciate the level of ingenuity and contrivance it took to produce it. He writes:

> The operating theatre was reasonably well equipped, in so far as was necessary for the procedures carried out there. The walls were covered in washable white tiles; there was an adjustable operating table, of a rather old-fashioned type but still in good condition, which allowed the patient to be placed in the main operative positions, and an electric sterilizer for surgical instruments; illumination was provided by several movable lamps and a large, fixed central light. On one wall, behind a wooden screen, wash basins with hot and cold running water were installed so that the surgeon and his assistance could scrub their hands.[7]

Many months of work, constant scrounging in "Canada," trading for favors: all of these were necessary for the installation of tiled walls, lighting, and the other accoutrements of a working surgical theater. Not until the boiler was "organized" from the Buna factory did the hospital have reliable hot water or a laundry.

Dr. De Benedetti's description of the wards and services that were available corroborate Stefan's testimony. Dr. De Benedetti recorded that the hospital had the following facilities:

- out-patient clinic for general medicine
- out-patient clinic for general surgery
- otorhinolaryngology and ophthalmology out-patient clinic
- dental surgery (in which fillings and the most basic prosthetic work were also carried out)
- ward for infective surgical cases
- general clinical ward, with a section for nervous and mental illnesses, equipped with a small electric shock therapy apparatus
- ward for infectious diseases and diarrhea
- recuperation ward—"Schonungs Block"—to which were admitted dystrophic and oedematous patients and certain convalescents

- physiotherapy surgery, with a quartz lamp for ultraviolet radiation and lamps for infrared radiation
- chemical, bacteriological and serological research unit[8]

Stefan reported that the staff at the hospital was working on setting up their own x-ray facility, but did not yet have the proper equipment. Dr. De Benedetti confirms that patients needing an x-ray had to be moved to Auschwitz, that is, Auschwitz I, the main camp, which had good x-ray facilities.

Having delivered the good news, Dr. De Benedetti started listing deficiencies: no waiting rooms, a serious bed shortage, dirty bed linens, poor hygiene rules, paper bandages, and a serious lack of medications. But what is he comparing the prisoner hospital to? Any comparison with even an inferior hospital in the hinterlands of Europe would condemn the HKB's facilities as substandard, even primitive. Compared to what the prisoners had before mid-1943, however, the Buna-Monowitz prisoner hospital was an immense improvement.

Dr. De Benedetti lauds the doctors, but condemns the staff as ignorant or contemptuous of "every hygienic, therapeutic and humanitarian principle."[9] The editor of the English language edition, Robert Gordon, picks up on Dr. De Benedetti's dismay and amplifies it: "the infirmary [sic] is in actual practice a place of mistreatment, neglect and meaningless regulation, of torture and violence meted out by its nurses. It is more akin to an antechamber of death than to a curing station."[10] This stereotypical view of what it "must have been like" in a concentration camp hospital is not supported by the narratives written even by Primo Levi himself. Each of the autobiographical works cited which describe a stay in the prisoner hospital refer to it in terms of respite, calm, and a moment of security. Clearly the chance-met nursing staff was untrained, but reference to torture and violence is mistaking the prisoner hospital with the camp itself.

What kind of assessment is possible of Dr. Stefan Budziaszek? Dr. De Benedetti's report, as well as the other descriptions of the hospital, revealed a working organization which functioned as a real hospital under astoundingly difficult circumstances. The credit for the transformation of a small infirmary to a working hospital must stand to Stefan's credit. The recruitment process of physicians and workers, the constant conniving and organizing to equip it, the balancing act of cooperative relations with the SS physicians—all are elements that he was able to manipulate. His organizational ability was prodigious. He repeatedly brought services together for the prisoners, starting in Jawischowitz, then Buna-Monowitz and the once again as Buchenwald disintegrated and then the displaced person's hospital in Celle. At Buna-Monowitz he pulled together physicians from Poland and later from all over Nazi occupied Europe to produce meaningful work under hopeless circumstances.

His relationship with the German Nazis who controlled the concentration camps was astoundingly difficult. He needed the cooperation of the SS men to construct the hospital. The prisoner hospital could not have happened without the external forces which forced the SS leadership to reassess their policy of exterminating workers. The arrival of SS Dr. Wirths was the pivotal moment. He pulled Stefan into the Buna-Monowitz camp and opened a window of opportunity. Yet Stefan could not stop the SS physicians, such as SS Dr. Fischer, from walking through the wards with his cursed notebook and consigning patients to death. The SS men were constantly bribed with services, but could always exert arbitrary and lethal power. These were third-rate men. Prominent and enterprising Nazis did not end up running the concentration camps. SS men were often corrupt. They were arrested and placed in prisons like those in Montelupich. A prominent camp official, the head of the Gestapo, Grabner, was arrested by the SS itself for theft. The camp was rife with Germans trying to take advantage or seek a bribe. These were weaknesses that created opportunities for the men manning the prisoner hospital as well as dangers for Stefan.

Dr. Antoni Makowski, who served as the *Blockälteste* and preserved copious records of the personnel of the hospital, talked of the need to lessen the social distance between the prisoners and their jailers. He stated it was crucial to provide gifts for the SS such as valuable objects found in the Canada warehouse. It was important to provide medical services to the SS such as Stefan's treatment of Vinzenz Schöttl. These acts "provided a gradual reduction of the distance between the SS men and the prisoners and a greater independence [*Unabhängigkeit und Selbständigkeit*] both in the hospital and in the camp."[11] Makowski also reports the systematic procurement of bricks, wood, cement, sinks, piping—stolen from the Buna factory and carried back to the hospital in the empty soup kettles.[12] The SS men, guards and SS physicians, could not have been ignorant about the source of the equipment for the construction and outfitting of the hospital. A large boiler could not have been moved from the factory and installed at the hospital without a complicit set of guards. Dr. Stefan Budziaszek, as the leader of the hospital, was the man who perforce had to keep these relationships in balance. As noted above, only Stefan and Hermann Langbein spoke openly after the war of the necessity of working with the SS in order to bring about change or improvement in the camp.

Yet Stefan also showed willful ignorance of resistance movements among the prisoners. He claimed that there were no such groups whereas we can see from Zając (Polish AK resistance movement), Wohl (Czech resistance), and Langbein (Communist resistance) that, on the contrary, there were numerous prisoner groups working to protect fellow nationals or coreligionists. Stefan was oriented toward placating and manipulating his superiors rather than forming relationships with prisoners. He formed long-lasting friendships with physicians in the prisoner hospital, but was focused on bureaucracy and policies rather than on the patients. He was perhaps too proud of coming to Buna-Monowitz in SS Dr. Wirths's personal car and enjoyed the status this conferred on him. It was not a trait to endear him to the men he replaced at the hospital. A late-comer physician such as Dr. Robert Waitz (#157,261) felt undervalued and was personally affronted for not receiving the respect he believed his due.

A series of confrontations define Auschwitz: older prisoners versus more recent prisoners, elite groups versus the regular prisoners, functionary prisoners versus laborers, cooperation with SS to gain leverage versus confrontations leading to shootings. So often these struggles are refashioned as "racial" in Auschwitz since the older, more privileged, more experienced survivors were the gentile Poles who fought strongly to maintain themselves and the newer groups became increasingly Jewish and had less leverage until they sorted themselves out. Primo Levi shows the trajectory newly arrived Jews experienced as he started as a brute laborer and ended up with some protection six months after his arrival. He supplied the HKB with equipment and he was a patient.

How effective was the hospital? Did it make a difference to the survival rate of Buna-Monowitz prisoners? Makowski's figures are the most complete though they do not cover all of 20 months of the reconfigured hospital. Between July 1943 and June 1944, while the hospital was under the leadership of Stefan, the prisoner hospital treated 15,707 prisoners. Of these, 766 died in the hospital and 12,342 returned to the camp. However, 2,599 were selected by SS physicians for transfer either to Auschwitz I or Auschwitz II-Birkenau. In the previous year while the hospital was being served by well-meaning but medically untrained personnel, 4,890 men were selected for transfer out of Buna-Monowitz. The reorganized prisoner hospital was able to spare some 1,200 lives.[13] The prisoner hospital also saved the physicians, physically and psychologically, by creating a worksite for them.

Stefan is vague about the number of selections which took place in the hospital. His narrative avoids calling the biweekly SS doctor's visits "selections." He want to recall only the significant campwide selections. All prisoner physicians struggled to create a triage system which would condemn only the dying to the gas chambers. In a regime run by the SS, this was not possible. The SS solved the problem of a high camp census by murdering 20% of the inmates. They controlled epidemics by condemning blocks of both healthy and diseased prisoners to death. There was never enough subterfuge or obfuscation possible to save all of the patients. Stefan and his coworkers could not save them all. He did, however, exert protean efforts to create a working hospital that returned patients to work rather than to Birkenau. The vast majority of all patients and physicians in the hospital were Jews. Both survivors and victims were Jews. Jewishness was not an overriding selection criterion used by the prisoner physicians.

The teleological deception of retrospect collapses the messy and contradictory reality of complex events like the Auschwitz concentration camps into the story in which the Shoah is the only event. Yet at the time in which the various Auschwitz camps functioned, the systematic death machine of Birkenau was not well understood even by the men in the camp. Each prisoner was facing possible death due to starvation or illness, a selection of the weakest to die in Birkenau. The actual dimensions of the atrocities, however, were unknown to the new arrivals. They had to learn about the implication of being incapable of work. Prisoners sometimes took weeks to understand that when they were separated from parents and children, that their families had been killed on arrival. The enormity of the Shoah only coalesced slowly, after the event, and it eventually became the dominant narrative.

The daily reality of workers in a site like Buna-Monowitz was not the confrontation of Jews and gentiles. It was the confrontation of prisoners and jailers. In the hierarchy of prisoners, prisoners sought allies and social groups which could give them a chance for survival. Primo Levi kept meticulous track of the survivors of his transport both while he struggled in Auschwitz and after liberation. Understanding and keeping track of friends was paramount. Survivors repeatedly refer to help that they received from other prisoners.

In Stefan's oral testimony his final remarks address the political fault lines which developed in the struggle for functionary, relatively safer work positions in the hospital setting. The issue was politics and not race. It was the Germans who made race the ultimate criterion for life or death. Prisoners had survival agendas which they expressed in terms of patriotism, political affiliations, personal and national loyalties.

> In conclusion, I want to mention that after the war, specifically during the Frankfurt Auschwitz trial against members of the SS active in Auschwitz, former prisoners, Jews, accused me of insulting and defamatory charges. In this only a couple of people were active, among them Kurt Posener, Robert Waitz, and Stefan Heymann. They wrote some news articles hoping to influence the press. As I explained earlier, the root of their hatred was very prosaic, stemming back to the camp, where I opposed the authority and management exerted by the clique of Buchenwald and Sachsenhausen prisoners over the hospital in KL Auschwitz III. Contrary to their opinion I will mention that to this day I maintain warm and collegial relations with prisoner doctors, Jews, and that the greatest hatred comes from nonphysicians whom I removed from decision-making roles in dealing with sick prisoners. I am pleased to know that the closest colleagues of my main antagonists do not join them in casting aspersions against me and at least in public are not joining this hunt. Ascribing to me such actions as participating in selections among the sick or identifying those trying to escape the camps—well, those actions only exist in the imagination of my enemies. (February 29, 1974)

NOTES

1. Szymborska, *Seventy Poems*, 76–77.
2. *Minerva Medica,* "Report On The Sanitary And Medical Organization Of The Monowitz Concentration Camp For Jews (Auschwitz—Upper Silesia)," November 24, 1946, Dr. Leonardo De Benedetti, Physician and Surgeon and Dr. Primo Levi, Chemist.
3. Primo Levi with Leonardo De Benedetti, *Auschwitz Report,* translated by Judith Woolf, edited by Robert S. C. Gordon (New York: Verso, 2006).
4. Levi, *Auschwitz Report,* 92.
5. Ibid., 56.
6. Ibid.

7. Ibid., 57.
8. Ibid., 63.
9. Ibid., 69.
10. Ibid., 13.
11. Makowski, *Häftlingskrankenbau in Monowitz*, 175.
12. Ibid., 18.
13. Ibid., 180.

AFTERWORD

> The joy of writing.
> The power of preserving.
> The revenge of a mortal hand.
>
> *Radość pisania.*
> *Możność utrwalania.*
> *Zemsta ręki śmertelnej.*

In 2012 I was contacted by Dr. Monika Freyer-Mohl, a physician in Switzerland, and the daughter of Dr. Herbert Mohl, who was imprisoned in Buna-Monowitz and worked at the prisoner hospital concocting medicines. Dr. Herbert Mohl survived the evacuation from Auschwitz as well as the Buchenwald period. He returned to Czechoslovakia after the war, as did fellow Czech prisoner Tibor Wohl. Dr. Monika Freyer-Mohl alerted me to Tibor Wohl's book, *Arbeit Macht tot*, which is a valuable source for the camp, the prisoner hospital, and the political tensions among prisoners. Dr. Mohl and his family emigrated to Switzerland in 1968. Tibor Wohl also emigrated in 1968: he went to West Germany. The two families maintained contact.

Monika talked to Tibor Wohl by phone on November 15, 2012. She mentioned my book project to him. Tibor Wohl, then in his 89th year, is certainly among the very few living witnesses to the events of Buna-Monowitz. She related Tibor Wohl's comment: "he remembers your father and referred to him as a decent man."

ACKNOWLEDGMENTS

Just as a child is raised by a village, a writer is formed by her community. Parental guidance, schooling, life experiences are all relevant. My professors at the University of Chicago, particularly Emile Karafiol and William MacNeill, formed the scholar; my colleagues at Lewis University formed the teacher. My dear colleague and friend Mark Schultz has offered his erudition and unending moral support. Peter Froehlich at the Purdue University Press was unstinting in his encouragement and provided advance readers of the manuscript. I am forever grateful for their generosity, their essential help and their support.

There is more to scholarly work than education and professional skills. I am also supported by a wonderful family and friends. My much loved daughter-in-law, the novelist Michele Bacon, read and reread *Saving Lives in Auschwitz* to help me avoid too much unfortunate academic prose. My compatriot and friend in the American Association of University Women, Marilyn Mayer Wiedemann, encouraged me with her critical reading and her deep conviction that Stefan's story needed to be told. My husband John has patiently lived through and supported me during numerous periods of intense work. This was essential.

While I never spoke with my father about his experiences, I know that at the core of this book is my feeling of indebtedness to him. I am here, my family is here, his great grandchildren are here because he persevered and struggled through a bestial period of European history. He survived. While my retelling of his survival is as accurate as I can make it, the omissions and errors that may remain are mine.

BIBLIOGRAPHY

PRISONER NARRATIVES

Buthner, Stefan (Budziaszek). Unpublished oral testimony. File IV-8520 -227/4091/73, Państwowe Muzeum Oświęcim-Brzezinka, recorded January 11, 1974.

Crome, Len. *Unbroken: Resistance and Survival in the Concentration Camps.* New York: Schocken Books, 1988.

Hoffman, Bedřich. *And who will kill you . . . The Chronicle of the Life and Sufferings of Priests in the Concentration Camps.* Poznań: Pallottinum, 1994. From a Czech original edition of 1946.

Jaworski, Czesław. *Apel Skazanych: Wspomnienia z Oświęcimia (Oświęcim, Brno, Monowice).* Warsaw: Instytut Wydawniczy PAX, 1962.

Kertész, Imre. *Fatelessness.* Translated from the Hungarian by Tim Wilkinson. New York: Vintage International/Random House, 2004.

Kirschner, Ann. *Letters to Sala: A Young Woman's Life in Nazi Labor Camps.* With an essay by Debórah Dwork and Robert Jan van Pelt. New York: The New York Public Library, 2006.

Lengyel, Olga. *Five Chimneys: A Woman Survivor's True Story of Auschwitz.* New York: Granada, 1972.

Levi, Primo. *The Drowned and the Saved.* Translated from the Italian by Raymond Rosenthal. New York: Vintage Books, 1989.

———. *Moments of Reprieve: A Memoir of Auschwitz.* Translated from Italian by Ruth Feldman. New York: Penguin Books, 1987.

———. *Survival in Auschwitz.* Translated from Italian by Stuart Woolf. New York: Simon & Schuster, Touchstone Edition, 1996.

Levi, Primo, and Leonardo de Benedetti. *Auschwitz Report.* New York: Verso, 2006.

Makowski, Antoni. "Häftlingskrankenbau in Monowitz (KL Auschwitz III)." *Hefte von Auschwitz* 15 (1975): 113–81.

Nansen, Odd. *From Day to Day. One Man's Diary of Survival in Nazi Concentration Camps*. Edited by Timothy Boyce. Nashville: Vanderbilt University Press, 2016.

Sztaba, Romuald. "Ze wspomnień lekarza w Gross-Rosen." in *Okupacja i medecyna*, 4th selection from "Przeględa lekarskiego—Oświęcim from 1963–1978." Warsaw: Książka i Wiedza, 1979.

Wanat, Leon. *Za Murami Pawiaka*. Warsaw: Książka I Wiedza, 1958.

Wiesel, Elie. *Night*. Translated from the French by Stella Rodway. New York: Bantam Books, 1982.

Wohl, Tibor. *Arbeit Macht tot: Eine Jugend in Auschwitz*. Frankfurt am Main: Fischer Verlag, 1990.

Zając, Mieczysław. *Powrót Niepożądany*. Krakow: Wydawnictwo Literackie, 1986.

SECONDARY LITERATURE

Allen, Michael Thad. *The Business of Genocide: The SS, Slave Labor, and the Concentration Camps*. Chapel Hill: The University of North Carolina Press, 2002.

Aly, Götz. *Hitler's Beneficiaries: Plunder, Racial War, and the Nazi Welfare State*. New York: Henry Holt/Metropolitan Books, 2006.

Bacon, Ewa. "Strategies for Long-Term Survival in Auschwitz-Monowitz," in *Emerging Issues in Holocaust Education*, edited by Kathleen McSharry. Greensburg, PA: National Catholic Center for Holocaust Education, Seton Hill University, 2009. 49–55.

———. "The Prisoner Hospital in Buna-Monowitz," in *History (1933–1948) What We Choose to Remember*, edited by Margaret Monahan Hogan and James M. Lies, C.S.C., 161–87. Portland: University of Portland, 2011.

Bauer, Yehuda. *Rethinking the Holocaust*. New Haven: Yale University Press, 2001.

Beischl, Konrad. *Dr. med. Eduard Wirths und seine Tätigkeit als SS-Standortarzt im KL Auschwitz*. Würzburg: Verlag Köninghausen & Neumann, 2005.

Borkin, Joseph. *The Crime and Punishment of I.G. Farben*. New York: The Free Press, 1978.

Buggeln, Marc. *Slave Labor in Nazi Concentrations Camps*. Translated by Paul Cohen. [German title *Arbeit & Gewalt: Das Aussenlagersystem des KZ Neuengamme*.] Oxford: Oxford University Press, 2014.

Clark, Jonathan. *Our Shadowed Present*. Stanford University Press, 2004.

Czech, Danuta. *Auschwitz Chronicle, 1939-1945: From the Archives of the Auschwitz Memorial and the German Federal Archives*. New York: Henry Holt/ Owl Book Edition, 1997.

Debski, Tadeusz. *A Battlefield of Ideas: Nazi Concentration Camps and their Polish Prisoners*. Boulder, East European Monographs. Distributed by New York: Columbia University Press, 2001.

Dickstein, Morris. "Sounds of Silence," Review of Yehuda Bauer's *Rethinking the Holocaust*. *The New York Review of Books*, January 28, 2001, 10.

Dixon, Jeremy. *Commanders at Auschwitz: The SS Officers Who Ran the Largest Nazi Concentration Camp, 1940–1945*. Atglan, PA: Schiffer Military History, 2005.

Dwork, Deborah, and van Pelt, Robert Jan. *Auschwitz 1270 to the Present*. New York: Norton, 1996.

———. *Holocaust, A History*. New York: Norton, 2002.

Fulbrook, Mary. *A Small Town near Auschwitz: Ordinary Nazis and the Holocaust*. Oxford: Oxford University Press, 2012.

Gilbert, Martin. *The Routledge Atlas of the Holocaust*. 3rd ed. New York: Routledge Press, 2002.

Goffman, Erving. *Asylums. Essays on the Social Situation of Mental Patients and Other Inmates*. New York: Anchor Books, 1961.

Gruner, Wolf. *Jewish Forced Labor under the Nazi: Economic Needs and Racial Aims, 1938–1944*. Cambridge: Cambridge University Press, 2006.

Hackett, David, ed. *The Buchenwald Report*. Boulder, CO: Westview Press, 1995.

Hartewig, Karin. "Wolf unter Wölfen? Die prekäre Macht der kommunistitschen Kapos in Konzentrationslager Buchenwald," in *Die nationalsozialistischen Konzentrazionslager*, edited by Ulrich Herbert, Karin Orth and Christopher Dieckmann. Vol. 2. Frankfurt am Main: Fischer Verlag, 2002.

Herbert, Ulrich. *Hitler's Foreign Workers: Enforced Foreign Labor in Germany under the Third Reich*. Translated by William Templer. New York: Cambridge University Press, 1997.

Höss, Rudolph. *Death Dealer: The Memoirs of the SS Kommandant at Auschwitz*. Edited by Steven Paskuly, translated by Andrew Pollinger. Buffalo, NY: 1992.

Iwańska, Alicja. *Polish Intelligentsia in Nazi Concentration Camps and American Exile*. Lewiston, NY: The Edwin Mellon Press, 1998.

Judt, Tony. *Postwar: A History of Europe Since 1945*. New York: Penguin Press, 2005.

Kłodzinski, Stanisław, and Niedoljadło, Eugeniusz. "Płk. Dr. med. Czesław Wincenty Jaworski." *Przegląd Lekarski* 34, no. 1 (1977).

Langbein, Hermann. *People in Auschwitz*. Translated from the German by Harry Zorn. Chapel Hill: University of North Carolina Press in association with the United States Holocaust Memorial Museum, 2004.

Lehnstaedt, Stephan. "Coercion and Incentive: Jewish Ghetto Labor in East Upper Silesia." *Holocaust and Genocide Studies* 24, no. 3 (2010): 400–30.

Lewis, Michael. *The Undoing Project: A Friendship That Changed Our Minds*. New York: Norton, 2017.

Lifton, Robert Jay. *The Nazi Doctors: Medical Killing and the Psychology of Genocide*. New York: Basic Books, 1986.

Longerich, Peter. *Holocaust: The Nazi Persecution and Murder of the Jews*. Oxford: Oxford University Press, 2010.

Lukas, Richard. *Forgotten Holocaust: The Poles under German Occupation, 1939–1944*. New York: Hippocrene Books, 1997.

———, ed. *Forgotten Survivors: Polish Christians Remember the Nazi Occupation*. Lawrence, Kansas: University Press of Kansas, 2004.

Oswald, Jan. *Die Ermittlungen im Fall "4 Js 798/64": Handlungsspielräume von Funktionshäftlingen in nationalsozalistischen Konzentrationslagern am Beispiel des Monowitzer Revierältesten Stefan Budziaszek alias Dr. Stefan Buthner*. Munich: GRIN. Dokumet Nr. V167959 aus dem GRIN Verlagsprogramm. 2006.

Pendas, Devin. *The Frankfurt Auschwitz Trial, 1963–1965: Genocide, History and the Limits of the Law*. New York: Cambridge University Press, 2006.

Radford, R. A. *Economica* 12 (1945). http://albany.edu/~mirer/eco110/pow.html.

Schwarz, Gudrun. "Frauen in Konzentrationslagern—Täterinnen und Zuschauerinnen," in *Die nationalsozialistischen Konzentrationslager, Band 2*, edited by Ulrich Herbert, Karin Orth, and Christoph Dieckmann. Frankfurt am Main: Fischer Verlag, 2002.

Sehn, Jan. *Concentration camp Oświécim-Brzezinka (Auschwitz-Birkenau)*. Warszawa: Wydawnictwo Prawnicze, 1957.

Setkiewicz, Piotr. "Häftlingsarbeit im KZ Auschwitz III-Monowitz. Die Frage nach der Wirtschaftlichkeit der Arbeit," in *Die nationalsozialistischen Konzentrationslager, Band 2*, edited by Ulrich Herbert, Karin Orth, and Christoph Dieckmann. Frankfurt am Main: Fischer Verlag, 2002.

———. *Z dziejów IG Farben Werk Auschwitz, 1941–1945*. Oświęcim: Państwowe Muzeum Auschwitz-Birkenau, 2006.

Shore, Marci. "The Jewish Hero History Forgot." *The New York Times*, April 18, 2013.

Steinbacher, Sybille. *Auschwitz, A History*. New York: HarperCollins, Ecco Edition, 2005.

Strzelecki, Andrzej. "Der Todesmarch der Häftlinge aus den KL Auschwitz," in *Die nationalsozialistischen Konzentrationslager, Band 2*, edited by Ulrich Herbert, Karin Orth and Christoph Dieckmann. Frankfurt am Main: Fischer Verlag, 2002.

Szymborska, Wisława. *Sounds, Feelings, Thoughts: Seventy Poems by Wisława Szymborska*. Translated by Magnus J. Krynski and Robert A. Maguire. Princeton: Princeton University Press, 1981.

Wachsmann, Nikolaus. *KL A History of the Nazi Concentration Camps*. New York: Farrar, Straus and Giroux, 2015.

Wagner, Bernd. *IG Auschwitz: Zwangsarbeit und Vernichtung von Häftlingen des Lagers Monowitz, 1941–1945.* Munich: K. G. Saur Verlag, 2000.

Wildt, Michael. *An Uncompromising Generation: The Nazi Leadership of the Reich Security Main Office.* Translated by Tom Lampert. Madison: University of Wisconsin Press, 2009.

1

APPENDIX: REGISTER OF PHYSICIANS

Name	Camp #	Position
Budziaszek, Stefan	20526	HKB eldest prisoner
Cremieux, Albert		physician
Cuenca, Leo	110941	physician
Drohocki, Zenon	169779	physician & barracks eldest
Eitinger		physician
Epstein, Berthold	79104	physician
Fischer, Bela		physician
Garfunkel, Israel	157057	physician
Grossmann, Franz	107566	physician
Happ, Hans	81314	dentist
Hermann, Willi	89075	dentist
Hirsch		physician
Hofstein, Jules	172702	physician
Holly, Imre	A 8107	physician
Jaworski, Czesław W.	31070	physician
Kaufmann		physician
Keketi, Eugen	A 8234	physician
Kindberg, Leon Michel	172729	physician
Kletz, Gaston	157101	physician
Kovac, Georg		physician
Lengyel, Moritz	A 8371	physician
Levy, Camille	167585	physician
Lubicz, Szymon	65686	physician

Name	Camp #	Position
Makowski, Antoni	131791	physician & barracks eldest
Mohl, Herbert	71182	physician
Ornstein, Hugo	43722	physician
Pejsa, Vaclac		physician
Rutkowski, Bronisław	79281	physician
Salpeter		physician
Samuel, Max	104868	physician
Samuelidis, Salomon	121104	physician
Schönzweig		physician
Schweikert, Rudolf	62890	dentist
Silber, Jonas	38968	physician
Spazierer		physician
Sperber, Karel	85512	physician
Stern, Andre		physician
Stern, Imre		physician
Sternberg, Aladar	A 8611	physician
Szczedryn, Aleksiej	RKG 11091	physician
Śliwiński, Tadeusz	68939	
Ullman		dentist
Waitz, Robert	157261	physician
Weisskopf, Rudolf	71261	physician
Weiner		physician
Wellers, Georges		chemist
Winter, Alfred	65342	physician

MONOWITZ: HELPERS AND ADMINISTRATORS

Name	Camp #	Position
Barczyk, Ryszard	101541	nurse (*Pfleger*)
Braunsberg, Anton		barber
Chirschtritt, Nathan	70291	camp administrator for food service
Czylok, Józef	114840	nurse (*Pfleger*)
Eisler, Eric		nurse (*Pfleger*)
Eliasz, Julian		nurse (*Pfleger*)
Feldbau, Jacques	157026	clerk
Fogel, Froim	69723	disinfector

Name	Camp #	Position
Frenkiel, Israel	68440	barber
Halbreich, Zygmunt	68233	nurse (*Pfleger*) & barracks eldest
Hanak		camp administrator for food service
Hahn, Heinz		nurse (*Pfleger*)
Hauser, Kei	70289	nurse (*Pfleger*)
Hess, Ludwig	68486	night guard
Heymann, Stephan	68488	main clerk
Kanarak		
Kaplan, Serge	139776	electrician
Kapler, Mieczysław	68506	surgical nurse
Klimek, Franz	60354	barracks eldest
Kmieciński, Franciczek	126246	disinfector
Kośmider, Tadeusz	624	barracks eldest
Kowalski, Jerzy	135668	nurse (*Pfleger*)
Kozdass, Otto	71344	barracks eldest
Kujawa, Ryszard	135678	nurse (*Pfleger*)
Kwaśny, Gustaw	114844	senior disinfector
Lay, Georg	71349	barracks eldest & senior disinfector
Leonhard, Hermann	152256	barracks eldest
Lindenbaum, Abraham		nurse (*Pfleger*)
Linhard, Karl	112117	barracks eldest
Lippman, Heinz	87467	barracks eldest
Lippman, Rudolf		clerk
Littwitz, Kurt	116968	nurse (*Pfleger*)
Luger, Joseph	60357	barracks eldest
Magiera, Szczepan	122988	nurse (*Pfleger*)
Maneli, Mieczysław		nurse (*Pfleger*)
Matheu, Karl		disinfector
Markowitsch, Erich	70110	nurse (*Pfleger*) & barracks eldest
Minc, Karel	68582	camp administrator for food service
Mucha, Roman	122804	dentist assistant
Munk, Honsa	71170	nurse (*Pfleger*)
Nakache, Alfred		masseuse
Niedojadło, Eugeniusz	213	nurse (*Pfleger*) & barracks eldest
Nowakowski, Edward	131730	locksmith
Pośpieszyński, Mieczysław	169710	disinfector
Poznański, Artur	104691	clerk

Name	Camp #	Position
Rączka, Eugeniusz	127647	nurse (*Pfleger)*
Rausch, Felix	68628	clerk
Rudziński, Tadeusz	124977	nurse (*Pfleger)*
Schuller, Otto	91143	nurse (*Pfleger)*
Schulmann, Hirsch	142533	disinfector
Schuster, Heinrich		HKB eldest
Schwarz, Hermann	71224	disinfector
Śliwiński		electrician
Stasik, Tadeusz	5870	nurse (*Pfleger)*
Sylman, Leon	68677	nurse (*Pfleger)*
Szachowski, Witold		nurse (*Pfleger)*
Tadlewski, Albert	157246	nurse (*Pfleger)*
Tannenwurzel, Chaim	114163	nurse (*Pfleger)*
Treister, Noach	68710	nurse (*Pfleger)*
Vesely, Karel		nurse (*Pfleger)*
Wassermann, Leopold	114865	disinfector
Wolf, Paul	71413	barracks eldest
Wohl, Tibor	71255	disinfector
Wörl, Ludwig	60363	HKB eldest
Wyszatycki, Władysław	124975	nurse (*Pfleger)*
Zając, Mieczysław		nurse (*Pfleger)*

Note: List from Antoni Makowski, *Häftlingskrankenbau in Monowitz,* 177–78.

2

APPENDIX: DEVELOPMENT OF HOSPITAL BARRACKS

Barrack #	Date of inception	Main function	Remarks
#18	Oct 42	out-patient clinic	
		secretary; pharmacy	
		surgery; lab; physiotherapy	
#19	Oct 42	ward for bed-ridden patients	
		post-surgical ward	
		ward for "Reichsdeutsche"	
#20	Feb 43	ward for infectious diseases, TB and skin diseases; Durchfall	
#15	June 43	ward for internal diseases	Stefan Budziaszek, Krankenbau-älteste
		dentist; out-patient clinic	
#16	June 43	surgical unit with sterile operating theater	
#17	Nov 43	second internal medicine ward	
		laryngology	
#22	Jan 44	ward for convalescent & weak patients	the Schonungsblock
#14	June 44	operating theater II	
#13	Jan 45	a second Schonungsblock	

Note: List from Antoni Makowski, *Häftlingskrankenbau in Monowitz,* 119.

3

APPENDIX: STEFAN BUDZIASZEK'S 1949 ARREST

[in German; typed]
Medical Doctor Budziaszek Stefan
Göttingen
Friedländerweg 3

January 25, 1949
[in Polish, typed]
Oświęcim

I met citizen Jan Bielski in Oświęcim in 1940 at Captain Bronikowski's, whom I was treating after his return from prison. From March 1940 I was constantly at the University Clinic in Krakow. At that time I belonged to Fr. Czesław Skarbka's conspiratorial group.

In the spring of 1941, already after Fr. Skarbka's flight from Krakow, I met Bielski several times in the apartment of Fr. Skarbka's sister near St. Anne's street in Krakow where a printing press and radio receiver were located.

After the arrest of Fr. Skarbka's sister I expected to be arrested any day, but a couple of weeks went by quietly. On a certain day I found out that Bielski had been arrested. Two days later the Gestapo came to the clinic to arrest me, though I managed to escape at the last minute.

Bielski was arrested in the apartment of Fr. Skarbka's sister, where he came to visit, not realizing that the sisters themselves had been arrested. The Gestapo settled in the apartment and arrested everyone who showed up.

On June 21, 1941, Bielski drove to Krosno and came to the apartment of P. P. Baranów, where I was hiding.

Bielski knew that I was hiding in Krosno and as he told me himself, he came to Krosno hoping to see me by chance and indeed found me at Baranów's,

No one knew about my hiding place, not my parents and not my friends.

After greeting me, Bielski told me he had come to warn me that the Gestapo was determined to seize me. He now told me of his own arrest, about his stay in Montelupich, where he claimed he was beaten and threatened that he and his whole family would be sent to the concentration camp if he didn't reveal my hiding place and Fr. Skarbka's.

I told him that I knew all this and that is why I had escaped from Krakow. Among other things I also told him that I had false papers in the name of "Mieczysław Szuster."

At the end of his stay, Bielski asked if one could buy cheap butter in Krosno. I asked the householder and if I remember correctly, we got 2 kg of butter. Bielski claimed he had no money on him and that he would repay me later. This he never did.

Bielski was very curious and asked for the details of my and Fr. Skarbka's flight, which thankfully I didn't tell him.

Bielski returned to Krakow on Saturday, June 21, 1941, and on Monday, early in the afternoon of June 23, 1941, a Gestapo officer and three underlings broke into Branów's apartment and arrested me. They came in a special car straight from Krakow, immediately used my actual name and my pseudonym, and already knew the layout of the apartment. During the interrogation, which lasted all night, I determined that they had accurate information about my trips to Bochno, that I drove Fr. Skarbka from Krzyżanowic, as well as the existence of a radio receiver and press on St. Anne Street.

At the time I thought that the Gestapo had gotten all these details from Fr. Skarbka's sisters. But a half-year later, when I became a prisoner doctor in the jail and had, comparatively speaking, freedom to move about, I found out from Fr. Skarbka's sisters and from priests who were arrested at the same time, that Bielski had spilled everything.

Additionally, SS man Siebert told me a couple of hours before my transfer to Auschwitz that Bielski told them everything. He revealed further that Bielski was released from jail and was guaranteed total freedom if he found my and Fr. Skarbka's hiding place.

Since he revealed my hiding place, he was released and got to keep his railroad job.

Only Bielski knew my false name and only he could reveal it to the Gestapo.

Signed:
Dr. Med. Stefan Budziaszek
[red stamp with the same name]

[handwritten in Polish and signed]
This statement is being sent to the hands of Florian Budziaszek, Oświęcim.

[in German, typed and signed: a notary seal and statement]
Nr. 41 of the document register for 1949

Göttingen, 31 January 1949
Dr. Wilhelm Busse, Notar

BIOGRAPHICAL NOTE

Ewa K. Bacon is Professor Emerita of history at Lewis University in Romeoville, Illinois. Her BA in psychology from Stanford University and PhD in history from the University of Chicago led her to a two-decade teaching career in globalization issues, Eastern European history, and genocide. In 2002 she received a copy of her father Stefan Budziaszek's testimony to the Oświęcim Museum about his imprisonment in the Auschwitz concentration camp system during World War II. Placed in the context of modern scholarship, his narrative brings a compelling story of prisoner agency to an audience now several generations removed from the events.

INDEX